The
SONG OF GOD

The
SONG OF GOD

A Summary Study of
Bhagavad-gita As It Is

His Divine Grace
KĪRTANĀNANDA
SWAMI BHAKTIPĀDA

BHAKTIPADA BOOKS

Readers interested in the subject matter of this book are invited to visit the New Vrindaban Community, Home of Prabhupada's Palace of Gold, Hare Krishna Ridge, Moundsville, W.Va., or to correspond with the Secretary.

c/o New Vrindaban
R.D. 1 Box 319
Moundsville, W.Va. 26041

1st Printing 12,000 copies

© 1984 Bhaktipada Books
All Rights Reserved

Printed in Singapore

Library of Congress Catalog Card No. 84-45783

International Standard Book Number: 0-932215-00-9

DEDICATION

To His Divine Grace
A.C. Bhaktivedanta Swami Prabhupada,
our beloved spiritual master
who saved the world from impersonalism
and voidism by presenting
Bhagavad-gita As It Is.

Contents

INTRODUCTION

From time immemorial, those interested in the science of transcendentalism have recognized *Bhagavad-gita* as the essence of the *Vedas* and the guiding scripture for the entire Hindu world. Although spoken five thousand years ago by Lord Krishna, the Supreme Personality of Godhead, *Bhagavad-gita* has been unknown in the West until recently. First translated into English two hundred years ago, it has been studied by Western writers and scholars—notably Emerson and Thoreau in America—and lauded as India's principal scripture.

Despite *Bhagavad-gita's* teaching of exclusive devotion to Krishna as the highest spiritual path, not one devotee of Lord Krishna emerged outside India. Why? There were plenty of translations, and the Sanskrit verses themselves have always been clear, for its "confidential knowledge" was certainly not related in obscure or coded language. There was another reason: by its spiritual nature, *Bhagavad-gita* remains enigmatic to anyone who is not completely devoted and surrendered to its Divine Speaker, Lord Krishna. Nondevotees, or those who are envious of Krishna—those who think that they are God, or who want to become God—cannot understand *Bhagavad-gita*, even though they be the greatest Sanskrit scholars. They are like bees trying to relish the taste of honey by licking the outside of a honey jar. The jar remained tightly sealed, until His Divine Grace A.C. Bhaktivedanta Swami Prabhupada began lecturing from a small New York storefront in 1966. At that time, he opened it to the world, and the nectar of transcendental knowledge flowed freely.

I was most fortunate to be present when that nectar flowed at those first lectures. At that time, since Srila Prabhupada had not yet published his lucid translation and commentaries (*Bhagavad-gita As It Is*, Macmillan, 1968), he had to read from a nondevotional, albeit popular, edition, but he often attacked the misleading commentaries. Although the Sanskrit translations in such mundane editions were academically acceptable, Srila Prabhupada could not recommend any of them "because the commentator has expressed his own opinions without touching the spirit of *Bhagavad-gita* as it is." That spirit is mentioned in every chapter, wherein Lord Krishna tells us, "Surrender unto Me." Being a pure devotee and perfect spiritual master, Srila Prabhupada taught such surrender and wholehearted devotion to Krishna by his every word and act. Today, following in his footsteps, thousands of Lord Krishna's devotees all over the world go out into the streets chanting Hare Krishna and preaching the real message of *Bhagavad-gita*.

By *Krishna*, we mean, of course, God. In Sanskrit, the word *Bhagavad*, or *Bhagavan*, means "the opulent one," and *gita* means "song." Hence *Bhagavad-gita* means "The Song of God." Only God is opulent, for He alone is the ultimate proprietor of everything, the possessor of all opulences in full: complete beauty, knowledge, fame, power, wealth, and renunciation. The English word "God," however, is not a name but an impersonal descriptive word meaning "He whom we invoke" in our prayers or petitions. In English, when we speak of "the Lord God," we refer to the Absolute Controller of everything, but we do not necessarily infer a personality. The word *Krishna*, however, is a name which invokes the Supreme Personality of Godhead. That is, Krishna means "the all-attractive person," who attracts all living entities by His infinite opulences. When we chant "Hare Krishna, Hare Krishna, Krishna Krishna, Hare Hare, Hare Rama, Hare Rama, Rama Rama, Hare Hare," we are calling out to that Supreme Person to please help us attain devotion to Him. The word *Rama* means "the Supreme Enjoyer," who is Krishna. Only God is the factual enjoyer; all others are enjoyed. The word *Hare* refers to the Lord's pleasure potency—His spiritual energy—by which we reach the Lord Himself.

Being infinite, God is called by countless names, but in our disciplic succession (*Brahma-sampradaya*), descending from Lord Krishna through Lord Chaitanya Mahaprabhu, we emphasize the name Krishna. This name is declared by Vedic authority to be the primal name of the Lord, the supreme Father of all living entities. We accept it as such. We have felt its transcendental potency act: the names of God, being nondifferent from God, bestow transcendental bliss. "If you chant offenselessly," Srila Prabhupada used to say, "you can have God dancing on your tongue." Therefore we invite the world to join us in chanting this supreme song of God, Hare Krishna.

In this, we are not at variance with the Judaeo-Christian tradition: "Our Father, who art in heaven, hallowed be Thy name." Nor are we violating the commandment, "Thou shalt not take the name of the Lord thy God in vain," for the sincere call of a devotee is not in vain, any more than the helpless call of a child for his mother. The name of God is hallowed, or honored, when it is chanted offenselessly with love and devotion. St. Paul also tells us, "Call upon the name of the Lord, and thou shall be saved." And the Psalmist exhorts, "From the rising of the sun unto the going down of the same, the Lord's name is to be praised."

Srila Prabhupada often referred to *Bhagavad-gita* as the most important scripture of all scriptures. Not that its essential message differs from other bona fide scriptures, but in it, we are introduced to the Supreme Personality of Godhead, and His devotee and friend, the valiant warrior Arjuna. "No other book is necessary," Srila Prabhupada used to say. "We need read nothing else." Of course, Srila Prabhupada himself presented other scriptures that more elaborately describe Lord Krishna's pastimes—nearly eighty volumes in all, including *Srimad-Bhagavatam*—but he always maintained that if we were ever stranded on that proverbial desert island, the one book to have would be *Bhagavad-gita*. "If we can just understand one chapter," he would say, "or just one verse, we will become fully Krishna conscious."

This present volume, *The Song of God*, is meant to serve as an introduction to Srila Prabhupada's *Bhagavad-gita As It Is*, though it is in no way to be taken as a substitute for that definitive work. Perhaps the reader may find it helpful to first read this summary study, and then turn to the corresponding chapter in Srila Prabhupada's book for further elucidation. This book arose out of a lecture series given in Bombay, India, during March, 1984. Some lectures were delivered at the homes of prominent Indian members of the International Society for Krishna Consciousness, and others at the famed Hare Krishna Mandir in

Juhu. Two months later, at New Vrindaban in America, the transcripts of the lectures were expanded into their present form. Throughout, I have tried to follow faithfully in Srila Prabhupada's footsteps, and if his voice can be heard in these pages, I consider the book successful. My only qualification is that I have tried to present his teachings without change. If one's personal opinions, or mental speculations, are inserted, the purity of the message is surely lost, and the whole endeavor becomes useless. Our greatest reward in devotional service is the satisfaction of assisting the *mahatmas*, great souls such as Srila Prabhupada, in broadcasting the glories of *Bhagavad-gita*.

I have also been assisted by many great souls, and I want to express my deepest gratitude for the tireless expert assistance of my editor and dear friend Sriman Hayagriva Das Adhikary, and to other faithful Krishna conscious friends, Umapati Das Adhikary and Hari Dhama Das Adhikary for proofreading, Nityodita Das for recording, and Sriman Nathaji Das (Dr. Narendra Desai of Bombay) for his generous financial assistance in publishing foreign language editions. All glories to Sri Sri Guru Gauranga!

Kirtanananda Swami Bhaktipada
New Vrindaban, July 24, 1984

The

SONG OF GOD

Arjuna said: O infallible one, please draw my chariot between the two armies so that I may see who is present here, who is desirous of fighting, and with whom I must contend in this great battle attempt. (*Bg.* 1.21-22)

CHAPTER ONE

Observing The Armies

The Sanskrit words *Bhagavad-gita* mean "Song of God," or, literally, "Song of the Opulent One." God is, of course, the supremely opulent one, because He possesses complete wealth, fame, beauty, knowledge, strength, and renunciation. *Bhagavad-gita* is a message spoken by the Almighty Lord for the enlightenment of His devotee, the valiant warrior Arjuna, and all mankind.

Some commentators try to reduce *Bhagavad-gita* to a mere allegory, wherein Arjuna represents the living being; the five Pandavas, the five senses; the material body, the battlefield; and Lord Krishna, the divine voice within each of us. Such comparisons may make interesting reading, but they obscure the real meaning. We must first accept *Bhagavad-gita* as it is: an actual conversation between the Supreme Personality of Godhead and His devotee on an actual battlefield, Kurukshetra, just north of modern New Delhi. Let us listen carefully to the words of that ancient dialogue, for they are vibrating eternally for our benefit.

As the First Chapter opens, King Dhritarastra asks the sage Sanjaya, "After assembling in the place of pilgrimage at Kurukshetra, what did my sons and the sons of Pandu do, being desirous to fight?" (1.1) This verse declares that there are two contending parties, the Pandavas and the Kurus, ready to fight at this holy place, where King Kuru had once performed great austerities. On the side of the Pandavas were Lord Krishna and His devotees, and on the other side were all the materialistic kings of the ancient world.

What took place five thousand years ago is taking place today, and each of us is faced with choosing sides. "Choose ye this day whom ye will serve," echoes across the sands of time. We may either choose to have Krishna, the transcendental Lord,

1

as our personal chariot driver, or choose to fight against Him by siding with the materialistic lords of this world. Being the Supreme Lord, Krishna is the loving Father who resides in everyone's heart. Moreover, He also appears externally, as the spiritual master, to give us directions. If we accept Him as the driver of our lives, the outcome of the battle is assured. "O son of Kunti," Krishna says, "declare it boldly that My devotee never perishes." (9.31)

Unfortunately, King Dhritarashtra was blind, physically and spiritually. His anxiety over the outcome of the battle is only another indication of his blindness. The outcome is certain, because the battle will be fought on the holy field of Kurukshetra under the direct supervision of the Supreme Personality of Godhead, Lord Sri Krishna, who is always accompanied by the Goddess of Fortune. By backing his nefarious sons, headed by Duryodhana, Dhritarashtra made Lord Krishna his enemy and thereby sealed his own doom.

Actually, Krishna is nobody's enemy. He is equally disposed to everyone. But if, by our envious attitude, we choose to make Him our enemy, He reciprocates. On the other hand, as soon as we become Krishna's devotees and sanctify our bodies by surrendering to Him, we receive His transcendental protection. "Just surrender to Me," Krishna says, "and I will give you all protection." (18.66)

Just as a modern general wants to assess the strength of the opposing army, Arjuna also wants to appraise his opposition. From the material point of view, the Kurus had a superior army. They had the best generals, the best strategists, the best weapons, the best of everything, but without Krishna, their assets were worth no more than a string of zeroes. All the zeroes in the world have no value, but if a one is placed before them, their value becomes immeasurable. Similarly, all our material assets are worthless zeroes without the Supreme One, Lord Krishna, without whom all material qualifications come to naught. The materialistic person does not know what is valuable and what is not, or what is powerful and what is not. He puts his trust in the temporary things of this world, not realizing that they are all fallible soldiers, unable to give him any ultimate protection.

Duryodhana was such a materialist, trying to evaluate every-thing according to his mundane vision. "Our strength is im-measurable, and we are perfectly protected by Grandfather Bhishma," he says, "whereas the strength of the Pandavas, care-fully protected by Bhima, is limited." (1.10) Trying to calculate everything by the tiny capabilities of a materialistic brain, Duryodhana counts his soldiers, evaluates his generals, and falsely concludes that his strength is immeasurable. Actually, the only immeasurable power on the battlefield was that of Lord Krishna, but because the Lord was driving Arjuna's chariot like an ordinary mortal, Duryodhana could not understand His su-preme power. "Fools deride Me when I descend in the human form," Lord Krishna says. "They do not know My transcendental nature and My supreme dominion over all that be." (9.11) This is the basic mistake of materialists. All of Krishna's energies are immeasurable and inconceivable. "With a single fragment of Myself, I pervade and support this entire universe," He declares. (10.42)

Unable to appreciate Lord Krishna's omnipotence, Duryodhana and his followers, the Kurus, had more faith in material things, in sense objects, specifically in an impressive display of troops and a noisy blowing of conch shells. Signific-antly, when the Kurus blew their conch shells, the sound is described as "tumultuous," indicating that it was loud and blar-ing, terrifying those subject to fear. "On the other side, the Lord Sri Krishna and Arjuna, stationed on a great chariot drawn by white horses, sounded their transcendental conch shells." (1.14) Note the difference: the conch shells of Lord Krishna and Arjuna are described as transcendental, for the paraphernalia of the Lord and His devotees is always on the transcendental platform. Devotees may appear to ride in the same kind of chariot or automobile, or use the same kind of weapon or typewriter, but whatever they touch becomes transcendental, because it is used in Krishna's service. When an iron rod is stuck into a fire, it becomes fiery. Similarly, although we are born into this material world, and although the body and its extensions appear material, as soon as we come in contact with Krishna—who is not in the least material, but always spiritual and transcendental—our lives become spiritual and transcendental. That is the secret of Krishna consciousness. Whatever we use for sense gratification is material and has all of the defects of material existence, but whatever we use for Krishna's service rises above all material qualities and becomes spiritual. The transcendental touch of the Lord makes the difference.

The effect of these transcendentalized objects is also different. "The blowing of these different conch shells became uproarious, and thus vibrating both in the sky and on the earth, it shattered the hearts of the sons of Dhritarashtra." (1.19) There is no mention that the sound of the Kurus' "tumultuous shells" shattered the hearts of the Pandavas. No. A devotee is fearless because he has Krishna at his side, but without God, our hearts are always full of fear. Consequently, the transcendental sound of that small band of devotees shattered the hearts of the enemy. Such is the nature of spiritual sound vibrations. We can shatter all of the forces of maya by the transcendental sound of the Hare Krishna mantra: Hare Krishna, Hare Krishna, Krishna Krishna, Hare Hare/ Hare Rama, Hare Rama, Rama Rama, Hare Hare. This is the sound coming from our transcendental conch shells today. It is so effective that we do not have to kill the demons physically; we can kill the demonic mentality by transcendental sound.

In the Fourth Chapter of *Bhagavad-gita*, the Lord says that He appears in every age "to deliver the pious and to annihilate the miscreants, as well as to reestablish the principles of religion." (4.8) In this present age, called Kali-yuga, the Lord has incarnated in the sounds of His holy names. This is the teaching of Lord Sri Chaitanya Mahaprabhu, who is Lord Krishna Himself come in the guise of a devotee to deliver this sublime message. All faithful servants of the Lord are enjoined to take this glorious sound to every nook and corner of the world. This is the only hope for peace and prosperity. The sound of the holy name is our only weapon, but it is quite sufficient. It is as powerful as the Lord Himself, and it is the authorized spiritual process for this age. We should not be fainthearted in the face of difficulties. By the order of guru and Krishna, anyone can distribute the blessing of this transcendental sound. The Lord can empower even the most insignificant person to act as powerfully as He Himself. That is Krishna's omnipotence. He can do anything.

Of course, Krishna bestows such potencies only on one who has pure love and faith, very rare qualities in this world. At the beginning of *Bhagavad-gita*, even the great Arjuna was not in that position, but by the instructions of Krishna, he became enlightened. At the start of the battle, he was acting like a conditioned soul. First, he asked Krishna, "Please draw my chariot between the two armies so that I may see who is present here, who is desirous of fighting, and with whom I must contend in this great battle attempt." (1.21-22) An eternal companion of Lord Krishna, Arjuna is certainly an eternally liberated soul, never subject to illusion. But because Lord Krishna desired to speak the transcendental knowledge of *Bhagavad-gita*, His eternal friend Arjuna played the part of an illusioned, conditioned soul. The Supreme Lord does not agree to speak to anyone and everyone. "That very ancient science of the relationship with the Supreme is today told by Me to you because you are My devotee as well as My friend; therefore you can understand the transcendental mystery of this science." (4.3) Unless we surrender to Krishna and become His devotee, Krishna will not speak to us, and even if He did, we could not understand Him. Krishna Himself says, "One can understand the Supreme Personality as He is only by devotional service." (11.54)

It was precisely because Arjuna had forgotten his constitutional position as servant of his Lord that he was in difficulty. When one forgets the transcendental position of Lord Sri Krishna, he is immediately covered by maya and subjected to illusion and distress. Arjuna was not content with the knowledge that Krishna, the Supreme Personality of Godhead, was his chariot driver and was fully protecting him. Consequently, he became like Duryodhana, an ordinary man who wants to calculate things by his own vision. This is natural for the conditioned soul. Therefore Arjuna wanted Krishna to drive his chariot to where he could see things for himself.

In truth, we cannot see anything by our own power. Even from the material point of view, our power of vision is never independent. It is said that we cannot see unless the sun sees first. Without light, what can we see? If the lights suddenly go off, we cannot see even our hand in front of our face. We are forced to admit that our vision is limited; unless we take help,

we cannot see. What, then, can we say of trying to see beyond
the range of the material senses? There is no use in trying to see
the spiritual realm with our present eyes. It is impossible. We
have to see through the eyes of scripture and the bona fide
spiritual master, who is called the transparent intermediary between man and God. We have to see by the teachings of the
genuine authority. This is the only way to see God.

Arjuna wanted to see for himself, but as soon as he tried,
he became bewildered. "Oh, how can I fight with my friends
and relatives? Even if I am victorious, how will I enjoy the fruits
of victory if my loved ones are slain?" Thus, due to the bodily
conception that shackles every conditioned soul, Arjuna began
to think like an ordinary man. Of course, everyone wants to live
in perpetual happiness with his family and friends, but since
the body itself is temporary, this desire is frustrated on the bodily
platform. By attempting to arrange our lives around the material
body, we become bewildered.

What causes such foolishness? Attachment for sense enjoyment. Due to this strong attachment, one loses all self-control.
"My whole body is trembling," Arjuna confesses, "and my hair
is standing on end. My bow Gandiva is slipping from my hand,
and my skin is burning." (1.29) When the power of discrimination
is lost, one gives up his divinely ordained duty. Since Arjuna
was a great warrior (kshatriya), it was his duty to protect the
weak and defenseless and to uphold the eternal principles of
religion. Deviation from such a duty is certainly a sign of weakness of heart, a result of the bodily conception of existence. At
this point, Arjuna is more concerned with his temporary blood
relationships than with his eternal spiritual connection with
Krishna. This is the greatest illusion. If one really loves his family
members and wants to serve them, he should know that real
service is on the spiritual platform. All other kinds of service
perish. Just as sticks floating on the river are carried by the
currents of the river—briefly meeting and then separating, never
to meet again—living beings also come together as father and
son, or brother and sister, and then in the course of time are
separated, never to meet again. Bhagavad-gita teaches transferral
of all affections to Krishna, who is everyone's eternal father,
friend, child, or lover. Whatever relationship we seek can be

found in Krishna—in perfection.

Still, Arjuna hesitates, saying, "Sin will overcome us if we slay such aggressors." (1.36) This means that he doesn't remember what sin really is. Krishna declares that those in the mode of ignorance do not know the difference between religion and irreligion, nor do they know what is to be done and what is not to be done. Arjuna didn't know that the real meaning of sin is disobedience to the orders of the Lord, the laws of God. The Supreme Personality of Godhead is seated before him telling him to fight, yet Arjuna thinks that fighting is sinful!

Arjuna is confusing religion with mundane morality, and this is a common mistake. Ethical codes and standards of behavior vary from country to country, and even from generation to generation. In India, it is considered immoral for a young girl to go out at night alone, but in the Western countries, this is allowed. In the Moslem countries, polygamy is allowed, but in many other countries, it is illegal. Social standards, or mundane morality, are always relative and never absolute, but the law of God is absolute, and sin, being a transgression of this law, is also absolute. Whatever God says is law, and His law is eternal. There can be no question of Krishna's being immoral; rather, Krishna sets the standard of morality. Being the source of all that exists, He is the Father of morality. No one is equal to Him, and no one is greater. That is the essence of all Vedic wisdom. As Krishna's friend, Arjuna should be aware of this, but due to family sentiment resulting from the bodily conception, he completely forgot himself.

Thus illusioned, Arjuna presents many other materialistic arguments to support his decision not to fight, saying, "With the destruction of dynasty, the eternal family tradition is vanquished, and thus the rest of the family becomes involved in irreligious practice. When irreligion is prominent in the family, O Krishna, the women of the family become corrupt, and from the degradation of womanhood comes unwanted progeny. When there is increase of unwanted population, a hellish situation is created both for the family and for those who destroy the family tradition. In such corrupt families, there is no offering of oblations of food and water to the ancestors. Due to the evil deeds of the destroyers of family tradition, all kinds of community projects and family welfare activities are devastated." (1.39-42)

These considerations are all top priorities for the materialist, who identifies himself with the temporary body, but for the spiritualist with transcendental vision, who realizes himself to be the eternal spirit soul temporarily within the body, they are insignificant. For such a realized person, even elevation to the topmost heavenly planet, Brahmaloka, is not very important. "From the highest planet in the material world down to the lowest," Krishna says, "all are places of misery wherein repeated birth and death take place." (8.16)

A devotee of the Lord does not care a fig for elevation to the heavenly planets, for he knows that he will have to come down again to earth. It is one of the universal laws: what goes up must come down. It may be today or tomorrow, or in a billion or trillion years, but eventually, everything that goes up, comes down. What is the use of working hard and piously for elevation to a heavenly planet, only to fall down again? However, when pious activities are performed for the satisfaction of the Lord, they are transformed into devotional service and are of eternal value. Krishna says: "O son of Kunti, all that you do, all that you eat, all that you offer and give away, as well as all austerities that you may perform, should be done as an offering unto Me." (9.27) In this way, everything becomes devotional and has permanent effect.

This is also the only intelligent welfare work. Devotional service is certainly superior to a temporary, stop-gap, do-good effort based on temporary values, an effort incapable of saving anyone from the ultimate danger—repetition of birth and death. It is not that Krishna's devotee deprecates morality or welfare work. On the contrary, a devotee is the most moral of moralists and the greatest of welfare workers. *Srimad-Bhagavatam* says that all the good qualities of the demigods develop automatically in the body of a devotee, without his extraneous endeavor. One can never become a pure devotee just by doing good works, however. There must be surrender to Krishna; then all good qualities manifest. A young girl should not expect a baby right after the wedding, but after serving her husband faithfully for some time, she may beget a child. Only a little faith in her husband and patience are required.

Similarly, we must have faith in Krishna, the all-knowing, all-powerful friend of every living being. Unfortunately, Arjuna has not yet realized this; therefore he continues to argue: "O Krishna, maintainer of the people, I have heard by disciplic succession that those who destroy family traditions dwell always in hell. Alas, how strange it is that we are preparing to commit greatly sinful acts, driven by the desire to enjoy royal happiness." (1.43-44)

Hearing by disciplic succession is certainly the way to real knowledge, but we have to be very careful to hear from the disciplic succession that comes from Lord Krishna, or God. It will not help us to hear from a disciplic succession based on mental speculation, family opinion, or mundane traditions. Although Krishna Himself was personally speaking to him, Arjuna was foolishly citing family tradition. How absurd! This is like holding up a candle to see the sun. There is no need of further light to see the powerful, self-luminous sun, nor is there a need to listen to anyone other than Lord Krishna or His bona fide representative. If one tries, he will be as bewildered as Arjuna "driven by the desire to enjoy royal happiness."

That's the real problem. Arjuna forgot that his only duty was to fulfill the desire of his transcendental friend, Sri Krishna; consequently, he was trapped by maya into thinking of royal happiness. Everyone has senses, but if these senses are not satisfied in the blissful service of the all merciful Lord, they will be compelled to engage themselves in the service of maya, or sense gratification. We are not dead stones. We cannot remain inactive, not even for a minute.

Everyone is seeking pleasure, but real pleasure can be experienced only on the spiritual platform. Arjuna was thinking in terms of royal happiness, but in truth there is no such thing. All mundane happiness is mixed with distress. Even a king is occasionally distressed, and is often in anxiety, thinking, "When will my enemy come to kill me?" In reality, everyone is in that position because material nature is going to kill us all. What is the possibility of happiness when we know that someone is coming to kill us? If we really want happiness for ourselves, our family, our society, or our friends, we must do something to stop the real miseries of life—birth, death, old age, and disease.

The only solution is to make Krishna happy. This should be our first consideration. If Krishna is satisfied, everyone is satisfied. Krishna is the root of existence, the cause of all causes, the alpha and omega. Srila Prabhupada used to say: "There is only one problem in the whole world—lack of Krishna consciousness." As soon as we say "consciousness," Krishna must be present, because God is the original source of all consciousness. Therefore, we are constitutionally meant to always think of Krishna favorably, with love and devotion.

Presently, we may not know how to think of Krishna favorably, but when the Lord sees that we sincerely want to know, He sends the bona fide spiritual master, His external manifestation, to show us the way. Therefore, thinking of the spiritual master's pleasure is as good as thinking of Krishna's. That is the verdict of Srila Vishvanatha Chakravarti Thakura, one of the great *acharyas* in Lord Chaitanya's line: "By the mercy of the spiritual master, one receives the benediction of Krishna. Without the grace of the spiritual master, one cannot make any advancement." And Lord Krishna says, "One who claims to be My devotee is not so. Only a person who becomes the devotee of My devotee is actually My devotee." (*Adi Purana*)

Thinking of the spiritual master's happiness is nondifferent from thinking of Krishna's because the spiritual master is the empowered representative of the Lord. God and guru may be compared to the two rails of a transcendental train track. A train cannot run on one rail. Guru and Krishna run side by side. Therefore we have to approach Krishna by means of His representative. The genuine spiritual master never claims to be God, but he is the most confidential servant of God. Together, guru and Krishna reveal the Supreme Absolute Truth.

We must surrender to Lord Krishna. This is the essential purport of this First Chapter. Arjuna had to surrender to Him by fighting, even though, because of material considerations, he thought it wrong to fight. In any case, fighting was necessary at Kurukshetra because the Supreme Lord Krishna had willed it. If we sincerely want to follow in the footsteps of Arjuna and achieve the same success in transcendental realization, we must also surrender to Krishna through His pure devotee. It is not important what we or others may think, or what we have imagined spiritual life to be. That is all mental speculation. The spiritual master is the representative of Krishna, and he alone can engage us in Krishna's loving devotional service, our only real duty.

From beginning to end, there is only one urgent message in *Bhagavad-gita*—surrender to Krishna. When Arjuna finally understood this, he said, "My dear Krishna, O infallible one, my illusion is now gone. I have regained my memory by Your mercy, and I am now firm and free from doubt and am prepared to act according to Your instruction." (18.73) As soon as we also realize this, our illusions will be dispelled, and we will see Krishna as He is. We will also see ourselves with Him as His eternal servants, His parts and parcels, eternal, full of knowledge and bliss. This is perfect self-realization. Hare Krishna!

As the embodied soul continually passes, in this body, from boyhood to youth to old age, the soul similarly passes into another body at death. The self-realized soul is not bewildered by such a change. *(Bg. 2.13)*

CHAPTER TWO

Contents of the Gita Summarized

Many Vedic literatures have been given to mankind for elevation to transcendental knowledge. Srila Vyasadeva, the incarnation of God especially empowered to transmit these literatures, divided the original single *Veda* into four. In addition, there are 108 *Upanishads*, eighteen *Puranas*, and also epics such as the *Ramayana* and the *Mahabharata*. Although it is but a small part of the *Mahabharata*, *Bhagavad-gita* contains the very essence of Vedic knowledge. It was spoken to deliver Arjuna from the illusion of maya, or ignorance, by which he misidentified himself with the material body and its extensions—family, society, and country. Under illusion, we too misidentify ourselves with the material body and its by-products.

In the Second Chapter, Lord Krishna assumes the position of Supreme Spiritual Master to dispel illusion and establish eternal truth. He tells His confused disciple, "My dear Arjuna, how have these impurities come upon you? They are not at all befitting a man who knows the progressive values of life. They do not lead to higher planets, but to infamy." (2.2)

Arjuna was supposed to be advanced in spiritual matters and know the progressive values of life. As a member of the royal *kshatriya* order, he should have known that he was not the material body. Arjuna, however, was speaking like an uncultured man, who identifies himself with the material covering. Therefore Lord Krishna asked, as if surprised, "How have these impurities come upon you?"

Because we are all originally pure living entities, this question is meant for everyone. The spirit soul is by nature pure, but presently, being attached to sense gratification, we identify ourselves with matter. Since Arjuna was also forgetting his

13

superior nature and misidentifying himself with gross matter, the Supreme Lord appeared surprised. Krishna has different energies: the material nature is His inferior energy; the spiritual nature, His superior energy; and living beings, His marginal energy. Constitutionally, living beings are infinitesimal portions of His superior energy, but because they have a tendency to become entangled in the inferior energy, or material nature, they are called marginal.

How has the superior energy become covered by the inferior? This is a great wonder that we can understand only by knowing that all of Krishna's energies are immeasurable and inconceivable. For us, even this inferior energy, material nature, is inconceivable. Therefore Krishna says, "This divine energy of Mine, consisting of the three modes of material nature, is difficult to overcome. But those who have surrendered unto Me can easily cross beyond it." (7.14)

These impurities of the modes of material nature are not at all beneficial for a Krishna conscious man, especially a twice-born man initiated by a bona fide spiritual master. Such initiation is a second birth, in which the spiritual master is considered to be the father, and Vedic knowledge the mother. After the second birth, the disciple is expected to give up the ways of a low-class man. Therefore in Krishna consciousness, there is no room for sinful activities, which exist on the gross bodily platform. The four pillars of sin are meat eating, illicit sex, intoxication, and gambling. If we want to be free from the illusion of matter, we have to keep strict guard against these causes of illusion.

Because Arjuna was playing the part of a conditioned soul, he displayed the symptoms of illusion, as evidenced here: "O Krishna, how can I counterattack, with arrows in battle, men like Bhishma and Drona, who are worthy of my worship? It is better to live in this world by begging than to live at the cost of the lives of great souls who are my teachers. Even though they are avaricious, they are nonetheless superiors. If they are killed, our spoils will be tainted with blood. Nor do we know which is better—conquering them, or being conquered by them. The sons of Dhritarashtra, whom if we killed we should not care to live, are now standing before us on this battlefield." (2.4-6)

This is the vision of a man overwhelmed by matter and

concerned only with what he can understand by physical perception. If a devotee wants to stay free from illusion, he must not let himself be controlled by the material senses; rather, he should accept guidance from the authorized sources— the spiritual master and the *Vedas*.

Transcendental knowledge descends through transcendental sound vibration. Those who actually hear from Krishna remain free from all material lamentation. Unfortunately, at this point, Arjuna was not listening to Krishna, but was looking about, trying to perceive duty and truth with his material senses. Therefore he was bewildered, as he admits: "Now I am confused about my duty and have lost all composure because of weakness. In this condition I am asking You to tell me clearly what is best for me. Now I am Your disciple, and a soul surrendered unto You. Please instruct me." (2.7)

Despite his confusion, Arjuna had the good intelligence to approach the real spiritual master and surrender unto Him. Today, we too are in a state of confusion because we cannot figure out the Absolute Truth by means of our material senses and our tiny brain power. We do not know who we are, why we are here, or where we are going, nor can we grasp the purpose of life. We remain perplexed, not knowing what is to be done or not to be done. This is bewilderment. In this condition, we should search out the Supreme Personality of Godhead, or His representative, the bona fide spiritual master, and surrender unto him, as Arjuna did. "Now I am confused," Arjuna admits. "I am asking You to tell me clearly what to do. I am Your disciple. Please instruct me."

This is the proper way to approach the spiritual master: with sincere inquiry and surrender. Why inquire, if we are not prepared to surrender? What is the use of making a show? Medicine is not effective left in the bottle. It must be taken. Similarly, we may hear transcendental instructions from Krishna or His representative, but they will not help us unless we follow them. True hearing, what Srila Prabhupada called "submissive aural reception," requires us to act according to what we hear. We listen carefully, then surrender to the instructions.

Krishna consciousness is a scientific process. First, we are attracted to it by meeting a bona fide spiritual master. After hearing from him, we must follow his instructions to cleanse all dirty things from our heart. If we do not follow his instructions, we cannot hope to cleanse our heart, nor become steady or fixed in Krishna consciousness, nor develop love of Krishna.

Interestingly enough, at this point in *Bhagavad-gita*, the sage Sanjaya states, "Krishna, smiling, in the midst of both the armies, spoke the following words to the grief-stricken Arjuna." (2.10) Krishna is situated in the midst of both armies. Since He always accompanies every living entity, He is available to both devotee and demon. At the battle of Kurukshetra, Krishna offered Himself to both sides, but the Kurus rejected Him. Only the Pandavas cared for Krishna, and only they were willing to listen to Him and follow His instructions. Consequently, they benefited. By listening to Krishna, they obtained everything auspicious, including the favor of the Goddess of Fortune, who eternally resides next to the Lord. Accompanying every one of us as the Supersoul within the heart, Krishna waits for us to turn our attention to Him so He can repeat what He told Arjuna five thousand years ago: "Surrender to Me only." This transcendental instruction is to be found in every chapter: "Surrender to Me, bow down to Me, become My devotee." By following this advice, we can have Krishna on our side.

Krishna is always smiling. Why? Because He is always in the transcendental position. "Fools deride Me when I descend in the human form. They do not know My transcendental nature and My supreme dominion over all that be." (9.11) Krishna is never subject to the modes of material nature. Even when He descends to the material world, He remains transcendental. Since He is not affected by anything material, He is never tainted by hankering or lamentation. This is one difference between Krishna and us. The conditioned living entity, although intrinsically spiritual, is affected by the modes of material nature. Therefore Arjuna was dejected, and Krishna was smiling. We also find that Krishna's representative, the bona fide spiritual master, is always smiling, for he is established in transcendental consciousness. Because he is always serving Krishna, he is not affected by material success or failure, and he is always able to give the same transcendental instructions that Lord Sri Krishna Himself gave on the battlefield of Kurukshetra.

Thus smiling, Lord Krishna spoke: "While speaking learned words, you are mourning for what is not worthy of grief. Those who are wise lament neither for the living nor the dead." (2.11) Because he is on the *brahma-bhuta* platform, a Krishna conscious person neither hankers nor laments. "One who is thus transcendentally situated at once realizes the Supreme Brahman. He never laments nor desires to have anything; he is equally disposed to every living entity. In that state he attains pure devotional service unto Me." (18.54) Knowing everyone to be spirit soul, he is joyful, and laments neither for the living nor the dead. Even if we lament from now until doomsday, we cannot prevent old age, disease, and death. Nor will it help to hanker for any other condition.

As soon as the living entity takes birth in this material world, he is forced to suffer or enjoy the results of his past activities. But whatever his condition, it is temporary. "O son of Kunti, the nonpermanent appearance of happiness and distress, and their disappearance in due course, are like the appearance and disappearance of winter and summer seasons. They arise from sense perception, O scion of Bharata, and one must learn to tolerate them without being disturbed." (2.14) In Krishna consciousness, one learns to tolerate all kinds of situations for Krishna's sake. Of course, the conditioned soul does not like to tolerate anything, for he is always thinking of sense gratification, but Krishna consciousness enables him to overcome this selfish mentality. Rupa Goswami says that if we don't give up unnecessary sense gratification, we cannot possibly become Krishna conscious. Therefore we have to learn to tolerate many things. In the beginning, this may be difficult, but we have to practice. Arjuna was reluctant to fight against his friends and relatives. He did not want to kill them, but Krishna said, "Tolerate it; just do it." This means following the instructions of the spiritual master, even if they are difficult, dangerous or seemingly unreasonable, because such tolerance brings us to the level of the pure spirit soul.

It is the soul that is eternal. Krishna says: "Never was there a time when I did not exist, nor you, nor all these kings; nor in the future shall any of us cease to be.... For the soul, there is never birth nor death. Nor, having once been, does he ever cease to be. He is unborn, eternal, ever-existing, undying and primeval. He is not slain when the body is slain.... As a person puts on new garments, giving up old ones, similarly, the soul accepts new material bodies, giving up the old and useless ones.... The soul can never be cut into pieces by any weapon, nor can he be burned by fire, nor moistened by water, nor withered by the wind.... It is said that the soul is invisible, inconceivable, immutable, and unchangeable. Knowing this, you should not grieve for the body." (2.12 ff.)

The soul, eternal, without beginning or end, cannot be affected by anything material; therefore one should not grieve for him. Interestingly, Krishna also concludes from this that we should not grieve for the material body either. Why? Because its existence is guaranteed impermanent, just as the soul's existence is guaranteed permanent. All material bodies are temporary. Why grieve for leaves that are destined to fall from the trees in autumn? Surely, in the springtime, new leaves will come. The body is always changing, just as the soul always remains as it is. The soul puts on new garments as they are needed, just as we change clothes every day. When the body becomes old and useless, the soul accepts a new material body. Why lament these inevitable changes?

Krishna then argues from another angle of vision: "If, however, you think that the soul is perpetually born and always dies, still you have no reason to lament." (2.26) The impersonalist Buddhists, as well as many modern so-called scientists, think that there is no soul and that with the dissolution of the body, consciousness ceases. That is, they consider consciousness just another stage of material evolution, arising from some combination of chemicals. For them, death ends everything. Extending their argument to its logical conclusion, Krishna says, "For one who has taken his birth, death is certain; and for one who is dead, birth is certain. Therefore, in the unavoidable discharge of your duty, you should not lament. All created beings are unmanifest in their beginning, manifest in their interim state, and unmanifest again when they are annihilated. So what need is there for lamentation?" (2.27-28)

That is, even if we think that there is no soul and that the person is born and dies, why lament? He exists for some time and then is gone. The body is only a pile of chemicals that are used and then thrown away. Why lament for chemicals? In modern warfare, millions of tons of chemicals are destroyed, but who laments the loss? Why, then, should we lament for the soul if it is material? Of course, Krishna does not accept this argument because he teaches that the soul is indestructible. "He who dwells in the body is eternal and can never be slain. Therefore you should not grieve for any creature." (2.30) Nonetheless, Krishna uses various atheistic arguments to substantiate His own statement that lamentation is unwise.

Krishna then argues from yet another viewpoint: "Considering your specific duty as a kshatriya, you should know that there is no better engagement for you than fighting on religious principles; and so there is no need for hesitation." (2.31) Here, Krishna explains that the warrior who fights on religious principles, for the right cause, is assured of success; either he wins and immediately gains the desired results, or he dies in battle and is at once promoted to the heavenly planets. Why, therefore, neglect one's duty? It is always auspicious to perform our duty, Krishna says, and inauspicious not to. "If you leave the battle," He cautions Arjuna, "people will always speak of your infamy, and for one who has been honored, dishonor is worse than death. The great generals who have highly esteemed your name and fame will think that you have left the battlefield out of fear only, and thus they will consider you a coward." (2.34-35)

We may think that this is a material consideration, but Krishna points out that even from the material viewpoint, we should perform our prescribed duty. Spiritual life is beneficial both materially and spiritually. Either Arjuna will be killed on the battlefield and attain the heavenly planets, or he will emerge victorious and enjoy an earthly kingdom. Therefore, Krishna urges him to get up and fight with determination: "Fight for the sake of fighting, without considering happiness or distress, loss or gain, victory or defeat, and by so doing, you will never incur sin." (2.38) After all material and spiritual considerations, this is Krishna's final conclusion: "Fight for the sake of fighting." We must transcend all considerations of happiness and distress, victory or defeat, loss or gain—everything—and just fight because Krishna wants us to. This is a call to transcendental con-

sciousness, the same basic message that runs throughout
Bhagavad-gita: "Surrender unto Me."

We must remember that the Supreme Personality of
Godhead is driving Arjuna's chariot, and, due only to ignorance,
Arjuna has forgotten the Lord's actual power and glory. Therefore, Krishna reminds him, "Fight for the sake of fighting. Fight
because I have asked you to." Surely there can be nothing inauspicious about that.

* * *

"Thus far I have declared to you the analytical knowledge
of sankhya philosophy. Now listen to the knowledge of yoga
whereby one works without fruitive result. O son of Pritha,
when you act by such intelligence, you can free yourself from
the bondage of works." (2.39)

Krishna now begins to explain the real science of yoga, the
linking with the Supreme. Every living entity in the material
world is bound by the shackles of his activities and has to suffer
or enjoy the reactions thereof. Due to his material desires, he
takes birth in the material world, where he tries to lord it over
the resources of material nature for sense enjoyment. He then
must take birth again to reap the results of his activities, auspicious or inauspicious. A person in Krishna consciousness, however, has nothing to do with either auspicious or inauspicious
work. This is what Krishna is explaining: the importance of work
without desire for fruitive result. This is what He calls knowledge
of yoga.

Yoga means yoking, or linking up, with the Supreme. It is
only because we have forgotten our eternal connection with the
Supreme that we think ourselves to be separate from Him, and
have therefore taken birth in this material world. We are all
eternally related to Krishna as His parts and parcels, but due to
the illusion of independence, we are acting without regard for
Krishna's desire. *Bhagavad-gita,* the science of *bhakti-yoga,* awakens us to our eternal, loving relationship with Krishna, the real
chariot driver of every living entity, who gives us perfect instructions on how to win the battle of life. He wants to take us across
the ocean of birth and death, back to His eternal abode, the

Kingdom of God, the realm of eternity, knowledge, and bliss.

To reassure Arjuna, Krishna next explains that in the attempt for Krishna consciousness, ultimate success is guaranteed. Success awaits us in our struggle to surrender to Krishna, but abandoning our desires for fruitive activity, we must work for Krishna's satisfaction. "In this endeavor, there is no loss or diminution, and a little advancement on this path can protect one from the most dangerous type of fear." (2.40) This wonderful verse assures the devotee of ultimate success. Even one percent advancement in Krishna consciousness is worth more than the whole world. Just working a little for Krishna is more auspicious than being a millionaire, or being the most beautiful or powerful person in the world. No material opulence can compare to the success of that one percent advancement, which can save us from the most dangerous type of fear—that is, falling again into a lower form of life wherein we can neither remember Krishna nor advance in Krishna consciousness. One may become the world's richest man, but since great riches are usually obtained illegally or immorally, one will have to suffer dreadful reactions. Similarly, those who have great bodily beauty usually become too attracted to bodily pleasures; thus they engage in illicit sex and have to suffer in the next life.

Any of the material opulences can entangle us more and more in the rising and descending cycle of birth and death. Therefore these opulences have to be directed toward Krishna. The humblest devotee sweeping the temple floor, or opening the door for devotees, or carrying some water for the Deity, is far superior to a materialistic king, president, or prime minister.

Krishna next declares: "Those who are on this path are resolute in purpose, and their aim is one. O Arjuna, the intelligence of those who are irresolute is many-branched." (2.41) This can be seen every day. Materialists can never be resolutely determined for anything, and their intelligence is many-branched because their aim in life is sense gratification. By nature, a person engaged in sense gratification is never satisfied. People gratify their senses one day, but a few days later they look for some new sense object to enjoy. Due to its restless nature, the mind runs here and there after the flickering pleasures of the senses. First, the mind tells us that we want something, then says, "No, this. Then, "No, that." Accepting and rejecting. In this way, the soul is dragged all over the material creation by the senses and their various objects, wandering here and there, trying to find happiness, ignoring the fact that death may come at any moment.

A person in Krishna consciousness, however, is called "fixed." His intelligence is steady, and he is resolute in purpose. Why? Because he is firm in his conviction that Krishna is the Supreme Personality of Godhead, the Supreme Enjoyer and the Proprietor of everything. He therefore tries to satisfy Krishna instead of his own insatiable senses. But Krishna is satisfied by only one thing—pure devotional service. Therefore a pure devotee of the Lord is single-minded, fixed in consciousness, and always satisfied. Transcendentally established, he can pass through the material world without becoming entangled in the various snares of maya, illusion.

Even if someone becomes a great Sanskrit scholar and studies the *Vedas* for many years, there is no certainty of his crossing the ocean of material existence. Krishna says, "Men of small knowledge are very attached to the flowery words of the *Vedas*, which recommend various fruitive activities for elevation to heavenly planets, resultant good birth, power, and so forth. Being desirous of sense gratification and opulent life, they say that there is nothing more than this." (2.42-43) Such people are involved in the ferris-wheel process, sometimes going up and sometimes coming down. Since their aim is sense gratification, they perform various auspicious activities, but they may, in the very process, make an inauspicious mistake. King Nrga, for example, was most charitable, giving thousands of cows, fully decorated with gold and silver ornaments, to qualified *brahmanas*. He also donated land, houses, jewels, grains, and many other costly items. Unfortunately, when one of the cows he had given away wandered back into his own herd, he unknowingly gave it to a second *brahmana*, thus committing an offense against the first *brahmana* by giving away his property. Consequently, according to the laws of *karma-kanda*, or fruitive activity, he was forced to accept the body of a lizard. Of course, by the grace of Lord Krishna, he was saved, but this incident shows that the path of fruitive activity is always dangerous, and therefore inauspicious.

Indeed, in all fruitive activities, there is danger at every step, but a devotee fixed in Krishna consciousness does not have to run such risks. As Lord Krishna explains: "All purposes that are served by the small pond can at once be served by the great reservoirs of water. Similarly, all the purposes of the *Vedas* can be served to one who knows the purpose behind them." (2.46) Later, Krishna says, "By all the *Vedas* am I to be known; indeed, I am the compiler of *Vedanta,* and I am the knower of the *Vedas.*" (15.15) Again: "Whoever knows Me as the Supreme Personality of Godhead, without doubting, is to be understood as the knower of everything." (15.19)

Having established knowledge of Himself as the ultimate goal of life, Krishna wants to show how we can realize this knowledge by applying it in our daily lives. "You have a right to perform your prescribed duty, but you are not entitled to the fruits of action. Never consider yourself to be the cause of the results of your activities, and never be attached to not doing your duty." (2.47) There are three kinds of activity: *karma,* or work that leads the soul upward; *vikarma,* which leads the soul downward; and *akarma,* which, having no material reaction, leads the soul to liberation from the cycle of birth and death. In the Vedic literatures, there are many prescriptions for activities that bring good results, and there are also many prohibitions against activities that bring inauspicious results, but neither of these can help one attain transcendental consciousness. Lord Krishna therefore advises Arjuna to make all of his actions akarmic; only then can he become free from the binding reactions of work. How can this be done? "Surrender the results to Me."

In pure Krishna consciousness, we can understand that only Krishna is the actual doer of all activities. Seeing this, we desire to act as His instrument only, and abandon forbidden or offensive activity. As soon as we think, "I am the doer," we are in illusion. Krishna, as the controller of material nature, is the real doer. "The bewildered spirit soul, under the influence of the three modes of material nature, thinks himself to be the doer of activities, which are in actuality carried out by nature." (3.27)

One who considers himself the doer is a madman, and he has to suffer in his ignorance. Misusing his minute independence by trying independently to enjoy the results of his actions, he verily reaps the results, both good and bad, and is reborn into this material world. Only by surrendering to Krishna can we become free from the bondage of work and repetition of birth and death. Therefore Krishna advises His disciple to be steadfast in yoga. "Perform your duty and abandon all attachment to success or failure. Such evenness of mind is called yoga." (2.48) Whereas a materialist works only for some reward, a yogi works without any desire for fruitive results. If a boss were to ask his employees to work for a week without pay, they would not agree. Every *karmi* (materialist) is working for some result. But if a devotee is asked to work for Krishna without reward, he will certainly do so. That is the difference between a yogi and a materialist. Sometimes we see that a neophyte devotee will err in this way, thinking, "I need a vacation," or, "This is my day off." This means that he is confusing devotional service with work. In pure Krishna consciousness, there are no vacations. Why? Because a devotee does not work.

Prabhupada used to say that in Krishna consciousness, there is no hard labor; there is only singing, feasting, and dancing. Whatever we eat is nectarean because it has been first tasted by Lord Krishna. Even fasting for Krishna is feasting for the devotee. Furthermore, the devotee is always engaged in singing the holy names of the Lord, Hare Krishna, the song of all songs. In this way, the devotee performs perfect yoga and always enjoys transcendental bliss. Therefore he never looks for remuneration for his endeavors. Of course, it takes a little intelligence to come to this platform.

Krishna then says: "The wise, engaged in devotional service, take refuge in the Lord, and free themselves from the cycle of birth and death by renouncing the fruits of action in the material world. In this way they can attain that state beyond all miseries." (2.51) We should not be foolish misers, hoarding material goods for sense gratification, nor, like animals, be content just to eat, sleep, defend, and mate. We must become thoughtful, and awaken to spiritual life by working in the spirit of renunciation.

Being a practical man, Arjuna asks Lord Krishna how it is possible to recognize a spiritualist. "What are the symptoms of one whose consciousness is thus merged in Transcendence? How does he speak, and what is his language? How does he sit, and how does he walk?" (2.54) Lord Krishna replies: "When a man gives up all varieties of sense desire arising from mental concoction, and when his mind finds satisfaction in the self alone, then he is said to be in pure transcendental consciousness." (2.55)

Lord Krishna then goes further to explain that the real essence of transcendental consciousness is manifest as freedom from the desire for sense enjoyment. Thus we return to the major theme of this chapter: We are not these bodies. Due to the desire for sense gratification, we mistakenly think, "I am this body, and these things are mine." This misconception is called maya, or illusion. Without being free from the desire for sense enjoyment, one cannot be in transcendental consciousness. He will certainly be agitated by the modes of material nature, and act under delusion caused by the bodily conception.

Freedom from the desires of the senses is attained in two stages. Krishna says, "The embodied soul may be restricted from sense enjoyment, though the taste for sense objects remains. But, ceasing such engagements by experiencing a higher taste, he is fixed in consciousness." (2.59) The neophyte devotee still has a taste for sense gratification, but by following the regulative principles given by the spiritual master, he engages in devotional service and avoids unnecessary or prohibited sense indulgence. In our Society for Krishna Consciousness, there are four main prohibitions: no meat eating, no illicit sex, no intoxication, and no gambling. There is also a positive injunction: remember Krishna always by chanting His holy names, at least sixteen rounds a day. When a devotee follows these principles, his heart becomes purified, and he gradually acquires the higher taste of spontaneous, loving attraction to the devotional service of the Lord.

Srila Prabhupada has explained that in the beginning, a disciple rises early in the morning and attends mangal-aratik only because he has been requested to do so by the spiritual master. After practicing this for some time, however, he automatically wakes up early in the morning and eagerly comes to the temple to see the Lord, bathe Him and dress His transcendental form, and render Him all kinds of service. This is a higher taste. In this state, the devotee becomes fixed in consciousness and freed from the endless waves of material desire.

Lord Krishna reminds Arjuna, however, that the senses are strong and difficult to control, and unless one is sincere and attentive, there is always the chance of a falldown. The only remedy is to think of Krishna always and act only for Him. Problems arise when our senses are not serving Krishna, for at such times the senses seek their own satisfaction. An idle mind is the devil's workshop, but senses engaged in service to the Master of the senses, Hrishikesha, are perfectly satisfied.

Lord Krishna explains how such falldowns come about: "While contemplating the objects of the senses, a person develops attachment for them, and from such attachment lust develops, and from lust anger arises. From anger, delusion arises, and from delusion, bewilderment of memory. When memory is bewildered, intelligence is lost, and when intelligence is lost, one falls down again into the material pool." (2.62-63) We should notice here that the whole descent begins with contemplation of sense objects. It is at this initial stage that a devotee has to pull himself back. As soon as we find ourselves contemplating the objects of the senses, we must use our intelligence to halt the process before attachment develops, because as soon as attachment arises, lust follows. Then it becomes most difficult to withdraw the mind.

We should therefore curb this process in the beginning by using our intelligence and power of discrimination. "Should I do this, or should I not?" We can use our intelligence to discriminate between what is favorable for remembering Krishna, and what is not. The guideline is the order of the spiritual master. "I won't do this because it's against the order of my spiritual master." As long as the intelligence discriminates, we have full liberty, full independence. We can bring ourselves back, or let ourselves go to hell. From the very beginning, there is freedom to decide: "No, I don't want to do this. I don't want to disobey my spiritual master. I don't want to become forgetful of Krishna. Let me engage in Krishna consciousness." If we make this intelligent decision, we can escape the whirlpool that leads to the degradation of the soul. "One who can control his senses by practicing the regulative principles of freedom can obtain the complete mercy of the Lord and thus become free from all attachment and aversion," Krishna says. (2.64)

The dualities of attachment and aversion, accepting and rejecting, and hankering and lamentation, are characteristic of material life. It is just like a football field where the conditioned living entity is kicked back and forth. Although we are constitutionally pure spirit soul, we are being kicked from one species to another due to our hankering and lamentation. Sometimes we go to a higher planet, sometimes to a lower. As long as we don't surrender to Krishna, the kicking process goes on.

The regulative principles lead to real freedom, which is realized in Krishna consciousness, not forgetfulness; in sense control, not indulgence; in liberation from material bondage, not in going down to hell. A sense indulger cannot understand this, for he equates freedom with doing whatever he wants, regardless of the consequences. Thus he engages in prohibited activities like illicit sex, intoxication, meat eating, and gambling. This is not freedom, but bondage. The more one breaks the laws of God, the more he becomes bound up by the laws of material nature. If we really want to become free, we have to follow the regulative principles of freedom, for through them, we become masters of our senses. When the senses are controlled, we can understand our actual nature, distinct from the body. When we understand that we are not the body, we realize that we are spirit soul, part and parcel of Krishna, and attain liberation. Thus, by following the regulative principles of freedom, we obtain the mercy of the Lord.

This divine mercy is indeed the birthright of all living beings, but due to ignorance, we fail to recognize it. Krishna describes the real position of freedom thus: "For one who is so situated in the Divine consciousness, the threefold miseries of material existence exist no longer; in such a happy state, one's intelligence soon becomes steady." (2.65)

Every living being in the material world is conditioned by the three modes of material nature and therefore suffers the threefold miseries: miseries arising from the body and mind; miseries inflicted by other living entities; and miseries inflicted by higher powers. These three miseries are symbolized by the prongs of the trident of Goddess Durga, material nature personified, who rides a tiger and presses her trident against the breast of the conditioned soul. It is not that Mother Durga is mean or sadistic. She is acting for our ultimate welfare. For instance, the pain we receive from the burning of fire is actually meant to protect the body from greater harm. If burning were not painful, a child might keep his hand in a fire and be consumed. The burning sensation is meant for our protection, to signal the brain that something is wrong, that the hand is in the wrong place. Similarly, the miseries of material existence are meant to convince the living entity that he is in the wrong place.

Since we are not meant for this material atmosphere, we can never be happy here, any more than a fish on land. A fish may be put in a palace, dressed in silks and given a golden crown, but the fish cannot be happy out of water. Nor can the eternal spirit soul be happy within matter, not even with the greatest riches. Regardless of the amount of sense gratification we acquire, we cannot be truly happy in material life because we are constitutionally spirit souls. We can be happy only in our element, at home in the eternal spiritual region of the kingdom of God. Therefore, only by surrendering to Krishna and accepting shelter at His lotus feet, through the medium of pure devotional service, can we be freed from the miseries of life.

Fortunately, those who engage in devotional service cease to be within the jurisdiction of the material world. Prabhupada used to say that his temples exist in Vaikuntha. This is a fact. Although they appear to be in this material world, they are not. Krishna has kindly transformed matter into spirit. As controller of all His energies, Lord Krishna has the power to turn matter into spirit, or spirit into matter, at His will. Simply by His will, a devotee engaged in Krishna consciousness, or devotional service, is liberated. He is already in the spiritual world of Vaikuntha, for he has attained the supreme spiritual peace.

Peace is much talked about, but it is not common or cheap. Lord Krishna concludes this chapter, the summary of *Bhagavadgita*, by giving the formula for attaining peace: "A person who has given up all desires for sense gratification, who lives free from desires, who has given up all sense of proprietorship and is devoid of false ego—he alone can attain real peace." (2.71)

This is the true path to peace. Before there can be peace externally, there first must be peace in our hearts and minds. As long as the desire for sense gratification is not subdued, there can be no peace within the heart, nor anywhere on earth, nor can there be good will among nations. World leaders may hold international peace conferences, but if they sincerely want peace, they must accept Lord Krishna's formula: control of the senses.

Of course, we cannot give up the desire for sense gratification artificially, but by dovetailing our senses in the service of the Master of the senses, Lord Krishna, we can feel transcendentally satisfied. By engaging our senses in Krishna conscious activities—such as eating spiritual food offered to the Lord with love and devotion, singing the most wonderful song of songs, Hare Krishna, the songs of the holy names, and hearing of the Lord's uncommon, wonderful activities—we become liberated from the desire for sense gratification. When a man fills his stomach, he automatically loses his hunger. Similarly, as soon as we render transcendental loving service to the Lord, we automatically satisfy our senses. In this way, we can attain peace and Krishna consciousness, make our lives perfect, and go back home, back to Godhead.

Arjuna said: O Janardana, O Keshava, why do You urge me to engage in this ghastly warfare, if You think that intelligence is better than fruitive work? My intelligence is bewildered by Your equivocal instructions. Therefore, please tell me decisively what is most beneficial for me. *(Bg. 2.1-2)*

CHAPTER THREE

Karma-yoga

Although Lord Krishna spoke *Bhagavad-gita* five thousand
years ago to His intimate friend and disciple Arjuna, we
can now understand that Arjuna was representing all
men in all countries and for all times. For the sake of Krishna's
speaking *Bhagavad-gita*, Arjuna became bewildered and illusioned by the bodily conception. Under this misconception,
driven by the desire for sense gratification, beginning with his
own body and then expanding to his bodily extensions in the
form of family, society, and country, Arjuna declined to fight.
But when he was enlightened by Lord Sri Krishna, that same
reluctant Arjuna became the Lord's most valiant warrior.

At the beginning of this Third Chapter, we find Arjuna still
indecisive. He can understand that Lord Krishna wants him to
fight, but he cannot comprehend how this fighting can have
auspicious results. In other words, he is still thinking in terms
of his own desires. *Bhagavad-gita* stresses that we have to relin-
quish all thoughts of personal sense gratification and think only
of what Krishna wants. Arjuna will understand this at the end
of *Bhagavad-gita* when he agrees to fight on behalf of Lord
Krishna. At the beginning of this chapter, however, he is still
confused. "O Janardana, O Keshava," he says, "if You think
that intelligence is better than fruitive work, why do You encourage me to engage in this ghastly warfare? My intelligence is
bewildered by Your equivocal instructions; therefore please tell
me decisively what is most beneficial for me." (3.1-2)

As long as there are questions or doubts, it is the duty of
the disciple to consult the bona fide spiritual master, the representative of Lord Krishna. Krishna, or His representative, is
expert in killing the demons of doubt. When Krishna was personally present five thousand years ago, He killed many demons.

31

Indeed, this is one of the main reasons He comes to earth. Doubts are compared to demons because they try to destroy our Krishna consciousness. Both demons and doubts are opposed to the supremacy of God. Everyone is attacked by the demons of doubt, but if we present these doubts to the spiritual master for their removal, we are sure to be victorious. When Arjuna presented his doubts to Lord Krishna, the Lord swiftly killed them.

Arjuna thought to avoid the inauspicious or sinful results of the war by becoming inactive; therefore he proposed going to the forest to retire from life. Explaining that no one can become inactive, the Lord does not approve of this. "All men are forced to act helplessly according to the impulses born of the modes of material nature; therefore no one can refrain from doing something, not even for a moment. One who restrains the senses and organs of action, but whose mind dwells on sense objects, certainly deludes himself and is called a pretender. On the other hand, he who controls the senses by the mind and engages his active organs in works of devotion, without attachment, is by far superior. Perform your prescribed duty, for action is better than inaction. A man cannot even maintain his physical body without work." (3.5-8)

By the same argument, Lord Krishna also refutes modern so-called philosophers and Mayavadis (impersonalists), who think that the best path is that of merging into the impersonal Brahman and becoming void, or zero. But since the soul is by nature active, it can never become inert. Anyone can easily perceive the active nature of the soul: matter, which is intrinsically dead, or inactive, moves and shows signs of life only when the soul is present within it.

Considering that the soul is so active that it can even animate dead matter, we should understand how energetic the soul must be when free from this material encumbrance. Since the liberated state *(brahma-bhuta)* is our true, active nature, Krishna says that we should abandon the vain attempt to become inactive or void. Instead, it behooves us to engage in activities of Krishna consciousness, in works of devotion.

According to the science of Krishna consciousness, inactivity—even if possible—could never truly satisfy us, for what we really want is eternal enjoyment and pleasure. It is our nature to have enjoyment, but no one can enjoy himself alone. We can, however, enjoy ourselves by serving Krishna, for in that service we find our real pleasure. Therefore Krishna instructs His dear friend Arjuna in this science of devotional service, frankly telling him to work on behalf of the Supreme. Arjuna should fight for Krishna's sake, not for his own sense gratification. As soon as we try to serve our own senses, we become entangled in the actions and reactions of material nature and have to suffer, but when we act only for the satisfaction of Krishna, we are freed from all such entanglements.

This Third Chapter deals with *karma-yoga* , or work that transcends merely doing one's duty for family, friends, society, and country. Herein, Krishna explains exactly what is meant by *karma-yoga:* sacrifice for the satisfaction of the Supreme Lord. "Work done as a sacrifice for Vishnu [Krishna] has to be performed, otherwise work binds one to this material world. Therefore perform your prescribed duties for His satisfaction, and in that way you will always remain unattached and free from bondage. In the beginning of creation, the Lord of all creatures sent forth generations of men and demigods, along with sacrifices for Vishnu, and blessed them by saying, 'Be thou happy by this *yajna* [sacrifice], because its performance will bestow upon you all desirable things.'" (3.9-10) We may work very hard as good businessmen or family men, but this will not prevent us from becoming entangled in the cycle of repeated birth and death. It is only by performing our duties for the satisfaction of Krishna that we can be relieved from this bondage.

We can still perform our duties toward our family, society, business, or whatever, and satisfy Krishna by working under His direction. On the battlefield of Kurukshetra, Arjuna was being personally directed by Krishna. Even his chariot was being driven by the Lord. Similarly, we have to accept the direction of Krishna through His representative, the bona fide spiritual master. Krishna very clearly says: "Just try to learn the truth by approaching a spiritual master. Inquire from him submissively and render service unto him. The self-realized soul can impart knowledge unto you because he has seen the truth." (4.34)

When we approach the spiritual master, we must carefully follow his instructions in order to learn the science of Krishna consciousness. Since working for the satisfaction of anyone means knowing what is desired, we have to know Krishna's will before we can please Him. Being the representative of Krishna, the spiritual master can teach us what Krishna's desire is.

Those who work only for their own satisfaction become bound by the actions and reactions of matter. Krishna therefore speaks of the Vedic process of sacrifice, which is meant to please the demigods, who, under His guidance, supply all necessities to man. Those who don't offer due sacrifices certainly become entangled because, like thieves, they take what is not theirs. In this present age, the sacrifice recommended by Lord Sri Chaitanya Mahaprabhu is *Hari Nama Sankirtan*, the chanting of the holy names of God. *Harer nama, harer nama, harer nama eva kevalam, kalau nastyeva, nastyeva, nastyeva gatir anyatha.* Here, the *Brihad Naradiya Purana* repeats three times for emphasis: "Chant the holy name, chant the holy name, chant the holy name. There is no other way, no other way, no other way to deliverance in Kali-yuga." In other words, the only sacrifice recommended for this age is the chanting of the holy names of the Lord. This one act satisfies everyone because it satisfies Lord Krishna. It is also clearly stated in *Srimad-Bhagavatam* that if Krishna is satisfied, all other personalities—including family members, fellow countrymen, demigods, and sages—are also satisfied, because Krishna is the root of all existence. When we satisfy the root, we satisfy everything. A tree is not satisfied by water sprinkled on the leaves, but when the root is watered, then the entire tree—leaves, twigs, and branches—is satisfied and nourished. When we offer sacrifice for Krishna's satisfaction by chanting His holy names, all obligations are fulfilled automatically and perfectly.

Lord Krishna stresses the spiritual value of sacrifice by citing an historical example: "Even kings like Janaka and others attained the perfectional stage by performance of prescribed duties. Therefore, just for the sake of educating the people in general, you should perform your work. Whatever action is performed by a great man, common men follow in his footsteps. And whatever standards he sets by exemplary acts, all the world pursues." (3.20-21) Even Krishna Himself follows this dictum: "There is no work prescribed for Me within all the three planetary systems.

Nor am I in want of anything, nor have I need to obtain any-thing—and yet I am engaged in work. For, if I did not engage in work, certainly all men would follow My path. If I should cease to work, then all these worlds would be put to ruination. I would also be the cause of creating unwanted population, and I would thereby destroy the peace of all beings." (3.22-24)

Krishna emphasizes here that everyone has some responsi-bility, both to himself and to others. If we want to solve life's problems, either individually or collectively, we have to follow in the footsteps of great authorities such as Lord Krishna or Srila Prabhupada. And if we really want to help others, we also have to become worthy leaders, that is, *acharyas*, teachers by example. There is no point in telling others to do one thing while we do another. It is said, "Your actions speak so loudly that I can't hear what you're saying." One cannot preach honestly if he himself is dishonest. No one can convince others to chant Hare Krishna if he himself doesn't chant. To become real *acharyas*, we have to follow in the disciplic succession from the previous *acharya*. This is the bona fide process for receiving and imparting transcendental knowledge. Therefore Lord Krishna says, "As the ancients did, you should also do."

Krishna originally spoke this science of self-realization (*Bhagavad-gita*) to the sun god Vivasvan, and Vivasvan spoke it to his son Manu, who spoke it to his son Ikshvaku. This is the proper way transcendental knowledge is imparted and received. Such knowledge is never a matter of mental speculation or whim-sical, philosophical concoction. *Srimad-Bhagavatam* tells us that at the beginning of creation, the Lord spoke Vedic knowledge to the first created living being, Brahma, from within Brahma's heart (*tene brahma hrda*).Then Brahma spoke it to his son Narada, who spoke it to Vyasadeva. This is the same process of transmis-sion. We have to hear from a bona fide authority in the disciplic succession from the Lord. But we should not just let the message go in one ear and out the other. This is not proper hearing. We must hear, understand, and respond. Srila Prabhupada called this "submissive aural reception." We must hear from the au-thoritative representatives of Lord Krishna, who are versed in Krishna consciousness, and we must be prepared to follow their instructions.

Krishna's ultimate instruction, and that of all bona fide suc-
cessors, is to surrender unto Him only. From beginning to end,
Bhagavad-gita teaches the renunciation of our own limited desire
and acceptance of the perfect desire of Krishna. In the beginning,
Arjuna declines to fight, and at the end, he agrees to fight according to Krishna's order. Every conditioned soul is born into this
material world due to his desire to enjoy separately from Krishna,
but this human form gives us a chance to come to full Krishna
consciousness by understanding that Krishna is our best friend
and perfect master. He is the perfect Lord, the knower of everything. Since He is our eternal well-wisher, we should surrender
to Him. Then He will guide us back home, back to Godhead.

Naturally, we may ask, "If Krishna is so good, kind, and
wonderful, why doesn't everyone surrender to Him?" Lord
Krishna answers: "The bewildered spirit soul, under the influence of the three modes of material nature, thinks himself to be
the doer of activities, which are in actuality carried out by nature." (3.27) Of course, Lord Krishna is the controller and proprietor of material nature, as He Himself says: "This material
nature works under My direction." (9.10) A shadow works under
the direction of the hand; whichever way the hand moves, the
shadow moves. Material nature functions in the same way under
Krishna's direction, but the bewildered spirit soul cannot understand this until he surrenders to Krishna. As soon as we want
to enjoy ourselves separate from Krishna, we become bewildered
by the material modes. Factually, nothing can be separate from
Krishna, for Krishna is the cause of all causes and all that is. In
truth, we are part and parcel of Krishna, but when we want to
enjoy independently, we forget this truth. Our real nature, as
spirit soul, is *sat-cit-ananda*—eternal, full of knowledge and
bliss—but due to our desire for sense gratification, we accept
the material covering as real. This leads to forgetfulness and
bewilderment by the three modes of nature.

"But one who is in knowledge of the Absolute Truth,"
Krishna says, "does not engage himself in the senses and sense
gratification, knowing well the differences between work in devotion and work for fruitive results." (3.28) Work in devotion is
devoid of desire for separate enjoyment; such work must be
unmotivated and uninterrupted. *Srimad-Bhagavatam* defines

the devotional standard: "Pure devotional service to the Lord must be unmotivated and uninterrupted in order to completely satisfy the self." (1.2.6) Clearly, work in devotion is very different from work for fruitive results. Devotional work is performed out of love, not for money to spend on sense gratification. Actual devotional service is work without expectations or pay checks. It is performed in a spirit of loving sacrifice.

When we come to understand the real meaning of Krishna consciousness and the transcendental nature of Lord Krishna, we become attracted to Krishna only and want nothing else, neither material benedictions, mystic powers, nor supermundane knowledge. The perfect examples of pure devotional attraction to Krishna are the *gopis* of Vrindaban. For Krishna, they were willing to abandon their families, society, and life itself. Since everything they did was for His satisfaction, they are considered the topmost devotees. What Krishna evoked from the *gopis* and what He demands from everyone is always the same: "Surrender unto Me."

"Therefore, O Arjuna, surrendering all your works unto Me, with mind intent on Me, and without desire for gain, and free from egoism and lethargy, fight." (3.30)

By inviting Arjuna to fight on His behalf, Krishna points the way to freedom from all material entanglement. As mentioned before, we are generally entangled in either auspicious or inauspicious activities and their results. Even if we are awarded birth in a heavenly planet, we have to return to earth and take birth again, perhaps in a degraded position. So, reaping the results of pious activities is not really a solution. Krishna clearly explains that all material planets, from the highest to the lowest, are places of misery where repeated birth and death take place. Whether we are sent to the highest heaven by our pious activities, or to hell by our impious activities, we are forced to take birth again and again. Only by surrendering to Krishna and acting for Him can we be freed from all this.

Krishna consciousness is very simple. If we surrender, we get one result, and if we don't, we get another. Krishna says, "One who executes his duties according to My injunctions, and who follows this teaching faithfully, without envy, becomes free from the bondage of fruitive actions. But those who, out of envy, disregard these teachings and do not practice them regularly, are to be considered bereft of all knowledge, befooled, and doomed to ignorance and bondage." (3.31-32)

Foolish people maintain that anyone can do whatever he likes, because at the end of this life, the body and everything else is finished. Or, they maintain that both pious and impious activities are equal, because at death everyone merges into the impersonal Brahman. But Krishna doesn't say this. Rather, He explicitly states that we reap the fruits of this life's actions in the next life. Every bona fide scripture teaches this basic law of karma: "What a man sows, that shall he also reap."

Krishna further explains that our mental attitude at the end of life determines our next birth. "Those who worship the demigods will take birth among the demigods; those who worship ghosts and spirits will take birth among such beings; those who worship ancestors go to the ancestors; and those who worship Me will live with Me." (9.25) The results are clearly not the same. Everything is not "all one." An intelligent man concerned about his future must surrender to Krishna. From the mundane point of view, this may seem dogmatic, arbitrary, unfair, or whatever, but once we understand our constitutional position as Krishna's eternal servants, we will acknowledge this as the only auspicious and intelligent course of action.

Next, Arjuna logically inquires why everyone doesn't resist sin and surrender to God. He asks, "By what is one impelled to sinful acts, even unwillingly, as if engaged by force?" (3.36) Why do we act contrary to our own interest and intelligence? Why don't we all become Krishna conscious and chant Hare Krishna?

Lord Krishna answers: "It is lust only, Arjuna, which is born of contact with the material modes of passion and later transformed into wrath, and which is the all-devouring, sinful enemy of this world." (3.37) In the remaining verses, Lord Krishna describes this lust in more detail: "Thus, a man's pure consciousness is covered by his eternal enemy in the form of lust, which is never satisfied and which burns like fire." (3.39) This is everyone's experience. Regardless of how much of anything we get, we always want more: more and more sex, more and more money, food, intoxication, or whatever. We can never be satisfied by sense gratification; rather, the senses become enraged, like a roaring fire on which we pour gasoline. By trying to satisfy our desires, we make them all the more voracious. They then entrap us more and more in material bondage, causing us to forget our real spiritual nature.

Since every warrior should know the location of his enemy, Lord Krishna tells Arjuna where this lust is situated. "The senses, the mind, and the intelligence are the sitting places of this lust, which veils the real knowledge of the living entity and bewilders him." (3.40) As long as this enemy, lust, is not brought under control, one cannot have true knowledge or understand that he is the soul instead of the body. This understanding of *aham brahmasmi*, "I am spirit," is real Vedic knowledge, but a person controlled by lust can never understand it, because he must identify himself with the body in order to gratify the gross senses.

We must try to understand our situation. In attempting to satisfy the bodily senses, we identify ourselves with the body, but even if we think that we are enjoying the senses, the body still dies, and this so-called enjoyment is cut short. Then, rebirth awaits us according to the activities and desires cultivated in this lifetime. Once dead, we cannot control our next birth. If, in life, we are addicted to sex, we may be awarded the body of a pigeon or some other creature capable of having prolific sex. If we like to eat indiscriminately, we may be awarded the body of a hog, capable of eating stool and enjoying it. But if we control our senses, we will at least be awarded a human body specifically meant for sense control, leading to self-realization.

Regulations are meant for human beings, not animals. If a man ignores a traffic light, he will be arrested, but a dog can cross the street at will without fear of apprehension. *Athato brahma jijnasa*, the *Brahma-sutra* admonishes, urging us to take up a higher occupation. We should contemplate Brahman, the spirit, and come to know what is eternal. Transcendental understanding begins when we learn to control the senses and inquire into life's ultimate purpose: Why am I here? Where am I going? How can I solve life's real problems? What is birth and death? A man under the control of lust can never know the answers to these urgent questions. He cannot even concentrate long enough to recognize them. "Therefore, O Arjuna," Lord Krishna says, "in the very beginning curb this great symbol of sin [lust] by regulating the senses, and slay this destroyer of knowledge and self-realization." (3.41)

We must be firmly convinced that knowledge and self-realization are impossible to attain unless we control lust from the very beginning. And where does lust begin? This was explained in the last chapter: "While contemplating the objects of the senses, a person develops attachment for them, and from such attachment lust develops, and from lust, anger arises." (2.62) Therefore, before the thought of enjoying sense objects arises, we should chant Hare Krishna and ask Krishna to give us strength to resist temptation. This is the point where we have full freedom. Before becoming entangled in lust, we should use our sense of discrimination and intelligence, thinking, "This is not good for me. It is against the orders of my spiritual master and is also prohibited in the scriptures." We should understand that as the Supersoul (Paramatma) in the hearts of all, Lord Krishna is the eternal witness. We should therefore pray, "Hare Krishna! Krishna, help me turn my mind from this enemy." Or, we should think, "My spiritual master wants me to render some devotional service. Now let me turn my mind to this service, for it is advised in the scriptures."

In the very beginning, we must resolve to become Krishna conscious, deciding in this very lifetime to use this human form to obtain what cannot be obtained in any other form. This is Lord Rishabadeva's instruction to his hundred sons: "My dear boys, of all the living entities who have accepted material bodies in this world, one who has been awarded this human form should not work hard day and night simply for sense gratification, which is available even to stool-eating dogs and hogs. Instead, one should engage in penance and austerity to attain the divine position of devotional service. By such activity, one's heart is purified, and when one attains this position, he attains eternal, blissful life, which is transcendental to material happiness and continues forever." (*Bhag.* 5.5.1)

Human life is specifically meant for self-realization, devotion to Krishna. Since this is possible only in the human form, we must learn to slay the enemy of self-realization, lust, knowing it to be our greatest enemy in life. This is Lord Rishabadeva's advice to his sons, Krishna's advice to Arjuna, and our spiritual master's advice to us. We cannot cheat anyone but ourselves. Knowing that this advice is for our eternal benefit, we must accept it. Hare Krishna!

The Blessed Lord said: I instructed this imperishable science of yoga to the sun-god, Vivasvan, and Vivasvan instructed it to Manu, the father of mankind, and Manu in turn instructed it to Iksvaku. This supreme science was thus received through the chain of disciplic succession, and the saintly kings understood it in that way. (Bg. 4.1-2)

CHAPTER FOUR

Transcendental Knowledge

When we speak of transcendental knowledge, we must first consider the reception of this knowledge and then turn to the actual subject matter. First, Lord Krishna describes the transmission and reception of knowledge through the *parampara* system, the chain of disciplic succession: "I instructed this imperishable science of yoga to the sun god, Vivasvan, and Vivasvan instructed it to Manu, the father of mankind, and Manu in turn instructed it to Ikshvaku. This supreme science was thus received through the chain of disciplic succession, and the saintly kings understood it in that way. But in course of time, the succession was broken, and therefore the science as it is appears to be lost." (4.1-2)

We should notice that transcendental knowledge begins with the Lord. It cannot possibly begin with anyone else. No man can manufacture a system of genuine transcendental knowledge, although the attempt has become fashionable today. People say, "I have found a new truth," or, "I have discovered a new way to the truth." This is not possible. Truth is truth eternally; therefore it is called *sanatana-dharma*, eternal truth.

Krishna Himself is the origin of truth because He is the Supreme Truth, the Absolute Truth. "There is no Truth superior to Me," He tells Arjuna. "Everything rests upon Me, as pearls are strung on a thread." (7.7) *Srimad-Bhagavatam* further states: *tene brahma hrda*. "It is He only who first imparted the Vedic knowledge unto the heart of Brahma, the original living being." (1.1.1) Not even Brahma can create truth, although he is the creator of the entire universe. Despite his elevated position, he has to learn the truth from Krishna. After hearing from Him, Brahma repeated the same truth to his son Narada, who imparted

43

it to Vyasadeva, who wrote down this Vedic knowledge for the benefit of all humanity.

This is the infallible process: hearing transcendental knowledge through the unbroken chain of disciplic succession. That knowledge must be transmitted as it is, without change. Whenever there is change, there is a break in the disciplic succession, and true knowledge can no longer be transmitted. If there is a break somewhere along an electric line, electricity can no longer be relayed. Similarly, transcendental knowledge must come in an unbroken chain, and Lord Krishna next explains how this chain can remain unbroken.

"That very ancient science of the relationship with the Supreme is today told by Me to you because you are My devotee as well as My friend; therefore you can understand the transcendental mystery of this science." (4.3)

Spiritual knowledge is a transcendental mystery that cannot be understood by mental speculation or mundane scholarship; rather, it is received by the divine grace of disciplic succession, transmitted from spiritual master to disciple when the disciple is qualified. That qualification is specifically mentioned here: "Because you are My devotee as well as My friend." Qualification does not come from academic scholarship or payment of money, but from surrender. By agreeing to become the devotee of Krishna, or the humble disciple of the spiritual master, one can receive actual transcendental knowledge.

Still thinking materially, Arjuna says, "The sun god, Vivasvan, is senior by birth to You. How am I to understand that in the beginning You instructed this science to him?" (4.4) The Lord replies: "Many, many births both you and I have passed. I can remember all of them, but you cannot, O subduer of the enemy." (4.5) Since Lord Krishna is omniscient, He knows all and remembers everything. He never forgets Himself. His transcendence and omniscience contradict and baffle the atheistic Mayavadi philosophers, who maintain that Krishna is a material creature under the control of the material energy. There is no difference between Krishna Himself and His body. Although the ordinary living entity may forget himself, the Supreme Lord does not. If Krishna were an ordinary man, what value could *Bhagavad-gita* have as scripture? *Bhagavad-gita* has value precisely because it was spoken by the Supreme Personality of Godhead. It is still being read thousands of years after being spoken at Kurukshetra, and millions of years after being delivered to the sun god, Vivasvan. If Krishna were forgetful, then forgetfulness, or maya, would be greater than God Himself. We must realize that God, Krishna, never forgets. Rather, it is the conditioned living entity who forgets.

Just to revive Arjuna's memory, and the memory of all mankind, Lord Krishna spoke *Bhagavad-gita* again at Kurukshetra. The transcendental relationship between the Supreme and the living entity is the essential subject matter of *Bhagavad-gita*, and its revival is the science of *bhakti-yoga*. By rendering transcendental loving service to the Lord, we reestablish our natural, eternal relationship with Him.

Lord Krishna then explains His own nature: "Although I am unborn and My transcendental body never deteriorates, and although I am the Lord of all sentient beings, I still appear in every millennium in My original transcendental form." (4.6) Just as the Lord Himself is different from us, His body is different from ours. Since our bodies are composed of matter, we take birth, grow old, suffer disease, and die. Krishna's body, however, is eternally transcendental. He was not born; properly speaking, He appeared. Krishna never grows old. Although He had sons and grandsons on the battlefield of Kurukshetra, He appeared as a fresh youth about twenty years old. His transcendental body never deteriorates. He is never controlled like ordinary living beings, but He is the Supreme Controller. In the Ninth Chapter, He explains that He is the controller of material nature (*maya dhyaksena prakrtih*). "This material nature is working under My direction." (9.10)

From time to time, through His own internal potency, Krishna descends into the material world. He comes by His own choice, to execute His own sweet will. When He descends, His transcendental body does not change. God does not metamorphose, as in certain Christian doctrines, into a mortal body of flesh, blood, and veins. No. Krishna does not take on "flesh." Rather, He appears in His same original, eternal, transcendental body, which is *asnaviram suddham apapa-viddham*: "without veins, pure, and uncontaminated." (*Ishopanishad*, 8)"Whenever and wherever there is a decline in religious practice, O descendant of Bharata, and a predominant rise of irreligion—at that time, I descend Myself." (4.7) Krishna does not come into this material world as we do, in order to enjoy sense gratification. He comes for transcendental purposes only. Krishna's senses are always fully satisfied because He is *atmarama*, complete in Himself. He doesn't need anything for His satisfaction. Everything in existence springs from but a spark of His splendor (10.41). When He wants to enjoy, He just expands Himself. Finished! He doesn't have to work hard for enjoyment, as we do. In His eternal spiritual abode, He is always fully satisfied. He comes here to reclaim the fallen, rebellious souls who are vainly trying to lord it over the material resources for sense gratification. Such gratification is ultimately impossible because living entities, being His parts and parcels, are also constitutionally spiritual. Consequently, the conditioned living entities, unable to truly enjoy this material nature, are always frustrated. Birth, death, old age, and disease forever baffle the conditioned soul in his attempts to attain perfect happiness. To rectify all this, the Lord Himself comes "in order to deliver the pious and to annihilate the miscreants, as well as to reestablish the principles of religion." (4.8)

Krishna's appearance coincidently serves a twofold secondary purpose: to annihilate the demons, who are always opposed to religious principles, and to reestablish those religious principles. But primarily, He comes to give pleasure to His devotees. Actually, the principles of religion can be reestablished by His servants, and the demons can be annihilated by material nature, which can destroy millions and billions of people with floods, earthquakes, and other natural disasters. The Lord has many energies for these subsidiary purposes, but only He Himself can give ultimate pleasure to His devotees, and to this end, He comes in His transcendental body and enacts His eternal pastimes.

Thus, the Lord engages in loving transcendental relations with His pure devotees, such as the residents of Vrindaban, His cowherd boy friends, or His parents, Nanda Maharaj and Mother Yasoda. He even plays the part of an ordinary child to satisfy His devotees' transcendental desire to have the Lord as their son. He also engages in loving exchanges as the perfect lover with the *gopis* of Vrindaban, or as the perfect husband with the queens of Dwaraka. In this way, the Lord satisfies His devotees as no one else can.

Next, Lord Krishna describes the pure nature of the living entity: "Being freed from attachment, fear, and anger, being fully absorbed in Me and taking refuge in Me, many, many persons in the past became purified by knowledge of Me—and thus they all attained transcendental love for Me." (4.10) The Lord Himself is always transcendental to contamination, but because the living entity is infinitesimal, he becomes contaminated by association with material nature, and his real knowledge of the soul becomes covered. By associating with Krishna, hearing about His pastimes and serving Him, we can revive our innate knowledge of Him and love for Him.

Krishna is the seed-giving Father of everyone, and knowingly or not, everyone is working under His direction. But the Lord has also given us independence, and to this end He has supplied both material and spiritual worlds. For those who want to remain in full Krishna consciousness and serve Him eternally, there is the kingdom of God. And for those who want to rebel against the authority of the Lord, there is the material universe of illusion. We are free to choose. Krishna does not force us to surrender, but He does invite us, and He reciprocates in terms of our surrender. Krishna says, "All of them, as they surrender unto Me, I reward accordingly. Everyone follows My path in all respects." (4.11) Krishna gives us full facility to satisfy our desires, but at the same time He imparts transcendental knowledge in books such as *Bhagavad-gita*, and through His representative, the bona fide spiritual master. We have independence. If we like, we can reject the Lord's authority and try to create "our own world," but we should know that without Krishna, our "creation" will be hell on earth.

This is not an exaggeration. Without Krishna, everything is hellish. As soon as the living entity rejects Krishna and His authority, he is forced to accept the dictates of material nature. Under the influence of the three modes of nature, one identifies with the material covering and degrades himself. Always striving for various kinds of sense gratification, he becomes an enemy both to himself and others. Still, Krishna gives him a chance to fulfill his desires, whether material or spiritual. This isn't to say that the results will be the same. It has already been pointed out that each action has its particular result. It is not "all one."

Unfortunately, in this world, men are more inclined to seek immediate pleasure in temporary, material things. Krishna says, "Men in this world desire success in fruitive activities, and therefore they worship the demigods. Quickly, of course, men get results from fruitive work in this world. According to the three modes of material nature and the work ascribed to them, the four divisions of human society were created by Me. And, although I am the creator of this system, you should know that I am yet the non-doer, being unchangeable." (4.12-13)

Although all living entities come into this material world for sense gratification, they are immediately put under the stringent control of nature's three modes, which act as taskmasters. This world is like a prison wherein the three modes serve as guards. Some living entities are confined to first class cells, and others to second and third class cells. In any case, everyone is confined, destined to suffer or enjoy the results of his past activities. Being our ever well-wisher, Lord Krishna advises us to surrender unto Him to get freed from the guardianship of the three modes and the bondage of repeated birth and death.

Although this system is created by Krishna, He is neither within it, nor controlled by it. Being the Lord of all, He is always transcendental to the modes of goodness, passion, and ignorance. This rigid system is created for our rectification, so that we can gradually elevate ourselves from ignorance and passion to goodness. Once established in goodness, we can receive transcendental knowledge and come to understand our eternal relationship with Krishna.

"There is no work that affects Me," Krishna says, "nor do I aspire for the fruits of action. One who understands this truth about Me also does not become entangled in the fruitive reactions of work. All the liberated souls in ancient times acted with this understanding and so attained liberation. Therefore, as the ancients, you should perform your duty in this divine consciousness." (4.14-15)

Divine consciousness is fixed by moment to moment surrender to Krishna. Krishna does not work for fruitive results like an ordinary man; He works for the benefit of all. Similarly, to become godly, we have to work for the benefit of all—that is, the benefit of Krishna, the origin of all. When we work for Krishna, we surrender our personal desires to Krishna to satisfy His transcendental desire. We can succeed only by following the path of the *acharyas*. "As the ancients did, so you should also do." There is no need to manufacture a new process. We have only to follow in the footsteps of the liberated souls. By trying to manufacture our own process, we become entangled, even if we are very clever. Krishna says, "Even the intelligent are bewildered in determining what is action and what is inaction. Now I shall explain to you what action is, knowing which you shall be liberated from all sins." (4.16)

When we speak of action, there are three factors to consider—prescribed action (*karma*), impious action (*vikarma*), and inaction (*akarma*). According to the *Vedas*, society is divided into four classes: *brahmanas* (intelligent class), *kshatriyas* (warrior or administrative class), *vaishyas* (mercantile and farming class), and *sudras* (working class). Then there are four stages of life: *brahmachari* (student life), *grihastha* (householder life), *vanaprastha* (retired life), and *sannyasa* (renounced life). The performance of duty according to these eight divisions (*varna* and *ashrama*) is called good karma. By such actions, we can be elevated in the modes of material nature. There are, however, reactions to these actions, but since the actions are pious, the reactions will be favorable. For instance, one can gradually be elevated to the topmost material planet, Brahmaloka, where life can be enjoyed for millions of years under most heavenly conditions. Still, whoever takes birth there must also die. Therefore Krishna says, *abrahma bhuvanal loka*: "From the highest planet in the material world down to the lowest, all are places of misery wherein repeated birth and death take place." (8.16) But even if one were to live for millions of years, he would not want to die. Therefore we must look beyond the heavenly planets for real peace and happiness.

If, however, one performs activities against scriptural regulations (*vikarma*), or fails to perform his duty, he is degraded to Patalaloka, the lowest planet. By Krishna's mercy, this hellish situation is not eternal; eventually, one takes birth again on a middle planet like earth, where once again he performs actions according to his desire.

Akarma refers to those activities devoid of reaction, pious or impious, performed in Krishna consciousness. Krishna advises Arjuna to work in such consciousness. Arjuna's confusion arose because he thought that to act according to Krishna's instructions would be vikarmic. From the mundane viewpoint, killing friends and relatives is most abominable. He further thought that immorality and the degradation of womanhood would result and therefore great sinful reactions would be incurred. But Krishna now tells him that when one follows His order, no sinful reactions follow. Action in Krishna consciousness is always akarmic. There is no reaction.

In summary, pious or impious activities do not lead to liberation but to rebirth in the material world. Only when we surrender to Krishna and act for Him, abandoning all desire for fruitive results, are we freed from all material reactions. "Abandoning all attachment to the results of his activities, ever satisfied and independent, such a man performs no fruitive action, although engaged in all kinds of undertakings." (4.20) "Fight for Me" is the transcendental conclusion.

Krishna next discusses the nature of sacrifice performed for His satisfaction. This was also discussed in the previous chapter. In the beginning, the Lord created men, demigods, and sacrifice. By sacrificing everything for Krishna, we are elevated to Krishna consciousness. Now Krishna describes the different kinds of sacrifice: sacrifice of the senses, of hearing, of the mind, and of the incoming and outgoing breath. Then He concludes, "All these performers who know the meaning of sacrifice become cleansed of sinful reaction, and, having tasted the nectar of the remnants of such sacrifice, they go to the supreme eternal atmosphere." (4.30)

By definition, sacrifice, performing a sacred ceremony (*sacrum facere*), means to satisfy Him for whom the sacrifice is performed. All sacrifice is ultimately meant for satisfying Lord Krishna, who is known as the *yajna-purusha*, or the Lord of all sacrifices, the original and ultimate cause of all existences. Watering the root of a tree is the proper method for watering the leaves and branches. By offering everything to Krishna, we can work without suffering reactions. Ideally, everything has to be sacrificed.

For instance, everyone has to eat, but if one eats without performing sacrifice, Krishna says, one "verily eats sin," and is a thief. (3.13) There is an entire process involved: Food is produced by rains, and rains are produced by sacrifice. When the demigods in charge of life's necessities are satisfied, prosperity results. Only a thief would try to enjoy the gifts of the demigods without performing sacrifices. Since a thief always worries about being punished, he can never be happy. Those who try to utilize the Lord's property without sacrifice are subject to punishment by the stringent laws of nature. Thieves are necessarily forced to suffer.

The sacrifice recommended for this age, and demanded of everyone, is *sankirtan-yajna*, the chanting of Hare Krishna. *Harer nama, harer nama, harer nama eva kevalam, kalau nastyeva, nastyeva, nastyeva gatir anyatha*: "In this age of quarrel and hypocrisy, the only means of deliverance is chanting the holy name of the Lord. There is no other way, no other way, no other way." For happiness and success in Kali-yuga, we have no alternative. "O best of the Kuru dynasty," Krishna tells Arjuna, "without sacrifice, one can never live happily on this planet or in this life: what then of the next?" (4.31) Just for mundane happiness, we have to perform sacrifice, and certainly much more is required for entrance into the kingdom of God.

"All these different types of sacrifice," Krishna says, "are approved by the *Vedas*, and all of them are born of different types of work. Knowing them as such, you will become liberated. O chastiser of the enemy, the sacrifice of knowledge is greater than the sacrifice of material possessions. After all, the sacrifice of work culminates in transcendental knowledge." (4.32-33)

Here, Krishna encourages the sacrifice of knowledge, and at the same time promises transcendental knowledge. This means that we must abandon or sacrifice all types of speculative knowledge, hear submissively from the spiritual master and the *Vedas*, and under their direction, engage in the Lord's devotional service. The result is transcendental knowledge and detachment combined in one.

Approaching a bona fide spiritual master is therefore imperative. "Just try to learn the truth by approaching a spiritual master," Krishna urges. "Inquire from him submissively and render service unto him. The self-realized soul can impart knowledge unto you because he has seen the truth." (4.34) This truth specifically relates to the proper performance of sacrifice, the very essence of Krishna consciousness. If we want to be free from the bondage of work and from birth and death, we have to follow the pure devotee who can show us how to work without attachment. Such pure *bhakti-yoga* can be taught only by the Lord's pure devotee. Krishna Himself has already said that to be in His disciplic succession, one has to be His devotee and friend. Logically, to know how to please Krishna by sacrifice, one has to be His pure devotee. We must search out such a pure devotee spiritual master who knows the science of satisfying Krishna by every word and deed.

Since the prescribed sacrifice for this age is *sankirtan yajna,* the chanting of the Lord's holy names, the bona fide guru promotes this chanting. Lord Chaitanya Mahaprabhu, Lord Krishna Himself, appeared about five hundred years ago, as the perfect spiritual master, to show us how to conduct this *sankirtan* movement. He requested us to take the holy name to every town and village of the world. We have to hear submissively, under the spiritual master's direction, and learn how to carry out Lord Chaitanya's mission for the benefit of all.

Hearing submissively entails following instructions and rendering service. The spiritual master doesn't want service for his own sake, though at times he allows the disciple to render him personal service for the disciple's own training. Being completely satisfied in himself, in pure Krishna consciousness, the spiritual master does not need personal service. Rather, since his mission is to save all conditioned souls, the greatest service that a disciple can render is to assist his master. This is also the way to please Lord Krishna. As the Lord Himself says at the conclusion of *Bhagavad-gita:* "For one who explains the supreme secret to the devotees, devotional service is guaranteed, and at the end he will come back to Me. There is no servant in this world more dear to Me than he, nor will there ever be one more dear." (18.68-69) Preaching *Bhagavad-gita* is our real service to humanity. After hearing from the spiritual master about the nature of the Absolute Truth, and after receiving Krishna's blessings and transcendental knowledge, we must repay the debt by distributing that knowledge to others. If we want to be faithful disciples, we have to assist our spiritual master in this mission.

Here is the key to understanding the truth: "And when you have thus learned the truth, you will know that all living beings are but part of Me—and that they are in Me, and are Mine." (4.35) This is the secret of transcendental knowledge: all living beings are part and parcel of Krishna. Since nothing can exist without Krishna, everything is meant for satisfying Him.

In the *Srimad-Bhagavatam,* as originally spoken to Brahma, the Lord says, "Brahma, it is I, the Personality of Godhead, who was existing before the creation when there was nothing but Myself. Nor was there the material nature, the cause of this creation. That which you see now is also I, the Personality of Godhead, and after annihilation, that which remains will also be Myself." (*Bhag.* 2.9.33) Therefore, since before, during, and after the creation, all that exists is Krishna, then everything is part and parcel of Krishna and therefore His property. *Ishavasyam idam sarvam:* "Everything animate or inanimate that is within the universe is controlled and owned by the Lord." This is the proclamation of *Sri Ishopanishad.* Everything is Krishna's, but in this material world, people are suffering the effects of action and reaction because they are trying to usurp Krishna's property. Of course, they can never succeed. Krishna takes away everything at death.

One in transcendental knowledge is obliged to inform others that they are also part and parcel of Krishna. And since whatever we possess is actually meant for Krishna's satisfaction, a devotee teaches everyone how to engage everything in Krishna's service. If we follow this simple principle, we can turn this material world into Vaikuntha, the kingdom of God. We can spiritualize everything by engaging it in Krishna's service. There is no need to change our business or residence. We can make our homes Krishna conscious by turning them into temples, installing the Deity of the Lord, offering food to Him, and gathering our family members before Him to chant His holy names. The very bodies of those dedicated to Krishna's service become spiritualized because anything engaged in Krishna's service ceases to be material; it takes on the qualities of spirit. Once spiritualized, we transcend all the miseries and defects of material existence. Therefore Krishna says, "Even if you are considered to be the most sinful of all sinners, when you are situated in the boat of transcendental knowledge [devotional service], you will be able to cross over the ocean of miseries." (4.36)

This is the spiritualizing effect of Krishna consciousness. As soon as we recognize everything as Krishna's property and ourselves as His parts and parcels, knowing that nothing can exist apart from Krishna, we find that all material miseries cease. After all, material miseries are inflicted by maya, Krishna's agent, just to remind us of our dangerous position in this material world. We are not meant to remain here. Our constitutional position is to serve the lord eternally in His kingdom, where everything is eternal, and full of knowledge and bliss. When we surrender to Krishna, Mayadevi no longer has to attack us with the trident of threefold miseries. Krishna Himself says, "As the blazing fire turns firewood to ashes, O Arjuna, so does the fire of knowledge burn to ashes all reactions to material activities." (4.37)

For Arjuna, there is no longer any question of auspicious or inauspicious reactions, since his fighting is under Krishna's direction, in full transcendental knowledge. "In this world," Krishna continues, "there is nothing so sublime and pure as transcendental knowledge. Such knowledge is the mature fruit of all mysticism, and one who has achieved this, enjoys the self within himself in due course of time." (4.38)

This mature fruit is full Krishna consciousness, *bhakti-yoga*, the topmost yoga. This is restated in the Sixth Chapter, wherein Krishna urges everyone to be a yogi: "And of all yogis, he who always abides in Me with great faith, worshipping Me in transcendental loving service, is most intimately united with Me in yoga and is the highest of all." (6.47)

Thus Krishna consciousness is the greatest gift, for it immediately enables one to cross the ocean of birth and death and attain transcendental love for Krishna. "A faithful man, who is absorbed in transcendental knowledge and who subdues his senses, quickly attains the supreme spiritual peace." (4.39) Of course, those who try to enjoy the senses can never have peace. This has already been discussed in the Second Chapter, wherein Lord Krishna says that real peace comes only when the senses are subdued. Materialists think that they can become happy by engaging in unrestricted sense gratification, but factually, the more we indulge the senses, the more they control us and force us to suffer the threefold miseries. Only by subduing the senses and surrendering to Krishna can we attain the supreme spiritual peace.

Lord Krishna continues: "But ignorant and faithless persons who doubt the revealed scriptures do not attain God consciousness. For the doubting soul, there is happiness neither in this world nor in the next." (4.40)

We have already noted that Lord Krishna is expert at killing these demons of doubt. Just by speaking this transcendental knowledge, Krishna eradicated all of Arjuna's doubts. A doubting man is never happy in this world nor in the next. First of all, in this world, instead of real happiness, there is only the mitigation of distress. Years ago, in primary school, we used to tell "moron jokes:" "Do you know why the moron kept hitting his head against the wall?" we would ask. Answer: "Because it felt so good when he stopped." In material life, we are all like the moron. As soon as we take birth, we begin the process of growing old, suffering disease, dying, and again taking birth according to our karma. To counteract this misery, we concoct so much unnecessary sense gratification, which in turn becomes the cause of future suffering. We must understand clearly that in this world there is no happiness, and for the faithless person who doubts both the word of God and God's very existence, there is no chance of attaining the Kingdom of God, the spiritual world of eternity, knowledge, and bliss.

"Therefore," Krishna says, "one who has renounced the fruits of his action, whose doubts are destroyed by transcendental knowledge, and who is situated firmly in the self, is not bound by works, O conqueror of riches." (4.41)

Significantly, Arjuna is called conqueror of riches in this verse. At one time, Maharaj Yudhisthira sent Arjuna and his brothers to the north to get gold for the *rajasuya* sacrifice. In previous ages, people had so much gold, silver, and jewels that they would make various utensils out of them, use them once, and throw them away. In fact, there was a place of sacrifice in the Himalayas where all the used utensils were discarded into a kind of golden junkpile. Because Arjuna fetched this gold, he is known as Dhananjaya, the conqueror of wealth. But here, Lord Krishna is explaining something that is more valuable than gold. He is presenting transcendental knowledge by which He Himself can be attained. Since we attain everything when we attain Krishna, that knowledge is of infinite value.

Lord Krishna concludes this chapter with a transcendental call to battle: "Therefore the doubts which have arisen in your heart out of ignorance should be slashed by the weapon of knowledge. Armed with yoga, O Bharata, stand and fight." (4.42)

In his illusion, Arjuna had cast down his powerful bow, Gandiva, but this is not the weapon Lord Krishna is talking about. Rather, he says, "Armed with yoga, stand and fight." Yoga is our real weapon. Yoga means linking with the Supreme, with Krishna, who says, "Declare it boldly that My devotee never perishes." (9.31) Arjuna was successful in the Kurukshetra battle not because he was a good archer—Karna was perhaps a better marksman—but because he had become invincible by linking himself to Krishna. With Lord Krishna as his chariot driver and his friend, he was assured of success.

This is the essence of transcendental knowledge: armed with yoga, we should stand up and fight. Fighting is necessary in the battle against evil. Krishna tells Arjuna that although He has already killed all the opposing soldiers, Arjuna still must take up his bow and "fight for the sake of fighting," detached from the results. Of course, it is our choice whether we fight or not; Lord Krishna has granted us this minute independence. At the conclusion of *Bhagavad-gita*, Krishna tells Arjuna, "Thus I have explained to you the most confidential of all knowledge. Deliberate on this fully, and then do what you wish to do." (18.63) Although Krishna is personally present, urging Arjuna to fight, He leaves the final decision up to him.

Today, He is still encouraging us to arm ourselves with the yoga of Krishna consciousness and fight. Our weapon is the holy name. By it, Lord Krishna is personally present on our tongues, and we are personally linked with Him. Where, then, is the possibility of defeat? Wherever there is Krishna and Arjuna, His pure devotee, there is no possibility of defeat. Krishna promises that His devotee will never be vanquished. For success, we must arm ourselves with yoga—that is, we must link ourselves to Krishna and abide by His order, as Arjuna did at Kurukshetra. Since the entire battle was engineered by Krishna, Arjuna had only to cooperate with Him to succeed.

Similarly, the *sankirtan* movement is Krishna's arrangement for success in this age. It is not our arrangement. Lord Chaitanya Himself has engineered everything and declared it successful: "My names will be chanted in every town and village in the world." Now we have only to stand up and fight on Lord Chaitanya's behalf. We are free to do it or not. If we agree, we get the credit for the success, but whether we participate or not, Lord Chaitanya's victory is an eternal fact. He is just inviting us to partake in the pastime of His glorious *sankirtan* battle.

This is a wonderful opportunity for the devotee, who derives great transcendental pleasure from striving on the Lord's behalf. To be a devotee means to be an instrument in the hands of the Lord and follow His orders. It is not that we are successful through our own efforts. This is not possible, for we are but frail men. We can be successful only if Krishna empowers us. Krishna is full of power. "Know that all beautiful, glorious, and mighty creations spring from but a spark of My splendor. With a single fragment of Myself, I pervade and support this entire universe." (10.41-42) If Krishna wants, He can empower anyone to become His representative, His instrument for reclaiming all fallen souls. If we surrender to the Lord, He will empower us to act wonderfully, just as He does. We have seen this in Srila Prabhupada's life, for by surrendering to Krishna and Lord Chaitanya, and by believing Lord Chaitanya's word, Srila Prabhupada appeared to act even more powerfully than Lord Chaitanya Himself. Lord Chaitanya travelled all over India to spread the holy names, but He never went outside India. That worldwide mission was undertaken by Srila Prabhupada.

Of course, Srila Prabhupada never took personal credit for his success. He always said that the Krishna consciousness movement was the power of the Lord at work. "My only credit is that I have acted faithfully on the order of my spiritual master and Lord Chaitanya," he often said. "I am only repeating what I have heard from the previous *acharya*, my Guru Maharaj."

In like manner, having full faith in guru and Krishna, we should take up Lord Chaitanya's order to spread the holy names

to every town and village. "On my orders, become guru," He
said. "Tell whomever you meet about this science of Krishna
consciousness." By sincerely following this order with full confidence, we become empowered by Him. Hare Krishna!

The humble sage, by virtue of true knowledge, sees with equal vision a learned and gentle brahmana, a cow, an elephant, a dog and a dog-eater [outcaste]. (Bg. 5.18)

CHAPTER FIVE

Karma-yoga—Action in Krishna Consciousness

Arjuna said: "O Krishna, first of all You ask me to renounce work, and then again You recommend work with devotion. Now will You kindly tell me definitely which of the two is more beneficial?" (5.1)

It may surprise us that Arjuna is still confused. He cannot quite understand Krishna's logic. How can Krishna expect him to fight the Battle of Kurukshetra and be renounced at the same time? To Arjuna's mind, these are contradictory instructions. Now, in this chapter, Lord Krishna will explain how renunciation and action in Krishna consciousness are neither contradictory nor mutually exclusive, but complementary.

Krishna says, "The renunciation of work and work in devotion are both good for liberation, but, of the two, work in devotional service is better than renunciation of work." (5.2) Of course, a person can abandon activity without being truly renounced. He can simply renounce external activity while meditating on sense gratification. In this case, such a person is called a pretender, a hypocrite. If one just gives up activity without doing something positive, what is the gain? When a child misbehaves, his teacher may tell him, "Stand in the corner and do nothing," but the teacher doesn't want the child to stand and do nothing indefinitely. This is just a way to stop the child's mischievous activity and to correct him. Eventually, the child must come out of the corner and engage in positive action to make progress in life. Similarly, a person may stop his sense gratification by renouncing activity altogether, but he is not properly situated on the spiritual platform until he begins devotional service. That rendering of service is his constitutional position.

From the beginning of *Bhagavad-gita*, Krishna has encour-

61

aged Arjuna to work on the platform of *brahma-bhuta*, fixing his intelligence in the understanding that the spirit soul is distinct from the material body (*aham brahmasmi*). "For the soul, there is never birth nor death," Krishna says. "Nor, having once been, does he ever cease to be." (2.20) True identity is "I am not the temporary body; I am the eternal soul." If we want to come to the platform of the soul, we have to learn of the activities of the soul. How is this possible? By approaching a spiritual master, we can come to understand the truth: "All living beings are but part of Me, they are in Me, and they are Mine." (4.35) Then we must act in awareness of this truth for the satisfaction of Krishna. The material body, for instance, has many parts—eyes, ears, nose, stomach, legs—which act together for the entire body's welfare. No part acts separately or independently. In like manner, all living beings are part and parcel of the Supreme Living Being, Lord Sri Krishna. When they work together under His direction, for His pleasure, and according to His purpose, they are situated on the spiritual platform and engaged in the activities of the soul. Acting on Krishna's behalf is devotional service.

Lord Krishna continues: "One who neither hates nor desires the fruits of his activities is known to be always renounced. Such a person, liberated from all dualities, easily overcomes material bondage and is completely liberated, O mighty-armed Arjuna. Only the ignorant speak of *karma-yoga* and devotional service as being different from the analytical study of the material world [*sankhya-yoga*]. Those who are actually learned say that he who applies himself well to one of these paths achieves the results of both." (5.3-4) This is affirmed also in the Seventh Chapter (7.19), wherein Krishna says that after many lifetimes of renunciation and cultivation of knowledge, one finally comes to the understanding that Vasudeva, Krishna, is everything. Understanding this, the *mahatma*, the great soul, surrenders to Krishna with all his heart.

Whether one follows the process of *jnana-yoga, hatha-yoga, bhakti-yoga*, or any other yoga, he ultimately has to come to the point of surrendering to Krishna. This is the essential teaching of *Bhagavad-gita*, from beginning to end: "Just get up, arm yourself with yoga, and fight for Me." Because Arjuna doesn't want to fight, when Krishna says, "Fight," Arjuna has to surrender his will to Krishna's. Sooner or later, we all have to surrender our desires to those of Krishna. In the conditioned state, our desires, separate from Krishna's, generally revolve around family, friends, and society, all of which are limited in scope. Setting all these mundane concerns aside for a moment, we must inquire about Krishna's desire, for He is the complete whole. What does He want us to do? We must find out and then surrender to His desire. We are meant for enjoyment in connection with the Supreme Personality of Godhead, not separate from Him. Surrender is the harmony of the beautiful song of God, *Bhagavad-gita*.

One who cultures knowledge, therefore, finally comes to understand that since Krishna is everything, everything should be directed to His satisfaction. In this knowledge, the path of renunciation and the path of works in devotion converge. By acts of devotion, the heart is purified, and by Krishna's grace, the devotee receives the knowledge whereby he understands that Vasudeva, Krishna, is everything. Regardless of the yoga path taken, the goal of knowledge is the same: *vasudevah sarvam iti*. The Supreme Lord is all there is.

Knowing this, the wise man acts for Krishna. Therefore Krishna recommends *bhakti-yoga:* "One who knows that the position reached by means of renunciation can also be attained by works in devotional service, and who therefore sees that the path of works and the path of renunciation are one, sees things as they are. Unless one is engaged in the devotional service of the Lord, mere renunciation of activities cannot make one happy. The sages, purified by works of devotion, achieve the Supreme without delay." (5.5-6)

Although the same goal can be attained through any yogic process, Krishna here stresses the indispensability of *bhakti-yoga*. Acting with senses purified by works of devotion, the sages "achieve the Supreme without delay," but those who try other paths frequently meet with delays. The difficulty of impersonal nondevotional processes is treated in more detail in the Twelfth Chapter, wherein Arjuna asks, "Which is considered to be more perfect: those who are properly engaged in Your devotional service, or those who worship the impersonal Brahman, the unmanifested?" (12.1) Again, Krishna says that whether one meditates on His impersonal Brahman feature, or directly worships

His personal form, one has to come to the Supreme Personality of Godhead. Krishna is ultimately a person; therefore He says that worship of His personal form is better. "For those whose minds are attached to the unmanifested, impersonal feature of the Supreme, advancement is very troublesome." (12.5)

At the time of realization, we have to abandon the impersonal conception because Krishna Himself is not impersonal. He is the Supreme Person. The impersonal Brahman is but the glaring effulgence of His transcendental body. Everything is emanating from that Supreme Person, just as sunshine emanates from the sun. In fact, the impersonal Brahman effulgence is often compared to sunshine, which spreads throughout the universe, while the sun disc itself is compared to the localized Paramatma feature of the Lord. But within the sun disc resides the sun god, who is the source of the sun's emanations.

Similarly, the source of everything is the Supreme Person. As the first words of *Srimad-Bhagavatam* proclaim: *janmady asya yato:* Lord Sri Krishna is the source of everything, the cause of all causes, the One from whom everything emanates, the Supreme Person from whom all subsidiary personalities arise. "I am the seed-giving father of all living entities," Krishna says in *Bhagavad-gita* (14.4). Even in mundane life, we can see that a son has the characteristics of his father. He cannot be a person unless his father is a person. Since all living entities are sons of Krishna, and all sons are persons, then Krishna must be the greatest, original person. Such realization comes easily to one who worships Krishna with love and devotion, knowing Him to be the Supreme Person. But this realization is very difficult for impersonalist meditators.

Therefore, Krishna emphasizes that the Supreme is attained "without delay" through the devotional process. Moreover: "One who works in devotion, who is a pure soul, and who controls his mind and senses, is dear to everyone, and everyone is dear to him. Though always working, such a man is never entangled." (5.7) He is not entangled because he renounces the fruits of his work. We are entitled to our work, but not to the results. Why? Because everything is actually accomplished by Krishna. On the battlefield, Krishna tells Arjuna, "I have already killed all these people. Just become My instrument." We are all instruments in the hands of the Supreme.

Why, then, do some people act impiously and others cultivate Krishna consciousness? Why do some people return to God's kingdom, and others go to hellish planets? Is it predestination, free will, brainwashing, environmental conditioning, or what? Philosophers and religionists never cease to argue these points. The answer, however, is given by Lord Krishna: "I am seated in everyone's heart, and from Me come remembrance, knowledge, and forgetfulness." (15.15) One man remembers Krishna and another man forgets Him, according to the desire deep within the heart.

The living entity has only fragmental independence; God alone is completely independent. Because we are God's eternal fragments, we have fragmental independence—that is, our independence is limited to desiring a finite thing in a finite way. "Man proposes, God disposes." We can choose to remember Krishna and become His servants, or forget Him and try to be lords of all we survey. Those who surrender to God and serve Him are known as devotees, and those who want to forget Him are known as demons. These two types of living entities are found everywhere.

We can choose our fate. We can hear the Lord's transcendental topics and surrender to Him, or we can avoid the devotees and never listen to discussions about Krishna. That is our minute independence, and Krishna doesn't interfere. He wants us to turn to Him so that He can give us a life of eternity, knowledge, and bliss, but we may obstinately choose to reject Him and refuse to chant His name. Then we forget Him more and more and glide merrily down the primrose path to hell. Such unfortunate living entities are therefore called "hell-bent."

The liberated souls who choose to remember Krishna are characterized thus: "A person in the divine consciousness, although engaged in seeing, hearing, touching, smelling, eating, moving about, sleeping, and breathing, always knows within himself that he actually does nothing at all. Because while speaking, evacuating, receiving, or opening and closing his eyes, he always knows that only the material senses are engaged with their objects, and that he is aloof from them." (5.8-9)

As soon as we are born into this material world, we take

birth under the influence of one or more of the material modes, and the body reacts to these modes, in goodness, passion, and ignorance. But as soon as one is liberated, he knows, *aham brahmasmi*: "I am spirit soul. I am not this body." Knowing this, he ceases to be controlled by the modes. Therefore, whether seeing, hearing, eating, sleeping, or whatever, he knows that only the material body is engaged in its activities and that he, as spirit soul, is separate. Knowing this, he engages himself spiritually in works of devotion, and his body follows along. When the soul is purified, the body is also purified. Under proper guidance, everything can be utilized in Krishna's service. Therefore, Krishna says, "The yogis, abandoning attachment, act with body, mind, intelligence, and even with the senses, only for the purpose of purification." (5.11)

As soon as one realizes his identity as spirit soul, he quickly abandons sense gratification. It is illusion to think that one can continue sense gratification and come to pure spiritual consciousness. Sense gratification and spiritual life are opposed and incompatible. They have never been and will never be successfully combined. Sense gratification is enjoyed only by one who identifies with the material body. The real yogi abandons sense indulgence and controls his senses to realize *Aham brahmasmi*: "I am not this body."

When one actually understands himself to be spirit soul, he acts with complete detachment for the satisfaction of the Supreme Lord, engaging his mind, intelligence and even his senses to this end. This is transcendental consciousness, *bhakti-yoga*. *Hrishikesa hrishikena sevanam:* The senses must serve the Master of the senses. And what are the results? Krishna says, "The steadily devoted soul attains unadulterated peace because he offers the results of all activities to Me, whereas a person who is not in union with the Divine, who is greedy for the fruits of his labor, becomes entangled." (5.12)

We become entangled in material life because we try to enjoy what is not ours. Since Krishna is the doer of everything, He is the proprietor of everything. In illusion, we erroneously think, "I've worked hard for this money, and therefore it's mine." But in reality, what is truly "mine?" It is said that "naked we come into the world, and naked we go out." Krishna is the source of all energy. We may think that we are working, but it is Krishna alone who works and supplies everything. We desire, and Krishna fulfills our desires by supplying whatever we need. Where do we think all this energy comes from? We eat food to get energy, but where does the food come from? Can it be manufactured by man alone, without the cooperation of the earth and sun? Who creates the earth and sun? With a little intelligent thought, we can understand that God is giving us all of the energy by which we are able to work in a certain way, according to our desire. The result of our work, therefore, is not ours: it belongs to God. Whatever we get factually belongs to God. When we try to enjoy it for ourselves, independently, against God's sanction, we turn into thieves and become entangled in material nature.

What is this unadulterated peace (*shanti*) of which Krishna speaks? In the material world, such perfect peace does not exist. There may be periods when nations are not at war, but this cannot be considered perfect peace. Unadulterated, unshakeable peace is possible only when one surrenders to Krishna and works with steady devotion on His behalf. It is worth noting that impersonalists interpret "union with the Divine" to mean merging into the Supreme and losing identity. But obviously this is not what Krishna means here. Union with the Divine means agreeing to work on God's behalf. Krishna is talking to Arjuna about working, not merging into the Supreme and losing his identity. How can anyone work with a lost, merged identity? Union means working for Krishna's satisfaction instead of becoming entangled in the results of one's activity. This is real oneness. Attaining real oneness does not consist of losing identity, but of becoming one in desire. By surrendering to the Lord, the devotee's desire becomes one with the Lord's, but the devotee does not lose his identity. Our identity is eternal, as Lord Krishna states at the very beginning of His discourse with Arjuna: "Never was there a time when I did not exist, nor you, nor all these kings; nor in the future shall any of us cease to be." (2.12) We are all individuals eternally. When we surrender to Krishna, we accept Krishna's desire, which is the best desire, for Krishna is the all-perfect, all-knowing, best friend of every living entity. Therefore when we surrender to Krishna, we can have unadulterated peace.

"When the embodied living being controls his nature and mentally renounces all actions," Krishna says, "he resides happily in the city of the nine gates (the material body), neither working nor causing work to be done." (5.13) This is the method for becoming peaceful and happy while in the material body. As long as we identify with the body and try to enjoy it, squeezing out every drop of pleasure at all costs, we will never be happy. Happiness is in knowing that the soul is distinct from the body, and that it resides in the body for a higher purpose. We may own an automobile, but if we were to identify with that automobile, thinking it to be nondifferent from ourselves, we would be considered crazy. If we but understand that the automobile is just a machine to get us from here to there, to help us go about our business, we can be free to actually enjoy the automobile. It is neurotic to think, "Oh, someone has hit *me!* Someone has dented *my* fender! *I* am scratched! What will *I* do?" Such neurotic people are certainly ridiculous. Similarly, while in these material bodies, we think, "*I* am growing old. *I* am suffering disease. *I* am dying. *I* am being born." All these material miseries are suffered by those who misidentify themselves with the gross body, which is temporary. The real *I* is eternal.

"The embodied spirit, master of the city of his body, does not create activities, nor does he induce people to act, nor does he create the fruits of action. All this is enacted by the modes of material nature. Nor does the Supreme Spirit assume anyone's sinful or pious activities. Embodied beings, however, are bewildered because of the ignorance which covers their real knowledge." (5.14-15) Due to ignorance of our real identity as spirit soul, part and parcel of Krishna, we accept this temporary, miserable material body. More or less, the body is always in a miserable situation, undergoing one of the fourfold miseries. How can anyone be happy, thinking, "I am being born, I am growing old, I am diseased, I am dying." Amid all this agitation, this tossing about, true peace and happiness are impossible.

In transcendental consciousness, knowing, *aham brahmasmi*. "I am spirit soul," we can enter the transcendental life of eternity, knowledge, and bliss. *Brahma-bhuta prasannatma:* "One who is thus transcendentally situated at once realizes the Supreme Brahman." (18.54) In this state, one becomes joyful, neither hankering nor lamenting. Since the soul is always complete in himself, always *atmarama*, what is there to hanker for? Since he is always transcendental, why should he lament?

Lord Krishna says, "When one is enlightened with the knowledge by which nescience is destroyed, then his knowledge reveals everything, as the sun lights up everything in the daytime." (5.16) This is a beautiful description of liberation, which is like the rising of the sun. Before the sunrise, we are in darkness, unable to perceive anything. Then gradually the darkness fades, the first hints of dawn are perceived, and the sun rises, dispelling the darkness, and turning everything into glorious color and variegatedness. Then our consciousness is awakened, and we can say, "Oh, now it is daytime! Now I can see everything clearly."

Similarly, by practicing sense control, engaging the senses in the Lord's service, and becoming detached from all material desires, we will suddenly realize the dawn of knowledge that we are spirit soul, separate from the body and its material activities. Then, as we step into the full light of Krishna consciousness, everything becomes clear, as in the daytime, and we receive full knowledge of everything. "When one's intelligence, mind, faith and refuge are all fixed in the Supreme, then one becomes fully cleansed of misgivings through complete knowledge and thus proceeds straight on the path of liberation." (5.17)

What impedes our progress down this joyful path? Material misgivings, false identification with the material body, family, business, and country, misuse of mind and intelligence, sloth, ignorance, and sense gratification—in one word, maya, forgetfulness of Krishna. All these create for us a hell on earth.

Our original, pure life is one of plain living and high thinking. Even on this earth, Krishna has provided everything we need for a happy life: a little land, a cow, and Krishna consciousness. When we have these, all of life's necessities are automatically provided. The cow provides health-giving milk, the bull tills the ground, and the earth yields grains and vegetables. With Krishna consciousness, we can chant Hare Krishna constantly, render devotional service, rest at the end of day, and feel satisfied and happy. This is plain living and high thinking. This is proper use of intelligence. This is self-realization.

It is certainly a misuse of intelligence to create a society of cats, dogs, and hogs, living merely to exploit the material body. When our intelligence is perverted in the mad scramble for sense gratification, we cannot control the mind, and when the mind is not controlled, it becomes our worst enemy. Actually, the mind should be our best friend in helping to control the senses and fixing them on the Supreme so that we can be conscious of Him. Unfortunately, under the dictation of the misdirected intelligence and mind, the senses run out of control and carry the living entity to hell. Thus the senses become a network of paths leading to death. Entangling us in the web of death, the senses occupy all our time, day after day, telling us, "See this, hear that, touch this, taste that, run here, run there, smell this, eat that," as Time keeps ticking on. And what is this Time? It is the form of Krishna that devours everything: Kala, the ultimate killer. "Time I am," Krishna says, "destroyer of the worlds." (11.32)

This human form of life is an opportunity given by God for self-realization, but Time is running out. We cannot say whether we will be granted more than one minute, five minutes, one year, or five years. Nothing is guaranteed except Death. In the world, there is only one certainty: our time is limited. "As sure as Death," we often say. All the money in the world cannot buy us one second of time beyond what is allotted. Therefore, those who are intelligent are eager to use this valuable human life to attain self-realization. Krishna says, "Out of many thousands among men, one may endeavor for perfection, and of those who have achieved perfection, hardly one knows Me in truth." (7.3) If we are fortunate enough to contact the Lord's pure devotee, who can teach us pure Krishna consciousness, we are the luckiest of men.

We have a great and rare opportunity to develop pure love of Krishna, for Lord Chaitanya Himself has given us special benediction in the age of Kali: the chanting of the Hare Krishna *mahamantra*. For this reason, Rupa Goswami says, Lord Chaitanya is "the most munificent, magnanimous incarnation." Lord Chaitanya has made easy that which in former ages was so difficult and rare: pure love of Krishna. We are most fortunate to have a human form and to contact Lord Chaitanya's movement.

Now we must use our intelligence to cultivate Krishna consciousness before Time takes away the chance. There is no guarantee of another opportunity in our next birth. We may have to pass through thousands and millions of births before getting another chance. After all, nature takes away what we don't use. If we don't use our arms, they will atrophy. If we lie in bed for months and don't use our legs, we will lose our ability to walk. This is nature's law. Similarly, nature has given us developed consciousness for understanding Krishna. If we use it for animalistic sense gratification instead, we will lose it and sink to animal life. Animals are given their specific bodies and consciousness to enjoy different kinds of sense gratification. That is the essence of their life. Therefore *Srimad-Bhagavatam* cautions us not to misuse this rare opportunity, the human form, by cultivating what is easily available to stool eaters, to dogs, hogs, and crows. Rather, we should strive for self-realization, the special purpose of human life. Proper use of human intelligence leads to Krishna consciousness. When that intelligence is developed, we will see everything spiritually.

And what is the vision of one spiritually situated in pure Krishna consciousness? Krishna says, "The humble sage, by virtue of true knowledge, sees with equal vision a learned and gentle *brahmana*, a cow, an elephant, a dog, and a dog-eater [outcaste]." (5.18) How is this? One with transcendental vision does not see the material, outward covering, which is like a dress; rather, he sees the spirit soul within, and he understands that soul to be part and parcel of Krishna. Established in this vision, he wants to serve every living entity. He does not see one person as his friend and another as his enemy, nor does he consider some fit and others unfit. He wants to distribute Krishna's mercy, the chanting of the holy names, to everyone.

"Those whose minds are established in sameness and equanimity have already conquered the conditions of birth and death. They are flawless, like Brahman, and thus they are already situated in Brahman." (5.19)

Liberation is possible even when one is still in the material body, as confirmed by Rupa Goswami. What is necessary is transcendental vision—that is, the ability to see Krishna everywhere.The liberated sage sees everything as Krishna's property, thinking, "Since nothing is mine, I can use nothing for my sense gratification. Everything is created, possessed, and enjoyed by Krishna. I am also part and parcel of Krishna, and I am His eternal servant." This is transcendental vision established in sameness and equanimity. One who thinks in this way has already conquered the conditions of birth and death, which exist for fruitive laborers. Such a sage gives up all the fruits of his labor for the Lord's satisfaction. He has transcended the conditions leading to birth and death.

Krishna further describes the transcendental sage: "A person who neither rejoices upon achieving something pleasant nor laments upon obtaining something unpleasant, who is self- intelligent, unbewildered, and who knows the science of God, is to be understood as already situated in Transcendence. Such a liberated person is not attracted to material sense pleasure or external objects, but is always in trance, enjoying the pleasure within. In this way, the self-realized person enjoys unlimited happiness, for he concentrates on the Supreme." (5.20-21)

Such a transcendental person is always in *samadhi*, or trance, regardless of his activities. *Samadhi* does not entail sitting in a corner with closed eyes. A person in full Krishna consciousness sees Krishna everywhere and acts, but only for Krishna's satisfaction. He is not a do-nothing. On the other hand, he is never attracted to material sense pleasure, for he is always enjoying the pleasure within, the pleasure of Krishna consciousness. Although he may be fighting a great battle, or running a big business, agricultural enterprise, or religious institution, he is always in trance, concentrating on the Supreme. Because of his fixed determination to serve Krishna, he cannot be deviated by anyone or anything.

Krishna further explains: "An intelligent person does not take part in the sources of misery, which are due to contact with the material senses. O son of Kunti, such pleasures have a beginning and an end, and so the wise man does not delight in them." (5.22) Everyone must admit that all material pleasures have a beginning and an end, regardless of their source. Every materialistic man, for example, takes great pleasure in his family, but when he eventually loses his family, that very source of pleasure becomes a source of pain. According to *Srimad-*

Bhagavatam, King Citraketu, who was very unhappy without a son, became the happiest man in the world when he finally begot a son by the grace of Angira Muni. But when that son was killed, the tables turned, and the King became the world's most miserable man. Such is nature's way. That which gives us the greatest pleasure, may also give us the greatest pain. This is true as long as we are attached to this material body, family, society, friendship, and love. Great pleasure incurs great suffering. Therefore Lord Krishna says that the wise man avoids seeking pleasure in the very sources of misery: the material senses. He distinguishes between the temporary and the eternal and never mistakes the two. Concentrating on the soul and its progress in Krishna consciousness, he delights in spiritual pleasures that have neither beginning nor end.

If we want to be intelligent, we must detach ourselves from the sources of misery and become attached to the source of real, eternal pleasure: Krishna consciousness, the transcendental loving service of the Lord. This doesn't mean that we neglect our family or business. Arjuna was incorrectly thinking that he would have to give up his duty as a soldier and go to the forest to cultivate Krishna consciousness. But Krishna explained how Arjuna could become fully Krishna conscious while on the battlefield. Similarly, He wants us to become fully Krishna conscious with our family and in our business, but first we must abandon attachment to these things by putting Krishna in the center. In the end, Arjuna fought only because it was Krishna's desire. We must also follow Krishna's desire by raising our family in Krishna consciousness, engaging wife and children in Lord Krishna's service, liberating our children by teaching them to chant Krishna's names, putting Krishna in the center of our business, working for Krishna, and giving the fruits of our labor to spreading the gospel of Krishna consciousness. In this way, we can be established in the transcendental position and avoid material entanglement.

Lord Krishna continues: "Before giving up this present body, if one is able to tolerate the urges of the material senses and check the force of desire and anger, he is a yogi and is happy in this world." (5.23) In the Second Chapter, Arjuna declined to fight because he thought it unbearable to kill his friends and relatives. There, too, Krishna said, "Tolerate it." (2.14) In the execution of Krishna consciousness, we may encounter many disturbances and difficulties, all of which must be tolerated. We shouldn't think, "Now I'm taking to Krishna consciousness. Life will be a bed of roses." No. Krishna has never promised this. We can't expect everything to go according to our desire, or everyone to be to our liking. There may be great difficulties to test our faith, and we must tolerate them by thinking of Krishna, chanting His names, and taking complete shelter of Him.

In Krishna consciousness, Lord Krishna is our chariot driver. He is in our hearts, and He is always with us. As the bona fide spiritual master, He appears before us to give us instructions and encouragement. But we must do our part by learning to tolerate the urges of the material senses. If the senses are controlled, the mind is controlled, and when the mind is controlled, the intelligence can concentrate on the Supreme Personality of Godhead. When our intelligence is fixed in Him, we have attained the transcendental position.

Lord Krishna continues: "One whose happiness is within, who is active within, who rejoices within and is illumined within, is actually the perfect mystic. He is liberated in the Supreme, and ultimately he attains the Supreme. One who is beyond duality and doubt, whose mind is engaged within, who is always busy working for the welfare of all, and who is free from all sins, achieves liberation in the Supreme." (5.24-25)

Here again, interior life and happiness are stressed. Pleasure, activity, joy, illumination, and contentment all come from within. This does not mean closing our eyes, sitting, and doing nothing. "Going within" means turning to the Supreme Lord (Paramatma) in our hearts and surrendering to His directions, which are available to us even in the conditioned state through His external representative, the bona fide spiritual master. There is no question of inactivity; rather, the enlightened man is always "working for the welfare of all." Arjuna was advised to work for everyone's welfare by fighting the battle of Kurukshetra. Similarly, Krishna wants the businessman to work for the welfare of all by making money to promote the Krishna consciousness movement. He wants the temple devotee to work for everyone's welfare by distributing knowledge of Krishna consciousness.

Everyone has some duty to perform, and when he performs it for Krishna's satisfaction, under the direction of Krishna from within and the spiritual master from without, he is truly working for the welfare of all.

Of course, many people talk about the importance of welfare work, but they generally refer to welfare work for the material body only. If the body is only a covering for the living entity, why concentrate on it? Why save only the shirt of a drowning man? First, we must save the living entity within the body. Then the rest will follow. Even if we somehow manage to feed and clothe the material body, take care of it, and educate it, what have we achieved if we don't liberate the soul within? "For what is a man profited, if he shall gain the whole world, and lose his own soul?" Christ asked. The body is destined to die. That is a fact. But what will happen to the soul? This is the important question asked by the transcendental welfare worker, who wants to care for the person trapped within the body. By providing for the soul, we automatically provide for the body.

Krishna takes care even of the material body of one surrendered to Him. "To those who worship Me with devotion... I carry what they lack and preserve what they have." (9.22) The soul includes everything. On the spiritual platform, nothing is left out. Even this material world is created by spirit. Being by nature dead, inert, matter itself cannot create anything. It is due only to contact with the spirit soul that matter now appears to be alive. When we actually come to the spiritual platform, we will see that we have everything and lack nothing.

Krishna says, "Those who are free from anger and all material desires, who are self-realized, self-disciplined and constantly endeavoring for perfection, are assured of liberation in the Supreme in the very near future." (5.26) To be freed from anger, one must be free from the desire for sense gratification. "While contemplating the objects of the senses, a person develops attachment for them, and from such attachment, lust develops, and from lust, anger arises." (2.62) Lust can never be satisfied. When fuel is poured on a fire, the flames blaze with greater force. Similarly, when we try to gratify the uncontrolled senses, they become all the more enraged and demanding. And because there can never be enough sense gratification to satisfy the plea-

sure capacity of the nonmaterial soul, we become angry. Therefore if we really want to uproot anger, we must control the
senses. We can get free from anger only by surmounting material
desires, and this is possible only by spiritualizing our desires.

It is the soul's nature to desire. No one can become desire-
less, but we can change the quality of our desire. When we plant
spiritual desires and nurture them carefully, material desires
have no chance to grow. The *gopis* were freed from all mundane
lust because they loved Krishna so much. We too must channel
all our desires toward Krishna. Then our desires will be transformed and spiritualized. If we want to be famous businessmen,
artists, speakers, politicians, or whatever, we can act on this
desire for Krishna. Desires can be spiritualized by engagement
in Krishna's service. Moreover, by acting in this way, we are
freed from karmic reaction. According to *Sri Ishopanishad*, we can
work indefinitely in Krishna consciousness without fear of reactions. "One may aspire to live for hundreds of years if he works
continuously in that way, because that sort of work will not bind
him to the law of karma." (*Isho.2*)

By working in Krishna consciousness, constantly endeavoring for perfection, we are guaranteed liberation in "the very near
future." Dedicating everything to Krishna, we should chant His
holy names. Who cannot do this? Even the world's poorest man
can chant Hare Krishna. It doesn't cost anything, nor does it
require any material qualification. One doesn't have to be a
highly learned Ph.D. Anyone can take to this process.

Lord Krishna continues, "Shutting out all external sense
objects, keeping the eyes and vision concentrated between the
two eyebrows, suspending the inward and outward breaths
within the nostrils—thus controlling the mind, senses, and intelligence, the transcendentalist becomes free from desire, fear,
and anger. One who is always in this state is certainly liberated."
(5.27- 28) Here, Lord Krishna speaks of freedom from material
desire. When desire is frustrated, it provokes fear and anger.
We can remove all these impediments by controlling the mind,
senses, and intelligence, and this we can easily accomplish by
engaging everything in Krishna's service. Our God-given intelligence is meant for understanding how to make the world
Krishna conscious. This is Krishna's desire, and it should be ours.

At the conclusion of *Bhagavad-gita,* Krishna says that no one is more dear to Him than the person who, on His behalf, teaches Krishna consciousness to others. If we really want to please the spiritual master and Krishna, we should use our intelligence to spread this transcendental knowledge. Humanity is presently suffering in the most hellish condition. People are living on the animal platform, if not lower than the animals. Striving hard to enjoy the material senses to the utmost, people are succeeding only in drawing death very near. Throughout the world, people are losing their opportunity for liberation; thus, countless human lives are being spoiled. Those who are compassionate want to rectify this situation by distributing Krishna consciousness to everyone. A Vaishnava is by nature compassionate upon all fallen souls. He is always using his intelligence to devise ways to make the world Krishna conscious. For instance, when he was still in India, Srila Prabhupada was thinking, "My countrymen are not interested in this message of Krishna consciousness. They do not want to hear me. Let me go instead to the West and try to convince some Americans. Now that everyone is imitating the Americans, if I can convince some sincere souls there and bring them back to India, maybe my countrymen will listen to them." Thus Srila Prabhupada used his intelligence to make the world Krishna conscious. When the intelligence is properly used, everything else follows. Once the mind, intelligence and senses are all serving Krishna, material life is finished, and the path of liberation is clear.

Lord Krishna concludes this chapter thus: "The sages, knowing Me as the ultimate purpose of all sacrifices and austerities, the Supreme Lord of all planets and demigods, and the benefactor and well-wisher of all living entities, attain peace from the pangs of material miseries." (5.29)

Every living being in this world suffers the pangs of material existence—birth, old age, disease, and death—due to misidentification with the material body. Those who are intelligent, those who are sages, want to use this life to solve this problem of suffering, both for themselves and others. That is the purpose of all Vedic sacrifice.

Krishna specifically states, however, that the sages who possess transcendental knowledge know Him to be the ultimate purpose of sacrifice, of austerities, of everything. Austerities should not be performed for some material benefit, but to know Krishna. Such austerities will truly relieve us from all material distress. Materially attached persons perform sacrifices for some temporary material end. Hiranyakasipu, the great demon of the Satya-yuga, performed austerities so severe that even the demigod Brahma was obliged to appear before him. Hiranyakasipu wanted to become immortal, but unfortunately he wanted immortality for his material body, and this is impossible. No one, not even Lord Brahma, can keep his material body indefinitely. Brahma therefore said, "Since I myself am not immortal, I cannot grant you this boon." Hiranyakasipu, being a great cunning demon, then tried to figure out an indirect way to receive the gift of immortality. Therefore he requested, "Grant me the boon of never being killed by day or night, neither by man nor beast, neither indoors nor outdoors, neither on the earth nor in the air, neither by water, fire, nor weapon...." He thus tried to think of every possible way to avoid death, and Lord Brahma granted all his requests. Hiranyakasipu finally concluded that he was unkillable and immortal, but he did not reckon that the Supreme Personality of Godhead is greater and more clever than anyone else. When the demon was raging against God in anger, the Lord appeared in His wonderful form as Lord Nrishingadeva and swiftly killed him. He killed him neither by day nor by night, but at twilight; neither inside nor outside, but in the threshold; neither as man nor beast, but in the form of Nrishingadeva, an awesome and transcendental half-man half-lion; neither on the ground nor in the air, but on His lap; neither with weapons, fire, nor water, but with His sharp claws. Thus without breaking any of Brahma's blessings, the Supreme Lord easily killed the demon.

God is transcendental to everyone. We cannot figure Him out with our tiny brains. No amount of futile mental speculation can approach Him. God is so great that we cannot even understand His material energy, which is but a fragment of His mystic power. God is full of all kinds of inconceivable potencies. We have only one recourse: Surrender unto Him. Since Lord Krishna is the ultimate goal of all sacrifice and austerity, why try, like Hiranyakasipu, to perform sacrifices for material benediction?

Why make sacrifices to obtain a good wife, or success in business? After all, these things are temporary. Lord Krishna clearly says that foolish people worship the demigods for such temporary blessings. Lord Krishna is the Supreme Lord of all the demigods, and the source of everything. By satisfying Him, we automatically satisfy the demigods and all other living entities.

Lord Krishna is the benefactor and well-wisher (*suhrdam*) of all living entities. In this world, no one can be the friend of everyone. A friend of the Pakistanis cannot be a friend of the Indians; or a friend of the Russians cannot be a friend of the Americans. The same with Turks and Greeks, Arabs and Jews, and on and on. In this world, there is rampant enmity on national, political, religious, and racial grounds. Moreover, people are killing and eating the poor animals. Sometimes people advertise themselves as the friends and well-wishers of everyone, but they continue to kill and eat animals. "Friend of everyone" also means friend of the animals. Materialistic endeavors to become the "friend of everyone" are bound to be frustrated.

Only Krishna or His pure devotee can be the friend and well-wisher of everyone. Being the seed-giving Father of every living entity, Krishna is everyone's best friend. He has everyone's welfare at heart. He is directing the wanderings of every conditioned soul, accompanying everyone as the Supersoul (Paramatma) in the heart. "The Supreme Lord is situated in everyone's heart, O Arjuna, and is directing the wanderings of all living entities, who are seated as on a machine, made of the material energy." (18.61) Whether the living entity is a dog, hog, ant, worm, or human being, the Lord is present in the heart, ready to give directions, waiting for us to turn our attention to Him. As soon as we do, He gives us full Krishna consciousness so that we may know Him perfectly. Through His mercy, we can come to know our true nature and our relationship with Him. This is real yoga: the knowledge of our relationship with Krishna. By rendering transcendental loving service, we can know that we are eternally related to Him as His servants and swiftly attain relief from the pangs of material existence. This is the real peace formula. Peace can be had only by surrendering to Krishna's will. Otherwise, there is no peace in this material world.

A man waiting in jail for his execution cannot be peaceful. Even if his life is extended for a day, week, or month, he cannot be peaceful. For peace, he must be reprieved. Only by understanding that we are not these bodies, but eternal spirit souls, part and parcel of Krishna, can we be pardoned from the death sentence of material existence. Then we can pass from death to eternal life with Krishna.

Peace can be found in Krishna and in knowledge of ourselves as spirit souls. Peace can be found in service to Krishna and to mankind by distributing Lord Krishna's sublime message, *Bhagavad-gita As It Is*. This message is the greatest gift we can give anyone. Lord Krishna has given it to us freely. Now we should freely deliver it to others. Hare Krishna!

A yogi is greater than the ascetic, greater than the empiricist and greater than the fruitive worker. Therefore, O Arjuna, in all circumstances, be a yogi. And of all yogis, he who always abides in Me with great faith, worshipping Me in transcendental loving service, is most intimately united with Me in yoga and is the highest of all. *(Bg. 6.46-47)*

CHAPTER SIX

Sankhya-yoga

In this chapter, Lord Krishna explains the essence and perfection of the *sankhya-yoga* system, a system of meditation—including mind control, breath control, and *asanas* (sitting postures)—set forth by Lord Kapiladev. Basically, the word *yoga* means yoking, or linking to the Supreme. In order to achieve this, we have to give up all other links. Therefore yoga is also related to renunciation.

In the conditioned state, due to lust for sense enjoyment, the living entities are yoked very tightly to matter, just as beasts are yoked to a great load. This material burden, including material desires, must be renounced for the sake of linking with the Supreme. Therefore Lord Krishna begins this discussion with a statement on renunciation. "One who is unattached to the fruits of his work," He says, "and who works as he is obligated, is in the renounced order of life, and he is the true mystic—not he who lights no fire and performs no work." (6.1)

As indicated here, the essence of renunciation is positive, not negative. This is also confirmed by Rupa Goswami, who defined renunciation as "engaging everything in the Lord's service." Materialists want to engage everything for sense gratification, believing this to be life's goal, but this path leads only to material bondage. Real liberation consists of devoting everything to Krishna. It is not sufficient to merely follow the four regulative principles (no meat eating, no illicit sex, no intoxication, no gambling). To be perfectly situated in yoga, one must come to the positive platform of Krishna consciousness, the platform on which everything is dovetailed in Krishna's service.

Lord Krishna continues: "What is called renunciation is the same as yoga, or linking oneself with the Supreme, for no one can become a yogi unless he renounces the desire for sense gratification. For one who is a neophyte in the eightfold yoga system, work is said to be the means; and for one who has already attained to yoga, cessation of all material activities is said to be the means." (6.2-3)

In the beginning stages, we may perform Krishna conscious activities mechanically, but this is not perfection. For perfection, we have to understand that the purpose behind renunciation is to link ourselves to the Supreme in positive Krishna consciousness. Here, "cessation of all material activities" means the abandonment of sense gratificatory action, not the cessation of devotional duties in Krishna consciousness.

"A person is said to have attained to yoga when, having renounced all material desires, he neither acts for sense gratification nor engages in fruitive activities." (6.4) Material desires, or desires for fruitive action, cause material bondage, but liberation is attained by sacrificing everything for Krishna. "All that you do, all that you eat, all that you offer and give away, as well as all austerities that you may perform, should be done as an offering unto Me." (9.27) This is the perfection of Krishna consciousness.

Next, Lord Krishna discusses the very instrument by which we can see Him: the mind itself. It is the mind that binds us to the material world and that leads us to liberation as well. "A man must elevate himself by his own mind," Krishna says, "not degrade himself. The mind is the friend of the conditioned soul, and his enemy as well. For him who has conquered the mind, the mind is the best of friends; but for one who has failed to do so, his very mind will be the greatest enemy. For one who has conquered the mind, the Supersoul is already reached, for he has attained tranquility. To such a man, happiness and distress, heat and cold, honor and dishonor are all the same." (6.5-7)

The perfection of yoga is to see Krishna in everything. Because the materialist sees everything in relation to his material body, he considers one thing favorable and another unfavorable, one thing pleasant and another unpleasant. Thus his mind is always accepting and rejecting things on the basis of the material body and sense gratification. Even the concept of good and evil become relative to the materialist's sense gratification. He will perform any evil, forbidden act as long as it gratifies his senses.

For one who has conquered his mind, however, good and evil are seen from the absolute point of view, in relation to Krishna. Because the yogi sees everything as the expansion of Krishna's energy, he sees everything as perfect and complete. This is confirmed by *Ishopanishad: Om purnam adah purnam idam.* The Supreme Lord is perfect and complete, and the perfect yogi sees everything in relation to Him. Therefore, for the yogi, the mundane conception of good and evil does not exist. For him, everything is Krishna.

This is not to say that the yogi performs forbidden acts in the name of monism, saying, "Everything is Krishna. There is no good or evil. Therefore I can do anything." No. His very vision is dependent on his mind's being perfectly controlled and centered on Krishna. Being on the spiritual platform, his mind immediately rejects all forms of sense gratification. It is therefore said that his mind is his friend. For the sense gratifier, however, the mind is the worst enemy. Only when the mind is controlled by service to Krishna can it become the perfect medium for seeing Him.

Sometimes Srila Prabhupada would say, "Don't try to see Krishna directly. Just try to see Krishna in your service." When the mind is completely engaged in serving Krishna, it becomes transparent. By nature, the mind is as transparent as pure water, but, like water, it becomes muddy when agitated. The mind is meant to deliver the conditioned soul from the material platform back to the spiritual platform, but this is possible only when it is engaged in Krishna's service and free from the mud of sense gratification. Once the mind is transparent, we can perceive the Supersoul, but as long as it is agitated by sense gratification, we can see only the mundane objects that gratify our senses. It is often said that "Beauty is in the eye of the beholder." Therefore, the yogi aspiring to see the Supersoul must have a controlled mind fixed in devotional service.

Real yoga aims at focusing the mind on the Supreme, whether the yogic process be the mechanical *astanga-yoga* system, or *jnana-yoga*, the cultivation of knowledge. *Bhakti-yoga*, however, controls the mind at once by engaging it in service to Krishna. *Bhakti-yoga* is therefore the perfection of yoga, and the best process of controlling the mind, as Lord Krishna confirms at the end of this chapter.

Next, Lord Krishna explains equality of vision: "A person is said to be established in self-realization, and is called a yogi [or mystic] when he is fully satisfied by virtue of acquired knowledge and realization. Such a person is situated in transcendence and is self-controlled. He sees everything—whether it be pebbles, stones or gold—as the same." (6.8) The real yogi sees Krishna in everything. Yoga is not a process meant for touching the nose with the toe, or standing on the head, or stopping the breath. If we don't come to the point of realizing Krishna in everything, then the performance of yogic exercises, or the cultivation of knowledge, or any other process is ultimately useless. Equanimity, or unity of vision, comes only when we see Krishna everywhere at all times. Once we see Krishna in everything, we can appreciate everything as Krishna's energy, and know its proper utilization as well.

Now that Krishna has established the value of yoga, He begins to describe the process itself: "A transcendentalist should always try to concentrate his mind on the Supreme Self. He should live alone in a secluded place and should always carefully control his mind. He should be free from desires and feelings of possessiveness." (6.10) Krishna begins by advising the yogi to go to a secluded place. This implies that yoga cannot be performed in a materialistic environment. By nature, the spirit soul is infinitesimal, and he tends to be influenced by those about him. By associating with materialistic people, he tends to become materialistic, and by associating with devotees, he becomes attracted to devotional service.

Formerly, yogis used to go to the forest because the mode of goodness prevails in the forest, whereas the mode of passion usually dominates the city. The temples of Vishnu (Krishna), however, are transcendental and as good as Vrindaban. Therefore yoga is best performed in the association of devotees in such temples. Because Krishna is here explaining the *astanga-yoga* system, which is a physical process of sitting postures (*asanas*) and breath control, He recommends a secluded place such as the Himalayas, where the yogi will not be disturbed by material vibrations. In today's cities, there are always radios blaring,

planes passing overhead, and many other disturbing materialistic noises that make meditation impossible.

Lord Krishna continues: "To practice yoga, one should go
to a secluded place and should lay *kusa*-grass on the ground and
then cover it with a deerskin and a soft cloth. The seat should
be neither too high nor too low and should be situated in a
sacred place. The yogi should then sit on it very firmly and
should practise yoga by controlling the mind and the senses,
purifying the heart and fixing the mind on one point." (6.11-12)
Today, it is fashionable to perform yoga to improve one's general
health, to reduce fat, and to better enjoy sex life. But this is not
real yoga. Yoga should be performed to purify the heart and fix
the mind on one point. "One point" does not mean a dot on
the wall, or some impersonalist mandala. "One point" means
Krishna, the one point that is the origin of everything. Unless
the mind is focused on the Supreme, it cannot concentrate on
one point. Yoga is a process of purification meant to enable us
to focus the mind on Krishna.

Lord Krishna continues: "One should hold one's body, neck,
and head erect in a straight line, and stare steadily at the tip of
the nose. Thus, with an unagitated, subdued mind, devoid of
fear, completely free from sex life, one should meditate upon
Me within the heart and make Me the ultimate goal of life."
(6.13-14) Again, the emphasis is on mind control to realize
Krishna as the supreme goal. Since Krishna is situated within
the heart of every living being, the Lord in the heart is the proper
object of meditation. The *astanga-yoga* system outlined here is
more or less mechanical, but the ultimate goal is Krishna consciousness.

"Thus practicing control of the body, mind, and activities,
the mystic transcendentalist attains to the kingdom of God [or
the abode of Krishna] by cessation of material existence." (6.5)

Unless the body, mind, and activities are controlled, yoga
cannot be performed. Real yoga is not performed just fifteen
minutes in the morning and evening and then forgotten in between. Of course, cheaters may promote such pseudo yoga for
money making, but this has nothing to do with self-realization.
The yoga that Krishna recommends must be practiced twenty-
four hours a day. Everything—body, mind, and activities—must

be controlled. Obviously, this is no cheap, easy process but a method that requires complete commitment.

Of course, for this difficult age of Kali, Lord Sri Krishna Chaitanya Mahaprabhu has recommended the chanting of the holy names. This is an easy and practical method by which the mind can be focused on Krishna and automatically controlled. We may not be able to search out a secluded place in the Himalayas, but we can visit the temple of the Lord, chant the holy names, focus the mind on Krishna, and immediately attain the transcendental position.

"There is no possibility of one's becoming a yogi, O Arjuna, if one eats too much, or eats too little, sleeps too much, or does not sleep enough. He who is temperate in his habits of eating, sleeping, working, and recreation, can mitigate all material pains by practicing the yoga system." (6.16-17)

These rules and regulations are intended to help us progress in Krishna consciousness. We are not interested in fad diets or life styles. Some years ago, when someone suggested that we eat only two *chapatis* a day, Srila Prabhupada said, "Why two *chapatis*? If a man can eat twenty *chapatis*, digest them, and work hard for Krishna, that is all right. But if he cannot digest what he eats, then even two *chapatis* may be sense gratification." The idea is to accept only what is necessary to keep the body in a healthy, fit condition for serving Krishna. When one eats too much, he becomes fat and unhealthy from being overweight, and he also tends to sleep too much. All this indicates overindulgence. On the other hand, if one eats too little, he becomes weak and thin, and unable to serve Krishna fully. Since the body is the property of the Lord, whatever is given to us by the Lord should be properly used for His service. If Krishna gives us automobiles, buildings, or temples, we should maintain them nicely for Him. It is sinful to enjoy them for sense gratification, or misuse them by not maintaining and utilizing them properly. The material body is also a facility given by Krishna, and meant for Krishna's service. We have neither the right to abuse it, nor the right to enjoy it for sense gratification.

"When the yogi, by practice of yoga, disciplines his mental activities and becomes situated in Transcendence—devoid of all material desires—he is said to have attained yoga." (6.18) In practically every verse, Krishna emphasizes the necessity of freedom from material desire. Since time immemorial, the conditioned soul has been covered with material desires for sense gratification, for himself and for his family and society. Yoga is the process by which all these selfish desires are sacrificed for the sake of the Supreme. Regardless of the type of yoga performed, the goal is surrender unto Krishna. Unless we have come to this point, we have not attained perfection in yoga.

Lord Krishna describes this perfect stage more elaborately: "As a lamp in a windless place does not waver, so the transcendentalist whose mind is controlled, remains always steady in his meditation on the transcendent Self. The stage of perfection is called trance, or *samadhi*, when one's mind is completely restrained from material mental activities by practice of yoga. This is characterized by one's ability to see the self by the pure mind and to relish and rejoice in the self. In that joyous state, one is situated in boundless transcendental happiness and enjoys himself through transcendental senses. Established thus, one never departs from the truth, and upon gaining this, he thinks there is no greater gain. Being situated in such a position, one is never shaken, even in the midst of greatest difficulty. This indeed is actual freedom from all miseries arising from material contact." (6.19-23)

The materially contaminated mind and senses drag the soul down to hell, but if they are purified, they become the vehicle for liberation. The *samadhi* mentioned here is not the inactive *samadhi* imagined by the impersonalists. Rather, it is complete absorption in Krishna's service. When purified, the mind does not think of sense gratification but of service to Krishna. And the senses follow; they do not engage in their own gratification but in Krishna conscious action. In this way, one never departs from the knowledge that all living beings are part and parcel of Krishna.

If we never want to forget Krishna, we must have a pure mind and transcendental senses. When the mind thinks of Krishna and the senses serve Him, relief from all material miseries follows naturally. All miseries arise from contact with matter and from the soul's misidentification with it. This misconception is called maya, or illusion. Krishna thus points the way to freedom: "One should engage himself in the practice of yoga with undeviating determination and faith. One should abandon, without exception, all material desires born of false ego and thus control all the senses on all sides by the mind. Gradually, step by step, with full conviction, one should become situated in trance by means of intelligence, and thus the mind should be fixed on the Self alone and should think of nothing else." (6.24-25) Again, trance is defined as the engagement of the mind in Krishna consciousness, not as a state of doing nothing.

"From whatever and wherever the mind wanders due to its flickering and unsteady nature, one must certainly withdraw it and bring it back under the control of the Self. Steady in the Self, being freed from all material contamination, the yogi achieves the highest perfectional stage of happiness in touch with the Supreme Consciousness." (6.26, 28) The individual self is happy when he is controlled by the Supreme Self, Krishna. Steadiness in the Self is the yoga of constant, undeviating Krishna consciousness.

"A true yogi observes Me in all beings, and also sees every being in Me. Indeed, the self-realized man sees Me everywhere. For one who sees Me everywhere and sees everything in Me, I am never lost, nor is he ever lost to Me. The yogi who knows that I and the Supersoul within all creatures are one, worships Me and remains always in Me in all circumstances. He is a perfect yogi who, by comparison to his own self, sees the true equality of all beings, both in their happiness and distress, O Arjuna!" (6.29-32)

Here, Lord Krishna describes the perfection of yoga as the ability to see Him in all living beings and to see everything in relation to Him. This true equality of vision cannot be realized by going out in the street and artificially proclaiming the equality of all men. Unless one has the spiritual vision to see Krishna within the heart of every living being, there is no question of seeing everyone equally. The material world is a place of duality: rich and poor, intelligent and dumb, beautiful and ugly, cultured and uncultured, human and animal. These are material differences that cannot be denied. But when by actual realization, attained through the cultivation of Krishna consciousness, the yogi understands himself to be spirit soul and not the material body, he can also understand that others exist on the same spiritual platform, be they man or beast. Seeing this, he feels ecstatic oneness in understanding that all living beings are part and parcel of Krishna. Then he can see the true equality of all beings, both in happiness and distress, as well as in any other duality.

At this point in the discourse, Arjuna expresses doubt about the practicality of this yoga system: "O Madhusudana, the system of yoga which you have summarized appears impractical and unendurable to me, for the mind is restless and unsteady. Truly, the mind is restless, turbulent, obstinate and very strong, O Krishna, and to subdue it is, it seems to me, more difficult than controlling the wind." (6.33-34)

Being a warrior, Arjuna doesn't have time to sit down and meditate for five or ten years, what to speak of sixty thousand years, like Valmiki. *Astanga-yoga* was the dharma for Satya-yuga, the golden age, when men lived for one hundred thousand years. After practicing this yoga for sixty thousand years or so, great yogis would finally succeed in seeing Krishna everywhere. Of course, on the battlefield, such lengthy meditation is impossible for Arjuna. Nor is it possible for anyone who lives for only a hundred years. Therefore Arjuna says that *astanga-yoga* seems to be an "impractical and unendurable" method for controlling the mind, which is more difficult to control than the wind. Although scientists brag of controlling nature, they have not been able to control the wind, let alone the mind. Who can control the mind? Since this yoga seems impossible, Arjuna has raised a doubt, but he is quickly reassured by the Lord.

"O mighty-armed son of Kunti," Krishna says, "it is undoubt edly very difficult to curb the restless mind, but it is possible by constant practice and detachment." (6.35) Since this discipline must be constant, the disciple must be determined to practice it constantly. Animals cannot be determined, but human beings can. At every turn, an animal is deviated by sense gratification. A dog may start to run toward his master, but if someone throws him a bone, he will be immediately diverted. Animals are trained and controlled through their desire for sense gratification, but a human being, due to superior intelligence, can decide to control his senses for a higher purpose. By exercising such control, he becomes even more determined.

In addition to constant practice, Lord Krishna mentions detachment. The two go together. If we constantly practice the
regulative principles of freedom with determination, we will
become detached from temporary, material things. Then the
cultivation of transcendental knowledge will automatically follow. In this way, Krishna says, the mind can be controlled.

Lord Krishna continues: "For one whose mind is unbridled,
self-realization is difficult work. But he whose mind is controlled
and who strives by right means is assured of success. That is
My opinion." (6.36) We should know that Lord Krishna's opinion
is not an ordinary one: it is the Absolute Truth. Since Krishna
Himself is the Absolute Truth, His body and opinion are also
Absolute. Although Krishna may sometimes appear to be an
ordinary human being, He is not. Therefore we should not mistakenly consider His opinion to be an ordinary one.

The "right means" of which Krishna speaks are those
methods prescribed by the *shastras* and the spiritual master. If
we control the mind and strive by right means, following the
orders of the guru, success is assured. On the battlefield of
Kurukshetra, for instance, Arjuna was both outnumbered and
outgeneraled. Materially speaking, his opponents had everything to their advantage, but to succeed, Arjuna had only to
follow the instructions of his guru, who was the Supreme Guru,
Lord Krishna Himself. Krishna was personally standing before
Arjuna as his teacher telling him to fight. Although Arjuna personally preferred not to fight, he sacrificed his own desires and
fought anyway. He just followed directions. Therefore, at the
conclusion of *Bhagavad-gita*, Sanjaya proclaims that wherever
there is Lord Krishna and His devotee Arjuna, there is victory.
It may be very difficult work to give up our sense gratification
and engage the senses in Krishna's service, but if we follow the
orders of guru and Krishna, victory will be ours. That is the
Lord's transcendental opinion, confirmed in the *Katha-upanishad*:

> *yasya deve parā bhaktir*
> *yathā deve tathā gurau*
> *tasyaite kathitā hy arthāḥ*
> *prakāśante mahātmanaḥ*

"Unto those great souls who have implicit faith in both the Lord and the spiritual master, all the imports of Vedic knowledge are automatically revealed." Faith, rightly placed, is our salvation.

Yet another doubt plagues Arjuna, caused by the fear of losing everything in the struggle to attain yoga: "What is the destination of the man of faith who does not persevere, who in the beginning takes to the process of self-realization but who later desists due to worldly-mindedness and thus does not attain perfection in mysticism? O mighty-armed Krishna, does not such a man, being deviated from the path of Transcendence, perish like a riven cloud, with no position in any sphere? This is my doubt, O Krishna, and I ask You to dispel it completely. But for Yourself, no one is to be found who can destroy this doubt." (6.37-39)

This is a most intelligent question. From the very beginning, Arjuna at least knew enough to approach Krishna about his doubts, admitting, "Now I am confused about my duty...tell me clearly what is best for me. Now I am Your disciple, and a soul surrendered unto You. Please instruct me." (2.7) Once again, Arjuna is admitting that "but for Yourself, no one is to be found who can destroy this doubt." Therefore Arjuna has rightly approached Lord Krishna to slay this demon of doubt. Indeed, whoever approaches the bona fide spiritual master in this way is assured of success. Doubts are always compared to demons, and Krishna can destroy any demon; therefore when doubts come before us, we should consult the spiritual master. Then these doubts can be slain on the basis of the supreme authority, the words and teachings of Lord Krishna.

Just see how Lord Krishna immediately slays this demon of doubt! "O son of Pritha," He says, "a transcendentalist engaged in auspicious activities does not meet with destruction either in this world or in the spiritual world. One who does good, My friend, is never overcome by evil." (6.40) Like the warrior engaged in battle for a righteous cause, the yogi can never lose. Either he is successful in his attempt and immediately attains the transcendental results, or he is elevated to the heavenly planets, due to his auspicious activities. "The unsuccessful yogi, after many, many years of enjoyment on the planets of the pious living entities, is born into a family of righteous people, or into a family of rich aristocracy. Or he takes his birth in a family of transcendentalists who are surely great in wisdom. Verily, such a birth is rare in this world." (6.41-42)

These are certainly consoling words. For a person striving to become Krishna conscious, nothing is inauspicious. Even if he fails, the outcome is good. Sometimes devotees ask why one must be reborn in the heavenly planets. Actually, this is not necessary. But as the fulfiller of everyone's desire, Krishna may make arrangements for the unsuccessful yogi to go to the heavenly planets to become purified of whatever material desires remain. After many years of enjoyment in the heavenly planets, the yogi understands that such enjoyment is not life's perfection. He then gets an opportunity to take birth in a family of advanced transcendentalists and once again continues to make spiritual progress. Krishna says, "On taking such a birth, he again revives the divine consciousness of his previous life, and he tries to make further progress in order to achieve complete success, O son of Kuru. By virtue of the divine consciousness of his previous life, he automatically becomes attracted to the yogic principles— even without seeking them. Such an inquisitive transcendentalist, striving for yoga, stands always above the ritualistic principles of the scriptures." (6.43-44) Herein, Krishna guarantees the ultimate success of every yogi, or devotee. Just by chanting Hare Krishna, the yoga for this age, our future perfection is assured. Nothing else is necessary. Just by sincerely chanting the holy names of the Lord, we can become perfect yogis.

Lord Krishna adds: "When the yogi engages himself with sincere endeavor in making further progress, being washed of all contaminations, then ultimately, after many, many births of practice, he attains the supreme goal. A yogi is greater than the ascetic, greater than the empiricist and greater than the fruitive worker. Therefore, O Arjuna, in all circumstances, be a yogi." (6.45-46)

The yogi is the topmost living being because he is striving to link himself to Krishna in transcendental loving service. Linking certainly does not mean merging into the impersonal Brahman, as Lord Krishna confirms in this chapter's concluding verse: "And of all yogis, he who always abides in Me with great faith, worshipping Me in transcendental loving service, is most intimately united with Me in yoga and is the highest of all." (6.47)

Real union with Krishna is a union of love. In love, there is no loss of individuality. Rather, conflicting desires are merged in the unity of common desire. For the lover, there is only one desire: the desire of his beloved. Through love, the desires of the lover and the beloved become one. When the devotee surrenders to Krishna, he naturally accepts the desire of Krishna. Thus the greatest yogi is one who surrenders utterly to Krishna, accepting Krishna's desire completely, and wanting nothing but His eternal service. Such a pure lover of God is certainly most intimately united with the Lord in transcendental loving service.

We can now understand that all other yogas culminate in *bhakti-yoga*, the yoga of loving devotion. *Bhagavad-gita* does not really teach many systems of yoga. It mentions different systems, but by showing that they all lead to loving devotional service, it ultimately teaches only *bhakti-yoga*. The perfection of *jnana-yoga*, for instance, is in understanding that Vasudeva, Krishna, is everything. After many births of cultivating knowledge, the *jnana-yogi* finally comes to this point and surrenders to Krishna. The perfection of the mystic yoga system comes when the yogi understands that Krishna is everywhere, within everything, and that everything is within Krishna. Understanding this, he surrenders to Krishna and becomes a *bhakta-yogi*, engaging in the Lord's transcendental service.

In the final analysis, there is only one yoga: unity with Krishna in transcendental loving service. Therefore at the conclusion of *Bhagavad-gita*, Lord Krishna advises: "Abandon all varieties of religion and just surrender unto Me. I shall deliver you from all sinful reaction. Do not fear." (18.66) If we want to attain yogic perfection, we have to accept the instructions of Krishna as they are. Sri Krishna Chaitanya Mahaprabhu has instructed us to chant the Hare Krishna *mahamantra:* Hare Krishna, Hare Krishna, Krishna Krishna, Hare Hare/ Hare Rama, Hare Rama, Rama Rama, Hare Hare. Similarly, Srila Prabhupada has said, "Chant Hare Krishna and be happy." There is no difference between Krishna and His name. If we just chant the holy name of Krishna with full faith in Lord Krishna and the spiritual master, we can be most intimately united with Krishna and thus attain the perfection of all yoga. Hare Krishna!

Unintelligent men, who know Me not, think that I have assumed this form and personality. Due to their small knowledge, they do not know My higher nature, which is changeless and supreme. *(Bg. 7.24)*

CHAPTER SEVEN

Knowledge of the Absolute

In the first six chapters of *Bhagavad-gita*, Lord Krishna explained the difference between matter and spirit, knowing which we can understand that the living being is not the material body, but spirit soul. He also explained the process of yoga leading to transcendental knowledge, understood in three basic stages: knowledge of oneself as nonmaterial, knowledge of God as the Supreme Controller, and knowledge of one's relationship with God in transcendental loving service.

Now, in this chapter, Lord Krishna begins to discuss His own divine nature, but first He sets down the qualifications for understanding Him: "Now hear, O son of Pritha, how by practicing yoga in full consciousness of Me, with mind attached to Me, you can know Me in full, free from doubt." (7.1) Unless we are in full Krishna consciousness and free from doubt, we cannot understand Krishna as He is. Actually, this subject matter is very difficult. It is not a very common or easy thing to study and understand God, the reservoir of all knowledge. Therefore Krishna says, "Out of many thousands among men, one may endeavor for perfection, and of those who have achieved perfection, hardly one knows Me in truth." (7.3)

It is not so difficult to realize *aham brahmasmi*, "I am not this body, but spirit soul." Just by philosophical analysis, we can understand that the body is changing and that the soul, who witnesses these changes, must be different from the body. Nor is it very difficult to realize the impersonal nature of the Absolute, which can be understood by mental speculation, utilizing the *neti neti* ("not this, not that") method. Searching for the eternal Truth, mental speculators go through the material universe saying, "God is not this, God is not that." Then finally, when they are exhausted by negating finite possibilities, they may come to understand that the Supreme is beyond everything. This kind of impersonal understanding is readily attainable.

What is truly difficult is understanding Krishna as He is. Although He appears as a human being, He is not human at all. Therefore He says, "Fools deride Me when I descend in the human form. They do not know My superior nature, and My supreme dominion over all that be." (9.11) Although this understanding is extremely difficult, it is possible by the grace of Krishna and His pure devotee. The *Padma Purana* also confirms that Krishna cannot be understood by the blunt material senses. But, being pleased with the transcendental loving service rendered by His devotees, Lord Krishna reveals Himself. "My dear Arjuna, only by undivided devotional service can I be understood as I am, standing before you, and can thus be seen directly. Only in this way can you enter into the mysteries of My understanding." (11.54) By the grace of the Lord and the instructions of His pure devotee, we can easily understand Him. Otherwise, understanding the infinite Supreme Person is most difficult, for He is unfathomable even to great sages and demigods. "You alone know Yourself by Your own potencies," Arjuna later declares (10.15).

Now, in this Seventh Chapter, Lord Krishna begins describing His different energies: "Earth, water, fire, air, ether, mind, intelligence, and false ego—altogether these eight comprise My separated material energies. Besides this inferior nature, O mighty-armed Arjuna, there is a superior energy of Mine, which is all living entities who are struggling with material nature and sustaining the universe." (7.4-5) As the Supreme Personality of Godhead, Lord Krishna possesses innumerable energies. Although we cannot calculate their number, the Lord Himself divides them into three principal categories for our understanding. First, there is the superior, spiritual, internal energy, of which the eternal kingdom of God is a manifestation. Secondly, there is the inferior, material, external energy, sometimes called the Lord's "separated energy." In one sense, of course, nothing can be separate from Krishna, but it appears that way. For instance, on a cloudy day, we appear to be separated from the sun, but factually the sun is still there giving light. Due to the intervention of clouds, the sun appears to be hidden. Similarly, the material energy is the Lord's deluding energy which hides from us Krishna's real identity as the Supreme Personality of Godhead. Because it veils Krishna from our vision, it is called separated, material, or inferior energy. Thirdly, there is the marginal energy, which is between the superior and inferior, and partakes of the qualities of both.

Specifically, the marginal energy refers to the living beings, the *jiva-atmas*. By nature, the *jivas* belong to the superior energy, but because they are infinitesimal in size (*anu*), they tend to be influenced, or covered, by the inferior material energy. Therefore they are called marginal, that is, existing between the inferior and superior. By their independence, or free will, they can align themselves with either the superior or inferior energies. When the marginal living entity turns his consciousness toward Krishna, he realizes himself to be part and parcel of the superior energy. And when he turns away from Krishna and tries to enjoy the separated material energy by engaging in sense gratification, he is captured by maya. Falsely identifying himself with the material nature, he permits his real spiritual nature to be covered.

Lord Krishna continues: "Of all that is material and all that is spiritual in this world, know for certain that I am both its origin and dissolution." (7.6) Krishna's real nature is the cause of everything. According to *Brahma-samhita: Isvarah paramah krishna sat-cit-ananda-vigrahah/ anadhir adir govindah sarva-karana-karanam.* "Krishna is the cause of all causes. He is the primal cause, and He is the very form of eternal being, knowledge and bliss." And, in the opening statement of *Srimad-Bhagavatam: Janmady asya yato.* Krishna, the son of Vasudeva, is declared to be "the transcendent reality, the primeval cause of all causes, from whom all manifested universes arise, in whom they dwell, and by whom they are destroyed." (*Bhag.* 1.1.1)

It is important to understand that although Krishna is everything, He is transcendental and independent. Although He is the cause of everything, He is aloof and is never entangled. "There is no Truth superior to Me," He tells Arjuna. "Everything rests upon Me, as pearls are strung upon a thread." (7.7) Here, Lord Krishna explicitly asserts His nature as the Supreme Absolute Truth and also the Supreme Person. The Supreme Absolute Truth is not impersonal; it is the Supreme Personality of Godhead Sri Krishna.

According to *Srimad-Bhagavatam*, the Supreme Absolute Truth is realized in three phases: Brahman, Paramatma, and Bhagavan. Brahman is the glowing effulgence of Krishna's transcendental body. Paramatma is Krishna's expansion in the heart of every living being. And Bhagavan is Krishna Himself, the Supreme Person. Realization of these three features has been compared to the threefold knowledge of the sun. A child first appreciates the sun as sunshine, the heat and light that give him daily enjoyment. Then, after going to school and hearing from a teacher, he learns that the sun globe, which is the life source for the whole solar system, is many miles away. If he becomes an advanced student of Vedic knowledge, however, he can understand that the sun god residing within the sun planet is the actual source of the heat and light. Similarly, the Absolute Truth is understood by neophytes as the impersonal, all-pervading spiritual energy called Brahman, then by the more experienced as the localized Supersoul in the hearts of all, and finally, by advanced transcendentalists, as Krishna, the Supreme Personality of Godhead. Just as the sun is the origin of the universe, so everything in existence depends upon the Supreme Personality of Godhead, Bhagavan Sri Krishna, the cause of all causes. He is the cause of both the material and spiritual manifestations, including the all-pervasive Brahman. Brahman is the energy, but Krishna is the energetic. "I am the basis of the impersonal Brahman," He directly states (14.27). Generally, impersonalists meditate on Brahman, but they should search out the source of Brahman, Krishna, who is greater than Brahman and superior to Brahman. That source, the cause of all causes, being the greatest of all, should be worshipped by all.

In the verses that follow, Lord Krishna reveals how He can be seen in all the attractive aspects of His creation. "O son of Kunti [Arjuna], I am the taste of water, the light of the sun and the moon, the syllable *om* in the Vedic mantras; I am the sound in ether and ability in man. I am the original fragrance of the earth, and I am the heat in fire. I am the life of all that lives, and I am the penances of all ascetics." (7.8-9) All living entities need water to live. Without water, the earth would be a lifeless desert. The taste of water is satisfying because of its purity. If water is salty or impure, no one wants to drink it. In its original, pure state, water represents Krishna. The sun and moon also represent Krishna. When we wake up in the morning, we are first aware of the sunlight, and in the evening there is moonlight. This means that we can be aware of Krishna both day and night. The impersonal vibration *om*, representing Brahman, also emanates from Krishna, the basis of Brahman. Indeed, Krishna is the origin of sound itself, which vibrates throughout the atmosphere. A man with unusual abilities or talents—a great artist, poet, musician, warrior, athlete, or whatever—certainly attracts attention. Those attractive abilities and qualities emanate from Krishna, the reservoir of all attractive qualities. Everything has some aroma or original fragrance: that too is Krishna. The pure, original feature of everything is Krishna, because Krishna is the origin of everything.

Such awareness of Krishna's presence in His creation should not be confused with the pantheistic or *sahajiya* approach that says, "Oh, everything is Krishna. Let me enjoy sense gratification." No. Since Krishna is the source from which all things flow, all things are meant for His glorification. What Krishna describes in this chapter is His various manifestations by which He can be seen and remembered. This is not sentimentalism, but a scientific process for developing Krishna consciousness.

"O son of Pritha," Krishna continues, "know that I am the original seed of all existences, the intelligence of the intelligent, and the prowess of all powerful men. I am the strength of the strong, devoid of passion and desire. I am sex life which is not contrary to religious principles." (7.10-11) The pure state of things, the greatest manifestation of things, represents Krishna. The strength of the strong is one of the opulences of Krishna, who is full in six basic opulences: wealth, strength, fame, beauty, knowledge, and renunciation. Sometimes we see that strength is misused by conditioned living entities who are controlled by passion and ignorance. Lord Krishna's strength, however, is pure and transcendental. Therefore, when strength, devoid of passion and ignorance, is used for the purpose of Krishna consciousness, it represents Krishna.

Similarly, sex life in accordance with the principles of Krishna consciousness represents Krishna. Some people think that the Hare Krishna movement is opposed to sex per se. No. Rather, we are opposed to the misuse of sex. According to dharma, religious principles, sex is to be used only for procreation, not for sense gratification. In every chapter of *Bhagavad-gita*, Krishna teaches that to be successful in human life, we must control the senses. Since the urge for sex is the strongest of all material desires, all the senses can be controlled if the sex life is controlled. Indeed, the shackles of material life are the shackles of sex. For this reason, Vedic culture stresses control of the sex urge. Human beings are expected to control the bestial instincts. If animals engage in sex in the middle of the road, no one will arrest them, but there are regulations and responsibilities for humans, and if people break the basic laws of decency, they are punished. Human beings are meant to be guided by a higher purpose: self-realization. We should therefore act in accordance with the regulations (dharma) set down by the Supreme Personality of Godhead, who is the friend and well-wisher of all.

Lord Krishna continues: "All states of being—be they of goodness, passion, or ignorance—are manifested by My energy. I am, in one sense, everything, but I am independent. I am not under the modes of this material nature." (7.12) The Supreme Personality of Godhead is never under the modes of material nature. He is always independent, although He is everything within and without. In the Ninth Chapter, He explains, "By Me, in My unmanifested form, this entire universe is pervaded. All beings are in Me, but I am not in them. And yet everything that is created does not rest in Me. Behold My mystic opulence! Although I am the maintainer of all living entities, and although I am everywhere, still My Self is the very source of creation." (9.4-5)

This is also Lord Chaitanya's teaching, called the *achintya-bheda-abheda-tattva* philosophy: "Everything is simultaneously and inconceivably one with and different from the Supreme Personality of Godhead. Just as sunshine is present throughout the universe, Lord Krishna is present everywhere by His impersonal manifestation. Lord Krishna is always residing in His supreme planet, Goloka Vrindaban, and from His transcendental position, His energy is inconceivably and simultaneously extending everywhere. All things depend on that energy for their existence, and whatever exists is nothing but that energetic expansion.

As stated before, *Srimad-Bhagavatam* asserts that before the creation, all that existed was Krishna (Narayana); during the creation, all that exists is Krishna; and after the annihilation, all that remains is Krishna. Still, despite all this, Lord Krishna has not changed His eternal identity. We should not foolishly think that because Krishna has expanded Himself everywhere, He does not remain where He is, or as He is. This misconception is due to material vision. In the material world, if we cut a cake into six pieces and give away three pieces, we have only half a cake left. Or if we distribute all six pieces, we have no cake left. But in the spiritual world, we can cut a cake into any number of pieces, distribute them all, and still have the whole cake. In spiritual mathematics, one plus one equals one, and one minus one equals one. Krishna is, of course, the one without a second. Therefore Krishna can distribute Himself everywhere and still remain as He is. This is confirmed in *Sri Ishopanishad: om purnam adah purnam idam:* "The Personality of Godhead is perfect and complete…. Whatever is produced of the Complete Whole is also complete in itself. And because He is the Complete Whole, even though so many complete units emanate from Him, He remains the complete balance." (*Isho.,* Invocation)

Krishna's pure devotees know Him as He is. Knowing His supreme feature as the Supreme Person, they are never deluded by the modes of material nature, but remain forever in the transcendental position, being linked to Him in transcendental love. Therefore Krishna says, "This divine energy of Mine, consisting of the three modes of material nature, is difficult to overcome. But those who have surrendered unto Me can easily cross beyond it." (7.14) This directly implies that those who don't surrender to Krishna can never cross over the ocean of material existence. One meaning of the word *guna* (mode) is "rope." Just as ropes tightly bind a captured criminal, the three *gunas,* modes of material nature, bind those who rebel against the Supreme Personality of Godhead. Those who do not surrender to Him can never get free. Furthermore, only a man who is already free from the *gunas*—the ropes of goodness, passion, and ignorance—can free those who are bound. Therefore Krishna either comes personally or sends His representative, the bona fide spiritual master, to liberate conditioned souls by untying the ropes of material nature. The transcendental message of *Bhagavad-gita*, repeated by the pure devotee, can liberate everyone from these modes. Lord Krishna certainly wants to see us all thus freed. "Rise above these modes, O Arjuna," He says. "Be transcendental to all of them." (2.45) This is possible only by surrendering to Krishna. Therefore the Lord says that those who are surrendered to Him can easily cross beyond the material ocean.

In the next verse, Lord Krishna describes the four kinds of men who are always bound by the *gunas* due to their refusal to surrender: "Those miscreants who are grossly foolish, lowest among mankind, whose knowledge is stolen by illusion, and who partake of the atheistic nature of demons, do not surrender unto Me." Of these four kinds of *duskritinas*, or miscreants, those who are grossly foolish are called *mudhas*, or asses, because they simply work hard day and night. If asked to hear about Krishna or visit Krishna's temple, they say, "I'm too busy. I don't have time. I have other duties. I must tend to my business and family." These hard-working asses are ignorant of the real purpose of human life—self-realization, or Krishna consciousness—which should come before everything else. Krishna consciousness should be our first business, not something we tend to in our spare time, or once a week. Do we eat just once a week, or sleep just once a week? Is Krishna consciousness less important? Just as we have to eat every day, we have to chant sixteen rounds of the Hare Krishna *mahamantra* every day, hear topics about Krishna, and associate with devotees. If we neglect our real, transcendental business, we become *mudhas*, simply working hard for nothing.

Factually, if only the ass could think about it, he wouldn't have to work hard to eat. Although grass grows everywhere, he still works all day for a little grass, or a little grain. He is therefore the very symbol of foolishness. God is feeding everyone, worker and nonworker alike. In India, we see that the poor living on the streets do not work, but still they eat something—some chapatis, a little *dal*—by the grace of God. And in America also, the unemployed are somehow provided for. We do not encourage laziness, or living at the expense of others, but we do discourage unnecessary labor for sense gratification, neglect of our spiritual lives, and distrust of the Lord as our supreme provider. In English, the very word "Lord" originally designated the "keeper of the bread" (loaf-ward). Why should we think that the Lord will not feed us if we become His devotees? He is feeding elephants, dogs, demons, beggars— everyone. Why not His devotee? Krishna says, "Just surrender unto Me. I shall deliver you from all sinful reaction. Do not fear." (18.66)

Lord Krishna promises, "For those who worship Me, I carry what they lack and preserve what they have." (9.22) The hardworking *mudha*, grossly foolish, devoid of faith in Krishna, cannot understand this. With his nose to the grindstone, he works hard all his life to amass wealth for sense gratification, claiming that he hasn't any time for Krishna consciousness or self-realization. Ironically, at the hour of death, Krishna comes as all-devouring Time and takes away every one of the *mudha*'s hard-earned sense objects.

Another kind of miscreant mentioned is the *naradhama*, the "lowest of mankind." Of the 8,400,000 species mentioned in *Padma Purana*, some 400,000 belong to the human division, and most of these are primitive and uncivilized. But the word *naradhama* specifically refers to those who are socially and politically developed, but religiously undeveloped. Most members of our modern so-called advanced civilizations are in this category. Laboring hard under the banner of material progress, and striving intensely to maintain and improve nonreligious institutions, they, like the *mudhas*, have no time for God. Although outwardly polished and technologically sophisticated, they are uncivilized savages within. Civilized human life begins with the religious institution of *varnashrama*. Making cloth and building skyscrapers are not necessarily hallmarks of an advanced civilization. Even animals have technology: beavers build dams, and spiders weave webs. Civilization is measured by the advancement of God consciousness, and that is the purpose of the *varnashrama* institution. Today, practically everyone is working hard for technological advancement only, and is therefore in the *naradhama* category, lowest among the human species. Working

hard for materialism and forgetting the soul, they can be compared to fools who carefully polish the birdcage, but let the bird
die of starvation. The spirit soul in the cage of the material body
requires spiritual food daily, but the *naradhamas* are too busy
polishing the cage. Letting the soul within die, they sacrifice
everything for so-called technological progress.

The third class of miscreant is the *mayayapahrita-jnana*, those
whose true knowledge has been nullified by their ignorant, puff-
ed-up mental speculation. This group includes the modern scientists, who try to use their education to lord it over material
nature. In reality, they simply become more and more entangled
in the laws of material nature. Such proud so-called intellectuals
hope to make everyone immortal in the future, but factually
their attempts have only succeeded in accelerating the death
process. In the past, men could be killed only one at a time with
clubs and swords. Now, millions of people can be destroyed
instantly by nuclear bombs. This is "scientific advancement."
Needless to say, no concrete progress has been made in solving
the real problems of life: birth, old age, disease, and death. As
in ancient days, the worldwide death rate still stands at exactly
one hundred percent. Whether we live to be thirty or ninety,
we still have to face death, although we don't want to. Disease
is still rampant. Despite the propaganda of modern medicine,
any fool can see that the hospitals are filled to overflowing, and
every year more are built. Despite contraceptives and abortions,
world population is rising. Real scientific progress means putting
an end to all these problems. But this they cannot do!

The fourth type of miscreant is called *asuram bhavam asrita*,
referring to those who avow demonic principles and are openly
atheistic. Being envious of the Supreme Personality of Godhead,
they are thrown again and again into demonic wombs. (16.19)
They will never be able to become Krishna conscious until they
give up their envious mentality and surrender to the Supreme
Personality of Godhead. Some of these demons openly declare
that there is no God, or that they themselves are God. Sometimes
they say that it is impossible for God to descend into the material
world, although they cannot give any good reasons for their
assertion. Due to envy, some are inclined to an impersonal conception of God. Not knowing God as He is, they concoct false

or blasphemous conceptions, and simply refuse to acknowledge the Absolute Personality of Godhead, or to surrender to Him.

Just as there are four types of miscreants who never surrender to Krishna, there are four types of pious men who do. "O best among the Bharatas [Arjuna]," Krishna says, "four kinds of pious men render devotional service unto Me: the distressed, the desirer of wealth, the inquisitive, and he who is searching for knowledge of the Absolute." (7.16) Often, people approach religion, or Krishna consciousness, with some motive. When there is a death in the family, when one loses a friend, or when there is marital difficulty, people suddenly turn to religion. In their distressed condition, they call out to Krishna, "Please help me!" Sometimes, when people are poverty-stricken, they approach God for some material benefit, saying, "Dear God. Please give me food, shelter, money." Others may look for God because they are simply inquisitive; they want to know what's out there. Then there are philosophic men who inquire after the Absolute Truth. Krishna says that of these four types of pious men, "the wise one who is in full knowledge, in union with Me through pure devotional service, is the best. For I am very dear to him, and he is dear to Me. All these devotees are undoubtedly magnanimous souls, but he who is situated in knowledge of Me, I consider verily to dwell in Me. Being engaged in My transcendental service, he attains Me." (7.17-18)

It is noteworthy that Krishna calls all four types *mahatmas*, or great souls. They are great souls because, regardless of their original motives, they have come to the right point. There are millions of distressed people who do not come to Krishna for shelter. Everyone wants more money, but only a few turn to Krishna, the Husband of the Goddess of Fortune. Even if one has a material motive, he becomes a *mahatma* just because he turns to God. The Lord will very quickly purify the desires of one who turns to Him with a material motive. When Dhruva Maharaj went to the forest to perform austerities, he had a material reason: to attain a kingdom greater than his grandfather Brahma's. For this, he chanted a mantra (*Om namo bhagavate vasudevaya*) under the direction of his spiritual master, Narada Muni. But when Lord Krishna appeared before him, Dhruva became purified of all material desires. When Krishna asked him want he wanted, Dhruva replied, "My dear Lord, now that I have seen You, I don't want anything." Because the vision of Krishna satisfied him completely, he automatically abandoned his desire for a material kingdom. In this way, Lord Krishna purifies those who turn to Him. There may be some ulterior motives in the beginning, but devotional service purifies the practitioner, and all impurities soon fall away.

Although Lord Krishna speaks of His devotee's being "in union with Me," and "dwelling with Me," there is no question of loss of individuality or identity. The devotee does not lose himself by merging into some impersonal aspect of God. No, individuality is retained. The devotee is in union with Krishna and dwells with Him because of oneness of desire. He certainly does not stop rendering devotional service, for that is his life and soul. Service automatically establishes the identity of the servant and the master. The eternal individuality of the spirit soul was proclaimed at the very beginning of *Bhagavad-gita:* "Never was there a time when I did not exist, nor you, nor all these kings; nor in the future shall any of us cease to be." (2.12) Krishna is eternal, and we are eternal. We are not Krishna, nor are we ever equal to Krishna. We are the infinitesimal parts and parcels of Krishna. *Nityo nityanam, cetanas cetananam. (Katha Up-anisad,* 2.2.13) Krishna is *nityo,* the supreme living entity, and we are also *nityo,* living entities. Amongst all living entities, both conditioned and liberated, Krishna is the one Supreme living Personality sustaining all others. Being infinite, Krishna can maintain everyone; being infinitesimal, we cannot maintain even ourselves. We can desire, but we cannot fulfill our desires. "Man proposes, God disposes." Krishna is always superior, and we are always subordinate. The conclusion is that we have to surrender to Krishna.

Lord Krishna continues: "After many births and deaths, he who is actually in knowledge surrenders unto Me, knowing Me to be the cause of all causes and all that is. Such a great soul is very rare." (7.19) The cultivation of knowledge may take many births, but when true knowledge comes, and we clearly understand that Krishna is everything, we naturally surrender to Krishna. There is no other conclusion. Whatever the process by which we come to knowledge—be it philosophical analysis, detached work, or devotional service—we ultimately must surrender. Without surrender, there is no knowledge. It may be now or after many, many births, but eventually we must come to understand that Krishna is everything, the cause of all causes, the complete whole, and that we are His parts and parcels. Since surrender must ultimately be there, and there is no avoiding it, why not surrender now? Why continue to suffer? We can put an end to all material miseries now by fully surrendering to Krishna. But if we continue trying to fulfill our selfish desires, we will have to suffer more and more.

Nor should we think that we can surrender to anyone we choose and get the same results. Krishna specifically states *mam prapadyante*: "Surrender unto Me." This is not blind surrender but surrender in perfect knowledge. In India we sometimes see people worshipping the demigods, but this is not advised here. Lord Krishna says: "Those whose minds are distorted by material desires surrender unto demigods and follow the particular rules and regulations of worship according to their own natures. I am in everyone's heart as the Supersoul. As soon as one desires to worship the demigods, I make his faith steady so that he can devote himself to some particular deity. Endowed with such a faith, he seeks favors of a particular demigod and obtains his desires. But in actuality, these benefits are bestowed by Me alone. Men of small intelligence worship the demigods, and their fruits are limited and temporary. Those who worship the demigods go to the planets of the demigods, but My devotees ultimately reach My supreme planet." (7.20-23)

Those who have material desires have distorted minds, not real intelligence. How can it be otherwise? Material desires are insatiable, and material sense pleasure is temporary. The intelligent man doesn't want to become entangled in the vicious cycle of trying to gratify endless sense desires. Those who worship the demigods always seek some temporary material benediction: success in business, a good wife, elevation to the heavenly planets, and so on. Since they seek the temporary, Krishna calls their intelligence small. They cannot be compared to the broad-minded *mahatmas*. Lord Krishna also speaks of this in the Ninth Chapter, wherein the Sanskrit words *brahmana* and *kripana* are used. *Brahmana* refers to one of broad intelligence who has understood the eternal, and *kripana* means "crippled-minded." Worshippers of the demigods are crippled-minded because, in their vain search for temporary happiness, they misuse the great opportunity of human life, the capacity for self-realization.

Purified or unpurified, those with broad intelligence take to Krishna's worship. This is also the conclusion of *Srimad-Bhagavatam: Akamah sarva-kamo va.* "Whether full of material desire or without material desire, a person with broad intelligence who wants liberation must by all means worship the Supreme Whole Personality of Godhead." (*Bhag.* 2.3.10) Regardless of one's desires, he should worship Krishna if he is truly intelligent. Why? Because the Supreme can grant whatever we want. "In actuality, these benefits [of the demigods] are bestowed by Me alone," Krishna says. Krishna can give us whatever we want. For Him, nothing is impossible. He is Bhagavan, the possessor of everything. The wise man knows that one who gets Krishna, gets everything, and that one who knows Krishna, knows everything. Why should he compromise? Why be content with some temporary material benefit when by worshipping Krishna we can attain the Supreme? Krishna says that if we choose, we can worship a demigod and thereby attain that demigod's planet, but we should know that "from the highest planet in the material world down to the lowest, all are places of misery wherein repeated birth and death take place." (8.16) Why continue transmigrating from one temporary situation to another? Why be content with second or third best? Why not strive for the Supreme? "My devotees ultimately reach My supreme planet," Krishna says. Goloka Vrindaban! Why settle for less?

Lord Krishna continues: "Unintelligent men who know Me not think that I have assumed this form and personality. Due to their small knowledge, they do not know My higher nature, which is changeless and supreme." (7.24) As stated before, Krishna is completely spiritual. When He descends to this material world, He does not incarnate as a mortal would. He never takes a body of maya. There is no difference between Krishna and Krishna's body. At the beginning stage of self-realization, we realize, "I am not this body," but Krishna never has to realize this because He and His body are identical. Krishna is *sat-cit-ananda*—eternal being, knowledge, and bliss—and His body is also *sat-cit-ananda*. Krishna's original feature is the form of the Supreme Person. As the original Supreme Personality of Godhead, He resides eternally in His spiritual abode, Goloka Vrindaban, where He enjoys Himself with His eternal associates. Lord Brahma has beautifully described Krishna's pastimes in this abode: *Cintamani prakara-sadmasu kalpa-vrksa-laksavrtesu.* "I worship Govinda, the primeval Lord, the first progenitor, who is tending the cows, fulfilling all desires in abodes built with spiritual gems and surrounded by millions of wish-fulfilling trees. He is always served with great reverence and affection by hundreds and thousands of goddesses of fortune." (*Brahma-samhita*, 5.29) Krishna is never impersonal or void; He is always full in six opulences: wealth, strength, fame, beauty, knowledge, and renunciation.

Sometimes people argue, "If Krishna possesses all fame, why isn't He known and worshipped everywhere?" Not knowing the extent of His opulences, and unaware that He is worshipped luxuriantly in the spiritual Vaikuntha planets, uninformed mundaners mistake Him for "a local deity of India." Such people do not realize that all men factually worship Lord Krishna, although the worship may be unconscious or even improper. "Whatever a man may sacrifice to other gods is really meant for Me alone, but it is offered without true understanding." (9.23)

"I am never manifest to the foolish and unintelligent," Krishna explains. "For them I am covered by My eternal creative potency (*yoga-maya*); and so the deluded world knows Me not, who am unborn and infallible." (7.25) Krishna is unmanifest to the deluded because He supplies whatever we want. "From Me come remembrance, knowledge, and forgetfulness." (15.15) If we want knowledge, Krishna will supply it, and if we want forgetfulness in order to pursue our own ways, Krishna will allow us to forget His supremacy.

We desire, and Krishna fulfills our desires. *Sri Ishopanishad* also affirms that He is "fulfilling everyone's desire since time immemorial." (*Isho.*,8) Enamoured with material things, the foolish can never know Him. For them, He is always covered by His glittering creative potency, maya. Bedazzled by this deluding energy, the foolish are placed under maya's control to work hard like asses. "By the sweat of thy brow," God told Adam, and so even today men must work like asses to acquire a few morsels of food. For what? To live and die like animals, and, in the end, because of animalistic desires, acquire an animal body. All this suffering is due to forgetfulness of Krishna.

"O Arjuna," Lord Krishna continues, "as the Supreme Personality of Godhead, I know everything that has happened in the past, all that is happening in the present, and all things that are yet to come. I also know all living entities; but Me no one knows." (7.26) Krishna cannot be known by mental speculation or by the blunt material senses. He can be known only by pure devotional service. When we render Him service, Krishna agrees to reveal Himself. He cannot be known by force. We cannot barge into the presence of the Supreme Personality of Godhead. Nor can we demand, "Krishna, appear! You must reveal Yourself to me." It is not our position to demand, but to serve. When Krishna is pleased with our service, He will automatically appear before us. This is the way to know Krishna. We should not try to see Him directly but should try to serve Him so sincerely that He becomes obliged and wants to show Himself to us. Krishna Himself said that He was so obligated to the *gopis* of Vrindaban that He could never repay them. Due to their service, the *gopis* could see Krishna daily, knowing Him as only a lover can. Such knowledge is not obtainable for those envious of Krishna, or for those trying to know Him by mental speculation.

"O scion of Bharata, O conqueror of the foe," Krishna addresses Arjuna. "All living entities are born into delusion, overcome by the dualities of desire and hate. Persons who have acted piously in previous lives and in this life, whose sinful actions are completely eradicated, and who are freed from the duality of delusion, engage themselves in My service with determination. Intelligent persons, who are endeavoring for liberation from old age and death, take refuge in Me in devotional service. They are actually Brahman because they entirely know everything about transcendental and fruitive activities." (7.27-29) Again, Krishna reminds us that if we really want to know Him, we have to render devotional service. By it, we can attain the transcendental position beyond the reach of the three modes, beyond desire and hate, and beyond the dualities of delusion.

Lord Krishna concludes: "Those who know Me as the Su-

preme Lord, as the governing principle of the material manifestation, who know Me as the one underlying all the demigods
and as the one sustaining all sacrifices, can, with steadfast mind,
understand and know Me even at the time of death." (7.30) The
success of this life is tested at the time of death. In the next
chapter, Krishna explains, "Whatever state of being one remembers when he quits his body, that state he will attain without
fail." (8.6) If we think of the demigods, we go to them; if we
think of our forefathers, we go to them; and if we think of
Krishna, we go to Him. In this way, death is our final examina-
tion, determining our future state of being. And our state of
mind at death will be determined by our life, for at death we
will remember what has been most dear to us in life. If Krishna
has become our dearmost friend, our refuge and our hope, we
will surely think of Him. Therefore devotees always chant His
holy name and remember His glorious pastimes at every moment. By thus remembering Krishna, we will be successful in
both life and death.

And how should we know Him? "As the Supreme Lord, as
the governing principle of the material manifestation." We
should know Him as the cause of all causes, as the real creator
behind all demigods. Brahma is but a secondary creator empowered by Lord Krishna. The primary creator is the Supreme
Personality of Godhead Himself.

When Nanda Maharaj was preparing a sacrifice for Lord
Indra, King of the heavenly planets, Krishna said, "Why prepare
this sacrifice for Indra? It is better to worship Govardhan Hill."
Nanda Maharaj replied that he didn't want to offend Indra, for
Indra sends the rain that nourishes the grass that nourishes the
cows, whose milk nourishes all men. "That's all right," Krishna
said. "Just worship Govardhan Hill." Therefore, under Krishna's
direction, Nanda Maharaj performed Govardhan *puja*. Angered,
the proud Indra sent torrents of rain to flood the whole region
of Vrindaban. Lord Krishna then lifted Govardhan Hill and used
it as an umbrella to protect His devotees. This transcendental
pastime demonstrates that there is never a need to worship the
demigods. Worship is meant exclusively for Lord Krishna, the
Supreme Personality of Godhead. The Lord will always protect
His devotees. This is His promise: "I will give you all protection.

Do not fear. My devotee will never perish." (18.66, 9.31)

Therefore a pure devotee puts his full faith in Krishna exclusively. He doesn't have faith in material nature, material progress, or the demigods. For him, Krishna is all in all. Always remembering Krishna, at the time of death he goes directly to Krishna's abode, Goloka Vrindaban, and lives eternally with His Lord. It is his faith that enables him to remember Krishna, even at the time of death.

By having faith in Krishna's words and in Krishna's representative, the bona fide spiritual master, we also have faith in Krishna. Appearing in this age as Lord Sri Chaitanya Mahaprabhu, Krishna has bestowed upon us this wonderful boon of *sankirtan-yajna*, the congregational chanting of His holy names. If we have faith in Krishna, we will follow this path set forth by Him. *Harer nama, harer nama, harer nama eva kevalam.* There is no other way to success in this Kali-yuga than chanting His names. Chant Hare Krishna and be happy!

One should meditate upon the Supreme Person as the one who knows every-thing, as He who is the oldest, who is the controller, who is smaller than the smallest, who is the maintainer of everything, who is beyond all material concep-tion, who is inconceivable, and who is always a person. He is luminous like the sun and, being transcendental, is beyond this material nature. *(Bg. 8.9)*

CHAPTER EIGHT

Attaining the Supreme

This chapter begins with Arjuna's inquiry into subjects that have not been discussed to his complete understanding. "O my Lord," he says. "O Supreme Person, what is Brahman? What is the self? What are fruitive activities? What is this material manifestation? And what are the demigods? How does this Lord of sacrifice live in the body, and in which part does He live, O Madhusudana? And how can those engaged in devotional service know You at the time of death? Please explain this to me." (8.1-2)

Because Arjuna is Lord Krishna's eternal companion, he should have known the answers to these questions. Actually, Arjuna is inquiring for our benefit, asking questions two or three times so that Krishna can elaborate and clarify everything for our enlightenment. Sometimes a question has to be asked repeatedly and answered from different angles of vision for proper understanding. These questions and doubts, however, are like demons; therefore Lord Krishna is addressed as Madhusudana, killer of the great Madhu demon, for the Lord is being indirectly petitioned to kill Arjuna's demons of doubt. In this chapter, therefore, the Lord answers all these questions elaborately.

Lord Krishna replies: "The indestructible, transcendental living entity is called Brahman, and his eternal nature is called the self. Action pertaining to the development of these material bodies is called karma, or fruitive activities. Physical nature is known to be endlessly mutable. The universe is the cosmic form of the Supreme Lord, and I am that Lord represented as the Supersoul, dwelling in the heart of every embodied being. And whoever, at the time of death, quits his body, remembering Me alone, at once attains My nature. Of this there is no doubt." (8.3-5)

117

Here, Lord Krishna concisely answers all of Arjuna's questions. The indestructible, eternal living entity is called Brahman. In the previous chapter, Krishna mentioned a superior energy "struggling with material nature." (7.5) This is the living entity in contact with material nature, laboring hard to "sustain the universe." The word *Brahman* also refers to the spiritual effulgence emanating from Krishna's transcendental body. This spiritual effulgence is full of living beings. In reality, there is nothing truly impersonal in the entire Kingdom of God. Under certain conditions, the impersonal feature of God is seen, but since everything is emanating from the Supreme Person, Lord Krishna, everything is ultimately personal. The very nature of the living entity is also spirit soul, not matter; therefore he is transcendental to the material world, and "his eternal nature is called the self."

In the material world, everyone mistakenly identifies himself with the material body, and this causes material contamination and suffering. All material miseries arise due to misidentification of the spirit soul (the self) with matter. "Action pertaining to the development of these material bodies is called karma," Krishna says. Identifying with the material body out of a desire to lord it over material nature for sense gratification, the living entity becomes entangled in the cycle of activity and reaction (karma). Pious activities bring good karma, and impious activities result in bad karma. In either case, the living entity has to suffer reactions and continue his material existence in the 8,400,000 species of existence.

"Physical nature is known to be endlessly mutable." That is, material nature is always in flux, always changing. Mundane scientists try to prevent old age and death, but their attempts are ultimately frustrated. Why? They are kicking against the stringent laws of material nature. Everything within the material world undergoes six basic stages of transformation: It is born, it grows, remains for some time, leaves some by-products, dwindles, and vanishes. No one can stop this process because in the material world, *Kala*, time, reigns supreme. "Time I am," Krishna says, "destroyer of the worlds." (11.32) Under the influence of time, everything is gradually wearing away. No one, not even the greatest material scientist, can stop this universal process.

In response to Arjuna's question about the Lord of sacrifice in the body, Lord. Krishna says that He Himself is "that Lord represented as the Supersoul, dwelling in the heart of every embodied being." This Supersoul is present to give directions to everyone. If we sincerely want to become Krishna conscious, the Supersoul helps us. In the *Chaitanya-charitamrita*, it is said that by the grace of Krishna, one gets guru, and by the grace of guru, one gets Krishna. As soon as the Lord sees that a person desires transcendental knowledge, He arranges for a guru. Lord Krishna exists internally in the heart as guru, and He manifests externally as guru as well. In this way, He gives unequivocal instructions.

Lord Krishna's nature is *sat-cit-ananda:* eternity, full knowledge, and bliss. If one gives up his material body remembering Krishna and no longer desiring sense gratification, he can go to the eternal kingdom of God, Krishna's abode, where everything is *sat-cit-ananda*. There, the living entity "attains My nature." That is, he attains eternity, full knowledge, and bliss.

Lord Krishna continues: "Whatever state of being one remembers when he quits his body, that state he will attain without fail." (8.6) Krishna is equal to everyone. He is not a friend of some and an enemy of others. A person's thoughts indicate his desire, and Krishna fulfills the desire of everyone. If we meditate on material sense gratification at the time of death, Krishna will give us another material body to enjoy the senses. According to the kind of sense gratification we desire, a particular type of body will be awarded. There are 8,400,000 species of life, and each one corresponds to a specific desire for sense gratification. Although we can enter these species according to our desires at the time of death, Lord Krishna mercifully urges us to think of Him only so that we can attain the highest goal: Krishna consciousness. Only Krishna is all goodness, eternity, complete knowledge and bliss. If we sincerely want to put an end to our material miseries, we must constantly meditate on Krishna during our lives and thus guarantee our thinking of Him at death.

"Therefore, Arjuna," Krishna says, "you should always think of Me in the form of Krishna and at the same time carry out your prescribed duty of fighting. With your activities dedicated to Me and your mind and intelligence fixed on Me, you will attain Me without doubt." (8.7)

Because Arjuna is still bothered by doubts, Krishna is reassuring him, emphasizing this point by adding "without doubt" (*asamsayah*). The outcome is certain. There is no chance of failure. If we meditate on Krishna, we will be successful. It is important to note here that Lord Krishna recommends meditating on Him in His personal form, "in the form of Krishna." This form is the origin of all other forms. As stated in *Srimad-Bhagavatam: krsnas tu bhagavan svayam.* "All incarnations are either plenary portions or portions of the plenary portions of the Lord, but Lord Sri Krishna is the original Personality of Godhead." (*Bhag. 1.3.28*) Krishna is the source of all forms and manifestations of God. Foolish scholars may define Him as "'the eighth avatar of Vishnu," but we should not think of Him in this way. Krishna is not an incarnation of Vishnu, nor a manifestation of the impersonal Brahman. No, He is the source of all divine manifestations. Therefore He urges Arjuna to think of Him "in the form of Krishna," for that is both easy and natural.

Krishna wants Arjuna to think of Him in the form of Krishna and, at the same time, fight. Thus Krishna affirms that inactivity, impersonalism, and voidism are inconsistent with real meditation on Him. Duties must never be given up. "At the same time, carry out your prescribed duty of fighting," He says. Krishna consciousness is a twenty-four hour a day way of living, not a once a week church visit, nor a daily twenty minute push-the-nose, stand-on-the-head pseudo-meditation. No. It is constant spiritual engagement. "Whatever you do, whatever you eat, whatever you offer and give away, as well as whatever austerities you perform, do it as an offering to Me." (9.27) Every detail of life must be lived in the divine consciousness of devotional service.

This process is sublime, and yet so simple that we can become Krishna conscious just by preparing food with love and devotion, offering it to Krishna, and eating the remnants. Everyone has to eat. This most basic daily act of eating can become a means to the highest goal. Even at work, we can become Krishna conscious. Here, Krishna urges Arjuna to fight because that is Arjuna's duty as a warrior. A *kshatriya* must protect the innocent and helpless. "Do your duty," Krishna says, "but at the same time meditate on Me." Some years ago, in

Vrindaban, a devotee complained, "Srila Prabhupada, I can't do this construction work because when I'm working, I can't remember Krishna." Prabhupada replied, "You just work for Krishna. Don't try to remember Krishna directly, but try to serve Krishna so nicely that Krishna remembers you." This is the way to remember Krishna, for Krishna is not different from His devotional service.

Since devotional service is Krishna's internal energy, it is Krishna. Just as there is no difference between Krishna and *prasadam*, there is no difference between Krishna and devotional service. Therefore, by meditating on His service, the devotee perfectly meditates on Krishna. When a wife cooks for her husband, her mind may be engaged in cooking and not directly in thoughts of her husband, but her service is better than that of a wife who, forgetting her duty and thinking of her husband, burns the food. The husband will be more satisfied with a wife who concentrates on cooking and then offers him the food with love. Not thinking of anything in return, we should perform our duty to our best capacity, offering everything to Krishna with love and devotion. This is the basic qualification of pure devotional service. It must be unmotivated and uninterrupted. *Ahaituky apratihata. (Bhag. 1.2.6)* We should not demand anything in return for our devotional service, not even salvation. Devotional service is not a business deal. The pure devotee does not say, "Krishna, I will do this for You, if You do this for me. Give me this day my daily bread, and then I'll render service." This is business, not love. Pure love consists in trying to serve Krishna without any motive, material or spiritual.

Lord Krishna continues: "He who meditates on the Supreme Personality of Godhead, his mind constantly engaged in remembering Me, undeviated from the path, he, O Partha [Arjuna], is sure to reach Me." (8.8) This is the real way to please Krishna. Krishna is more pleased by a devotee's sincere desire to serve Him than by any amount of Vedic prayers or Vedic study. The real purport of the *Vedas* is that we should surrender to Krishna and serve Him, for this is our constitutional position as part and parcel of Krishna. The parts are meant to serve the whole.

Lord Krishna next elaborates on the way His devotee should think of Him: "One should meditate upon the Supreme Person as the one who knows everything, as He who is the oldest, who is the controller, who is smaller than the smallest, who is the maintainer of everything, who is beyond all material conception, who is inconceivable, and who is always a person. He is luminous like the sun, and, being transcendental, is beyond this material nature." (8.9) Clearly, Krishna is never impersonal. He is the Supreme Person full of inconceivable potencies. Materialistic philosophers want to reduce God to the understanding of their tiny brains, saying that unless they can see or understand God, He doesn't exist. This is foolishness. Our power of sight is limited. We cannot even see the inside of our eyelids. All of our other senses are also limited. But God and His energies are unlimited. He is full of inconceivable potencies. In this verse it is said that He is older than the oldest, but we should not think of Him, or portray Him, as an old man. That is a material conception. Although He is the oldest, He is ever-new and ever-fresh. By mundane calculations, He was about a hundred and twenty-five years old when He spoke *Bhagavad-gita*, but He appeared like a youth of twenty or so.

We should not try to subject God to material processes such as aging. He defies all mundane calculations. Although He is greater than the greatest, He says in this verse that He is smaller than the smallest. The *Vedas* describe the living entity as "one ten thousandth of the size of the tip of a hair." Because the Supreme Lord can enter into the heart of the infinitesimal living being, He must be even smaller. Certainly He is not visible to our limited vision, but this does not mean that He is not there. We cannot directly see atoms, or the force of gravity, or the wind, but still we cannot deny their existence, for we see their effects. Visibility, therefore, is not prerequisite to existence. Radio and television waves are released into the atmosphere, and no one can hear or see them by unaided senses, yet we accept their existence because we perceive their effects with proper instruments. Similarly, the Supreme Lord, although present within every atom of His creation, cannot be directly seen by everyone, but He can be perceived by the devotee whose senses are purified. *Mayadhyakshena prakrtih.* "This material nature is working under My direction, and it is producing all moving and unmoving beings. By its rule, this manifestation is created and annihilated again and again." (9.10) Matter is by nature dead, but because God has entered into it, there is life, movement, and consciousness. Only a fool says that he cannot see God. God is omnipresent and all-pervasive, yet He is independent. His personal identity is never lost. These are but indications of the inconceivable potencies of God.

In the following verses of this chapter, Lord Krishna explains how a *jnana-yogi*, or an impersonalist, can also meditate on Him.

"One who, at the time of death, fixes his life air between the eyebrows, and in full devotion engages himself in remembering the Supreme Lord, will certainly attain to the Supreme Personality of Godhead. Persons learned in the *Vedas*, who utter *omkara* and who are great sages in the renounced order, enter into Brahman. Desiring such perfection, one practices celibacy. I shall now explain to you this process by which one may attain salvation." (8.10-11) To attain impersonal Brahman, one can recite the Vedic mantras, chant *omkara*, and practice celibacy. Brahman realization is the first stage. "I am the basis of the impersonal Brahman," Krishna says (14.27). Beyond this is Paramatma realization of the Supersoul in every living entity. And beyond this is full realization of Bhagavan Sri Krishna, the Supreme Personality of Godhead, the Supreme Absolute Truth.

Lord Krishna continues: "The yogic situation is that of detachment from all sensual engagements. Closing all the doors of the senses and fixing the mind on the heart and the life air at the top of the head, one establishes himself in yoga. After being situated in this yoga practice and vibrating the sacred syllable *Om*, the supreme combination of letters, if one thinks of the Supreme Personality of Godhead and quits his body, he will certainly reach the spiritual planets." (8.12-13)

Here it is clearly stated that while chanting the sacred syllable *Om*, one should remember the Supreme Person. *Om* is not confined to impersonal realization. Srila Prabhupada pointed out that "the impersonal sound of Krishna is *Om*, but the sound Hare Krishna contains *Om*." Chanting Hare Krishna is better than chanting *Om* because by chanting Hare Krishna, we can directly remember Krishna. In this age of Kali-yuga, the direct method of chanting the *mahamantra* is always recommended: Hare Krishna, Hare Krishna, Krishna Krishna, Hare Hare, Hare

Rama, Hare Rama, Rama Rama, Hare Hare. In this way, we immediately remember Krishna and attain full realization of Brahman, Paramatma, and finally all-inclusive Bhagavan, Lord Sri Krishna Himself.

Lord Krishna says, "For one who remembers Me without deviation, I am easy to obtain, O son of Pritha, because of his constant engagement in devotional service." (8.14) Here, Lord Krishna definitely asserts the superiority of *bhakti-yoga*. His calling Arjuna "son of Pritha" is significant because Pritha (also known as Kunti), Arjuna's mother, was such a pure devotee that Lord Krishna Himself was always at her beck and call. Women are generally considered less intelligent and not very learned in Vedic knowledge, but because of Queen Kunti's devotion, Lord Krishna was always indebted to her. Whenever she was in difficulty, she would cry out, "Hey Krishna! Hey Govinda!" And the Lord would always respond. By reminding Arjuna of his great mother, Krishna is indirectly telling him, "Become My devotee and surrender unto Me, and I will save you." This is advice for us all. When in difficulty, we should always remember the Lord and cry out to Him. Krishna says, "I am very easy to remember, and I am easily obtained by a pure devotee." By engaging in devotional service, we can easily remember Krishna, who always saves His devotees.

Lord Krishna continues: "After attaining Me, the great souls, who are yogis in devotion, never return to this temporary world, which is full of miseries, because they have attained the highest perfection." (8.15) Perfection in life is not found in material opulence, but in complete detachment from the material world. Perfection lies in not having to return to this place of misery. The truly great souls never return here. "This is no place for a gentleman," Srila Bhaktisiddhanta Saraswati used to say. Knowing this world to be a place of birth and death, the great souls always render devotional service, and thus become automatically liberated. "From the highest planet in the material world down to the lowest, all are places of misery wherein repeated birth and death take place," Krishna says. "But one who attains to My abode, O son of Kunti, never takes birth again." (8.16) We are born into this material world due to our material desires. Advancement even to Brahma-loka, the highest material planet, does not assure liberation. Quite the contrary, after exhausting the fruits of pious activity on Brahma-loka, one falls down again to this earth, where he suffers repetition of birth and death. Lord Krishna therefore reminds Arjuna that, being the son of Kunti, he should aspire to become a pure devotee like his mother and achieve ultimate success.

Lord Krishna next describes the lifetime of Lord Brahma, who presides over Brahma-loka: "By human calculation, a thousand ages taken together is the duration of Brahma's one day. And such also is the duration of his night. When Brahma's day is manifest, this multitude of living entities comes into being, and at the arrival of Brahma's night, they are all annihilated. Again and again the day comes, and this host of beings is active; and again the night falls, O Partha, and they are helplessly dissolved." (8.17-19)

What is the point in elevating ourselves to the highest material planet, Brahma-loka, if it is repeatedly being manifest and destroyed? What happiness can there be in such a temporary situation? Although Brahma lives for more than three hundred trillion earth years, his situation is considered miserable because it is temporary. How much more miserable, then, is this brief life on earth! Still, people are so unintelligent that they are not willing to make any sacrifices for eternal, blissful life with Krishna. What fools these mortals be!

In contrast to this ephemeral material universe is the eternal spiritual sky, which Lord Krishna describes next: "Yet there is another nature, which is eternal and is transcendental to this manifested and unmanifested matter. It is supreme and is never annihilated. When all in this world is annihilated, that part remains as it is." (8.20) We are here assured of another nature, beyond this material nature, which is sometimes manifested and sometimes not. At the end of Brahma's day, the conditioned individual souls (*jivas*), enter into the body of Vishnu. When Lord Brahma's day arrives again, all the *jivas* are again manifest, and another age begins. In this way, there is always coming and going—the great flux of material life. In contrast, the eternal nature, the spiritual nature of the Kingdom of God, is never annihilated. It is therefore eternally peaceful, without anxieties (Vaikuntha). Those who are intelligent desire to go there.

Lord Krishna continues: "That supreme abode is called un-manifested and infallible, and it is the supreme destination. When one goes there, he never comes back. That is My supreme abode. The Supreme Personality of Godhead, who is greatest of all, is attainable by unalloyed devotion. Although He is present in His abode, He is all-pervading, and everything is situated in Him." (8.21-22) The only way we can pass beyond the material world to the spiritual world is by unalloyed devotion. We cannot expect to enter into the spiritual world as long as we have the slightest desire for material enjoyment. The Kingdom of God is as pure as the Supreme Personality of Godhead Himself; there-fore those who go there must be just as pure. Their sole desire must be to render the Lord transcendental loving service.

Lord Krishna states that the Supreme Person is "greatest of all," meaning that no one can ever become equal or superior to Him. We are all eternally God's sons and servants. Only the illusioned think that they can become equal to God by merging into the impersonal Brahman. Because we are eternally frag-ments of God, we can never become equal to Him. But by sur-rendering to Him and rendering unalloyed devotional service, we can attain His eternal, superior nature and return to the spiritual sky, the Kingdom of God.

"O best of the Bharatas," Lord Krishna continues, "I shall now explain to you the different times at which, passing away from this world, one does or does not come back. Those who know the Supreme Brahman pass away from the world during the influence of the fiery god, in the light, at an auspicious moment, during the fortnight of the moon and the six months when the sun travels in the north. The mystic who passes away from this world during the smoke, the night, the moonless fortnight, or in the six months when the sun passes to the south, or who reaches the moon planet, again comes back. According to the *Vedas*, there are two ways of passing from this world: one in light and one in darkness. When one passes in light, he does not come back; but when one passes in darkness, he re-turns." (8.23-26) Here, Lord Krishna points out the different ways we can pass from this world. In either case, passage is troublesome. The easiest course is to become a devotee. Then successful passage is guaranteed. "The devotees who know these two paths, O Arjuna, are never bewildered. Therefore be always fixed in devotion." (8.27)

Krishna Himself assures his devotees success. Others, however, have to depend on the success of their fruitive activities, a path that is always uncertain. Those who perform such pious or impious activities are often bewildered. Being full of material desires, they can never be certain of the outcome of their actions. In the Second Chapter, Lord Krishna instructed Arjuna: "In the minds of those who are too attached to sense enjoyment and material opulence, and who are bewildered by such things, the resolute determination of devotional service to the Supreme Lord does not take place." (2.44) As long as we have a desire to enjoy this material world, there is every chance of being bewildered. Even if we perform all kinds of pious activities, there is always a chance that due to some misfortune, we will be defeated. As mentioned before, King Nrga had to take birth as a lizard due to having unwittingly given the same cow in charity twice. For a devotee, such problems do not exist. He is never bewildered by the complexities of fruitive activity. Therefore we should always be fixed in devotion.

Lord Krishna concludes: "A person who accepts the path of devotional service is not bereft of the results derived from studying the *Vedas*, performing austere sacrifices, giving charity, or pursuing philosophical and fruitive activities. At the end, he reaches the supreme abode." (8.28) According to Srila Prabhupada, this verse summarizes both the Seventh and Eighth Chapters of *Bhagavad-gita*. A devotee automatically attains whatever can be acquired by yoga, severe austerities, celibacy, or any other process. A devotee does not have to strive separately to become expert in any of these disciplines. By rendering devotional service to Krishna, he becomes expert in everything. It is also said that the devotee receives knowledge as a concomitant factor. By the grace of the Lord, all the good qualities of the demigods become automatically manifest in the body of a pure devotee.

If we just surrender unto Krishna, we don't have to worry about acquiring anything. The Lord Himself becomes our protector and supplier. There is nothing to fear. "Abandon all varieties of religion and just surrender unto Me. I shall deliver you from all sinful reactions. Do not fear." (18.66) A devotee never has anything to fear. He can fearlessly discharge his duty anywhere. When Arjuna finally understood that he was being protected by Krishna, he also became fearless and fought with full determination. Similarly, when we understand the science of Krishna consciousness, knowing Krishna to be the real doer of all activities, we become fearless and ready to act as Krishna's instrument. We can undertake any task on Krishna's behalf. It is not that we act whimsically, or think that we are very great or powerful, or take false pride in thinking that we can do anything. No. Rather, having full confidence in the order of our spiritual master, we execute that order to the best of our ability, fully confident that the Lord will empower us to accomplish the order. Alone, we can do nothing, but with Krishna we can do anything. Our only concern should be to fulfill the order of Krishna's representative, the bona fide spiritual master.

Lord Chaitanya Mahaprabhu has ordered us to distribute the holy name to every town and village in the world, and we are completely confident that this can be done, although from the material point of view, it may seem impossible. Materially speaking, it was impossible for the Pandavas to defeat the Kurus, but because Krishna was empowering them, they succeeded. Similarly, it is possible to defeat materialism and atheism and reestablish Krishna consciousness throughout the world, for this is the desire of Lord Krishna Chaitanya. In disciplic succession, our spiritual master has also ordered it. We have only to get up and fight, and let Krishna empower us by surrendering to His will. Hare Krishna.

The Supreme Lord said: My dear Arjuna, because you are never envious of Me, I shall impart to you this most secret wisdom, knowing which you shall be relieved of the miseries of material existence. *(Bg. 9.1)*

CHAPTER NINE

The Most Confidential Knowledge

"**M**y dear Arjuna," Lord Krishna says, "because you are never envious of Me, I shall impart to you this most secret wisdom, knowing which you shall be relieved of the miseries of material existence." (9.1)

Lord Krishna is imparting this secret wisdom to Arjuna because Arjuna is a surrendered devotee and friend. This is a point that was also made in the Fourth Chapter: "That very ancient science of the relationship with the Supreme is today told by Me to you because you are My devotee as well as My friend; therefore you can understand the transcendental mystery of this science." (4.3)

The real transcendental knowledge of *Bhagavad-gita* cannot be grasped by a nondevotee. One may be a very erudite Sanskrit scholar and know the grammatical construction of every *sloka*, or one may study *Bhagavad-gita* for a lifetime, but the inner meaning will remain a locked secret unless one becomes Krishna's devotee. Even then, Lord Krishna reveals Himself fully only to the pure devotee who has become nonenvious.

We must understand that we have fallen into this material world due to envy of Krishna. Wanting to enjoy like the Lord, wanting to be God ourselves, we have left the Lord's association in the Kingdom of God. Out of kindness, Krishna has given us this material creation as a facility. Here, everyone has a chance to imitate God by trying to lord it over material resources for sense gratification. Of course, far from enjoying, we are suffering. Only by surrendering to Krishna can we become nonenvious, attain transcendental knowledge, and return home, back to Godhead. In this way, we can gain immediate relief from all material miseries, which result from our misidentification with the gross and subtle material body. As soon as we abandon this bodily misconception, we realize our spiritual nature as sat-cit-ananda, eternal being, perfect knowledge, and bliss. *Brahma-bhutah prasannatma/ na socati na kanksati.* (18.54) When the soul realizes his eternal nature, he becomes ever joyful. "He never laments nor desires to have anything." After all, hankering and lamenting are dualities that torment the conditioned soul on the material platform.

Due to his nonenvious attitude, Arjuna is qualified to receive this most confidential knowledge. Of course, when we speak of most confidential knowledge, we imply that there is knowledge less confidential, and this is a fact. Today, knowledge is so meager that if a group of university students were asked, "What is education?" they could not answer. Education, from Latin *educare*, means "to bring out." Real education is not a question of adding something in the way that one adds certain mundane facts to his consciousness when learning history, science, or a foreign language. Nor is education something acquired, handed down from one person to another, or memorized by rote. Education is self-realization, knowledge of our inmost selves, something brought out from the deepest recesses of our consciousness, something very important evoked and remembered, something we have forgotten. Real education is remembrance of Krishna and our eternal relationship with Him.

Unfortunately, schools and colleges today do not teach this remembrance of our eternal Friend. Instead, they teach mundane knowledge: eating, sleeping, defending, and mating. The improvement of facilities for these animal activities is called technology, and this is all that is being taught. Universities offer courses in underwater basketweaving, mushroom identification, the sex life of snails, stick fighting, and many other equally absurd subjects, but their curricula neglect the transcendental science of the soul, whereby the student can learn the difference between matter and spirit, and alleviate the problems of birth and death.

Actually, mundane training should not be called knowledge or education at all. In truth, knowledge and education refer to God and the soul. Anything else is called nescience.

Human life should transcend the animal platform. *Atatho brahma jijnasa.* Human life means coming to the platform of Brahman, the platform of the spirit soul. Preliminary knowledge begins when we can distinguish between spirit and matter. Beyond this is *raja-vidya*, the king of education, and *raja-guhyam*, the king of knowledge, which Lord Krishna now imparts.

"This knowledge is the king of education, the most secret of all secrets. It is the purest knowledge, and because it gives direct perception of the self by realization, it is the perfection of religion. It is everlasting, and it is joyfully performed." (9.2)

Elementary knowledge distinguishes between matter and spirit. More confidential knowledge reveals the existence of God as the Supreme Creator. And the most confidential knowledge gives direct perception of the self by realization of our relationship with the Supreme Self, God. This most confidential knowledge, which is the perfection of religion, is not found in some formula or ritual. Nor does it belong to some church, institution, temple or synagogue. The perfection of religion is love of God—that's all. Srila Prabhupada used to say that we can test our religion by seeing how much we have developed love of God. Many people say, "I love God," but how can we know? We can tell simply by seeing who is most addicted to God, who is God-intoxicated and God-absorbed. If someone says, "I love God," but never talks of God nor goes to God's temple nor reads the books of God, then he is bluffing. The characteristics of one who loves God are described here: "Always chanting My glories, endeavoring with great determination, bowing down before Me, these great souls perpetually worship Me with devotion." (9.14)

This, then, is the king of education. It is everlasting. It is undeviating, uninterrupted Krishna consciousness. It is not something performed for a certain period and then abandoned. Being envious of Krishna, Mayavadis claim that *bhakti-yoga* is good for attaining a certain stage, but ultimately should be given up. That is, they believe that Krishna is maya and can be left behind. But in *Bhagavad-gita*, the perfection of religion is declared everlasting. Love of God is eternal. "Never was there a time when I did not exist, nor you, nor all these kings; nor in the future shall any of us cease to be." (2.12) Krishna is eternal, we are eternal, and our relationship with Krishna in transcendental love is eternal. Our loving service to Krishna is everlasting, without end, and joyfully performed. By nature, the soul is *sat-cit-ananda*, forever full of bliss and knowledge.

The performance of devotional service is actually bliss, or *ananda*. In the neophyte stage, a devotee may have some difficulties. Because some lingering material desires may create a conflict of interests in his heart, the neophyte may say, "Oh, this is so hard to practice!" However, in the liberated stage, when Krishna is directly perceived, the devotee experiences the overwhelming desire to serve his Lord. This service brings the greatest joy. "The stage of perfection is called trance, or *samadhi*, when one's mind is completely restrained from material mental activities by practice of yoga. This is characterized by one's ability to see the self by the pure mind and to relish and rejoice in the self. In that joyous state, one is situated in boundless transcendental happiness and enjoys himself through transcendental senses. Established thus, one never departs from the truth, and upon gaining this, he thinks there is no greater gain. Being situated in such a position, one is never shaken, even in the midst of greatest difficulty. This indeed is actual freedom from all miseries arising from material contact." (6.20- 23) One who has Krishna, has everything.

Before further explaining this king of education, Lord Krishna warns us: "Those who are not faithful on the path of devotional service, cannot attain Me, O conqueror of foes, but return to birth and death in this material world." (9.3) The king of knowledge and education is devotional service to Krishna. However, we are cautioned once more against hankering after material enjoyment. As Krishna warned in the Second Chapter: "In the minds of those who are too attached to sense enjoyment and material opulence, and who are bewildered by such things, the resolute determination of devotional service to the Supreme Lord does not take place." (2.44) Faith in Krishna and the spiritual master is the foundation. Then, there must be good association. If one associates with a pure devotee and follows his instructions, he can gradually be cleansed of all bad habits, but if he remains addicted to sinful activities, he can never become steady in Krishna consciousness. Those who think that they can sin and still become Krishna conscious are living in a great illusion, simply deceiving themselves. Sin and Krishna consciousness cannot go together. If we are determined to become Krishna conscious, we must renounce material hankering and sense gratification, and control the mind and senses. Then we can become steady in devotional service and conquer birth and death.

Lord Krishna continues: "By Me, in My unmanifested form, this entire universe is pervaded. All beings are in Me, but I am not in them." (9.4) Here, Krishna explains how He pervades everything by His impersonal energy. In the last chapter, we discussed the three principal divisions of energy: material, marginal, and spiritual. Krishna is everywhere by virtue of His impersonal energy (Brahman), but despite His omnipresence, His identity as Krishna is not lost. Although He is present in every living entity as the Supersoul (Paramatma), He still exists in His spiritual abode (Vaikuntha) as Bhagavan. "And yet everything that is created does not rest in Me," He says. "Behold My mystic opulence! Although I am the maintainer of all living entities, and although I am everywhere, still My Self is the very source of creation." (9.5) Krishna always remains the complete Personality of Godhead.

Again, the example of the sun is appropriate. Although the sunshine is perceived everywhere, the sun itself has not lost its identity. It remains in its own position as the source of light. Similarly, although Lord Krishna is present everywhere by His energy, He is still the source of everything. "As the mighty wind, blowing everywhere, always rests in ethereal space, know that in the same manner all beings rest in Me." (9.6) Krishna is the maintainer of everyone. *Nityo nityanam, cetanas cetananam.* Among all eternals, He is the supreme eternal, maintaining everyone. We are Brahman, and Krishna is Parambrahman. We are eternal spirit soul and Krishna is the eternal Supreme Spirit Soul. He is the source from which we flow. No one is equal or superior to Him. We are eternally subordinate to Him, as the parts are subordinate to the whole.

Lord Krishna continues: "O son of Kunti, at the end of the millennium, every material manifestation enters into My nature, and at the beginning of another millennium, by My potency I again create. The whole cosmic order is under Me. By My will it is manifested again and again, and by My will it is annihilated at the end. O Dhananjaya, all this work cannot bind Me. I am ever detached, seated as though neutral. This material nature is working under My direction, and it is producing all moving and unmoving beings. By its rule this manifestation is created and annihilated again and again." (9.7-10)

Since Krishna is the source of creation, He never comes under its laws. By the king's order, a prison is built and maintained by government agents. Because the king is the primal cause of the prison, he is never subject to its laws. He can come to visit, and leave at his own sweet will. Similarly, the Supreme Personality of Godhead has innumerable energies, and by one of them, His material energy, He creates this cosmic manifestation, maintains it for some time, then dissolves it within Himself. Although He sometimes comes into the material world by His own desire (internal potency), He is never under the control of material nature. "This material nature is working under My direction," He says. We should never forget that Krishna's transcendental nature is supreme. Only less intelligent persons think that because He has entered the prison, He is a prisoner.

"Fools deride Me when I descend in the human form," Lord Krishna says. "They do not know My transcendental nature and My supreme dominion over all that be." (9.11) Having no information of Krishna's eternal spiritual body, and seeing that all material bodies are perishable, Mayavadi impersonalists think that Krishna has a temporary body and is therefore an ordinary mortal, though admittedly very great. They do not know that His body is totally different from ours. His body is not in the least material but wholly spiritual. As mentioned before, there is no difference between Krishna and Krishna's body. Just as He is *sat-cit-ananda*, His body also is *sat-cit-ananda*, the eternal form of knowledge and bliss. (*Brahma-samhita*, 5.1) Envious fools, bereft of real knowledge, consider Krishna to be just another powerful man. Due to their envy, their dormant spiritual knowledge remains covered by the curtain of maya. In this state, they can never know Krishna as He is. Nor do they ever approach a spiritual master, who can deliver knowledge of Krishna. Indeed,

Krishna Himself declares that "Those who are envious and mischievous, who are the lowest among men, are cast by Me into the ocean of material existence, into various demoniac species of life. Attaining repeated birth amongst the species of demoniac life, such persons can never approach Me. Gradually they sink down to the most abominable type of existence." (16.19-20)

The fate of the demonic is further described in the next verse of this Ninth Chapter: "Those who are thus bewildered are attracted by demonic and atheistic views. In that deluded condition, their hopes for liberation, their fruitive activities, and their culture of knowledge are all defeated." (9.12) Here, Krishna speaks particularly of materialists who try to figure out the Absolute Truth by empirical philosophic speculation. Puffed up with mundane knowledge, drunk with intellectual pride, they try to elevate themselves to some heavenly condition, or at least release themselves from any higher authority or control. But because they are not Krishna conscious, they are defeated by material nature.

Without Krishna, we are always defeated. We may perform pious activities and go to the highest heaven, but without Krishna consciousness, we will be defeated. In the end, death will come to take away whatever we have attained. The only function of material nature is to defeat the conditioned soul in his attempts to perform pious activities, cultivate knowledge, amass wealth, progress socially, enjoy sense gratification, attain liberation, or whatever. Material nature is there to baffle and frustrate the demonic mentality struggling vainly against Krishna. Only by surrendering to Krishna can we cross over the ocean of material suffering, birth and death. Therefore, out of great compassion for all, in every chapter of *Bhagavad-gita*, Lord Krishna instructs, "Surrender to Me."

"O son of Pritha," Krishna continues, "those who are not deluded, the great souls, are under the protection of the divine nature. They are fully engaged in devotional service because they know Me as the Supreme Personality of Godhead, original and inexhaustible." (9.13) In this verse, Lord Krishna speaks of the *mahatmas*, the great souls. The word *mahatma* cannot be applied to a politician by votes. It cannot be acquired by any material endeavor—not by becoming a PhD, rich man, philanthropist, hospital worker, or national leader. Here, Krishna defines *mahatma* as one who is not deluded, who knows Him and fully engages in His devotional service. This is the secret of becoming a *mahatma:* knowing Krishna as He is and serving Him. Such a *mahatma* is also mentioned in the Seventh Chapter: "After many births and deaths, he who is actually in knowledge surrenders unto Me, knowing Me to be the cause of all causes and all that is. Such a great soul is very rare." (7.19) Knowing that Krishna creates everything, maintains everything, and destroys everything, the great soul surrenders unto Him and agrees to work on His behalf. According to *Bhagavad-gita*, there is no way to become a *mahatma* apart from surrendering to Krishna.

Lord Krishna continues to describe the activities of the great souls: "Always chanting My glories, endeavoring with great determination, bowing down before Me, these great souls perpetually worship Me with devotion." (9.14) This process is very wonderful because it is so simple and easily available to anyone in any material condition. The glories of God can be chanted in any part of the world by even the poorest man. One doesn't have to come from India or America, China or Pakistan, nor from an aristocratic or highly educated family. There are no material impediments. One need only hear submissively from the Lord's pure devotee and then repeat what he has heard. That is perfect chanting of God's glories.

Krishna speaks of "endeavoring with great determination" (*drdha-vratah*). We shouldn't just chant today and forget about it tomorrow, or take a month's vacation from praising God. Krishna consciousness is not such a cheap thing. Actually, it is very dear, for it can be purchased only by surrendering everything to Krishna at every moment of our lives. For this, we must endeavor with great determination. Although surrendering is difficult, the all-merciful Lord helps His sincere devotee from within as the Supersoul, and from without as the bona fide spiritual master. When Krishna sees a sincere attempt at surrender, He directs His devotee in such a way that complete surrender becomes possible. That is, He Himself helps the devotee along the path of purification.

At this point, Lord Krishna ceases to speak of His devotees, the *mahatmas*, and turns to those impersonalists who also try to realize Him: "Others, who are engaged in the cultivation of knowledge, worship the Supreme Lord as the one without a second, diverse in many, and in the universal form." (9.15) The universal form, which is fully discussed in the Eleventh Chapter, is a manifestation of Krishna for the impersonalists, who cannot understand how the Supreme Absolute Truth can be a person.

Krishna refers to such men as "others" (*anye*) to distinguish them from the *mahatma* devotees mentioned in the previous verse. These others may eventually come to Krishna when they have abandoned their impersonalist conceptions. This is fully explained in the Twelfth Chapter, wherein Krishna clearly tells Arjuna that it is better and easier to worship Him in His personal form than in His unmanifest impersonal aspect. Both personalist and impersonalist transcendentalists ultimately come to the same point (Krishna), but the impersonalist path is very difficult, both in practice and realization. In life, we have no experience with the impersonal, unmanifested, formless Absolute. From our very birth, we experience personalities and forms. Therefore meditation on the impersonal and formless is often frustrating, because it is no more than the opposite material conception. Therefore, at the time of complete realization, one must give up his impersonalist ideas, for God is ultimately realized as *sat-cit-ananda vigraha*, the Supreme Personality of Godhead. Everyone who desires perfect knowledge must come to the point of realizing Krishna, the Supreme Person. That is indicated here.

Still, by enumerating His diverse energies, Krishna describes ways in which He can be perceived through impersonalist meditation. In this way, the impersonalist may understand that all these innumerable manifestations are nothing other than Krishna: "It is I who am the ritual, I the sacrifice, the offering to the ancestors, the healing herb, the transcendental chant. I am the butter and the fire and the offering. I am the father of this universe, the mother, the support, and the grandsire. I am the object of knowledge, the purifier and the syllable *om*. I am also the *Rig*, the *Sama*, and the *Yajur Vedas*." (9.16-17) In the Fifteenth Chapter, Krishna also states that "I am the compiler of Vedanta, and I am the knower of the *Vedas*." (15.15) Krishna is everything, but until we surrender unto Him, we cannot realize this. Therefore only a devotee can be in full knowledge, realizing

Krishna as the Purusha, the Father of everyone. Krishna is also the grandsire, Brahma, born out of the navel of Vishnu.

"I am the goal, the sustainer, the master, the witness, the abode, the refuge, and the most dear friend. I am the creation and the annihilation, the basis of everything, the resting place, and the eternal seed. O Arjuna, I control heat, the rain, and the drought. I am immortality, and I am also death personified. Both being and nonbeing are in Me." (9.18-19) When one becomes a *paramahamsa*, perfect in Krishna consciousness, his vision becomes perfect, and he sees Krishna in everything. Impersonalists can never have perfect vision, for despite their seeing everything as one, they cannot see Krishna. The pure devotee does not see anything separate from Krishna. He sees Krishna in all things, and Krishna Himself simultaneously. Such vision is possible through loving surrender. Srila Prabhupada once gave a good example of this: "If you come into my apartment," he said, "and see my watch on the table, you immediately think, 'This is Prabhupada's watch.' A person who does not know me, or who has no love for me, will think, 'Oh, a Rolex watch,' or, 'My watch.' But because you are my devotee, the watch immediately reminds you of me." Similarly, a pure devotee sees that everything is Krishna's and that Krishna is everything. As Krishna says in the Sixth Chapter: "A true yogi observes Me in all beings and also sees every being in Me. Indeed, the self-realized man sees Me everywhere. For one who sees Me everywhere and sees everything in Me, I am never lost, nor is he ever lost to Me." (6.29-30) This is perfect vision.

Lord Krishna continues: "Those who study the *Vedas* and drink the soma juice, seeking the heavenly planets, worship Me indirectly. They take birth on the planet of Indra, where they enjoy godly delights." (9.20) Worship of demigods, such as Indra, brings only flickering happiness. In the Seventh Chapter also, Krishna pointed out the ephemeral nature of the results of such worship: "Men of small intelligence worship the demigods, for their fruits are limited and temporary. Those who worship the demigods go to the planets of the demigods, but My devotees ultimately reach My supreme planet." (7.23) Even if we are elevated to Brahma-loka, we have to undergo the miseries of birth and death. Such so-called happiness may appear "like nectar at first, but poison at the end." (18.38)

"But those who worship Me with devotion, meditating on My transcendental form—to them I carry what they lack and preserve what they have." (9.22) The devotee is never at a loss, neither in this life nor in the next, for Krishna comes personally to take charge of him. Even at the critical time of death, Krishna is there to help His devotee. This was pointed out at the conclusion of the last chapter. Impersonalists and yogis have to worry about the conditions under which they leave this planet—the position of the sun and moon, darkness and light—but the devotee doesn't have to concern himself with these things. If we always think of Krishna, He arranges everything. When Krishna became Arjuna's chariot driver, Arjuna didn't have to worry about the outcome of the battle. Krishna assured him that his enemies "are already put to death by My arrangement, and you, O Savyasacin, can be but an instrument in the fight." (11.33) The pure devotee is content to be Krishna's instrument, and happy to surrender unto the Lord. He neither hankers nor laments, for he knows that Krishna is his best friend and the real doer, supplying what he lacks and preserving what he has. In all circumstances, through thick and thin, Krishna is his constant companion.

Krishna continues: "Whatever a man may sacrifice to other gods, is really meant for Me alone, but it is offered without true understanding." (9.23) True understanding means knowing Krishna to be the cause and origin of everything, including all the demigods. He alone is the origin of Brahma, Shiva, Indra, Ganesh, Durga, and all others. He alone stands supreme. Just as in the Judaeo-Christian tradition, the first commandment states, "I am the Lord thy God.... Thou shalt have no other gods before Me," so in the *Bhagavad-gita*, Krishna stresses that worship is reserved for the Supreme Personality of Godhead. It is only the less intelligent, desirous of some material benefit, who worship the demigods. In the West, of course, we usually do not find overt demigod worship, but we do find a great deal of worship of powerful men, such as the President or the boss, celebrities, so-called sex symbols, movie idols, musicians, athletes, and so on. Living entities who minutely partake of Krishna's opulences of fame, beauty, wealth, power, knowledge, and renunciation, are often objects of worship. Factually, a man worships what he spends his time with, serves, adores, emulates, or admires. It is not unusual to see people worshipping famous, wealthy, intellectual, powerful men, beautiful women and children, and even pet dogs. These are all "other gods," though certainly not possessing the great qualities of Brahma and Shiva. Such worship, in the modes of passion and ignorance, only indicates the fallen, degraded condition of modern man.

"I am the only enjoyer and the only object of sacrifice," Lord Krishna declares. "Those who do not recognize My true transcendental nature fall down." (9.24) Even though a person may get some temporary benefit by worshipping a demigod, he eventually falls down because he doesn't recognize Lord Krishna's transcendental position as the Supreme Personality of Godhead. In such ignorance, a person cannot enter the world of Vaikuntha, where everything is eternal, full of bliss and knowledge.

Lord Krishna continues: "Those who worship the demigods will take birth among the demigods; those who worship ghosts and spirits will take birth among such beings; those who worship ancestors go to the ancestors; and those who worship Me will live with Me." (9.25) Krishna is equal to everyone. He supplies everyone's desire. If we want to go to the demigods, ghosts, spirits, or ancestors, we may. And if we want to go to Krishna, we may. The intelligent want to go to Krishna and therefore cultivate love for Him. Why? Krishna is the source of everything, and those who know Krishna, know everything. Life with Krishna is eternal; life with anyone else is temporary. Lord Krishna alone can give us full protection. There are many stories of the demigods' inability to give their devotees protection. Even Lord Shiva, unable to protect himself from the demon Vrkasura, ultimately had to take shelter of Lord Krishna. Krishna can give anyone protection, and He can give anyone liberation. He alone is called Mukunda, granter of liberation. No demigod is called Mukunda, for no demigod can grant liberation. We have already mentioned that Lord Brahma could not grant immortality to Hiranyakasipu. No demigod—much less man!—can give us immortality or ultimate protection. Only Krishna, the Supreme Personality of Godhead, can grant all boons, both material and spiritual, now and forevermore.

"If one offers Me with love and devotion a leaf, a flower, fruit or water, I will accept it." (9.26) Of course, being *atmarama*, self-satisfied, Krishna does not need anything. Still, He is looking for our love and devotion. A leaf, a flower, some fruit, and some water are available to any man in any part of the world; therefore no one can say, "I can't find anything to offer Krishna." When these insignificant things are offered with love and devotion, Krishna agrees to accept them. Of course, it is not very satisfactory if a rich man says, "Let me offer Krishna a glass of water, while I eat *puris, halavah,* and *kachoris.*" We have to offer Krishna the best of whatever we have, out of love, for He is the real proprietor of everything. Then we should take the remnants as His *prasadam,* or mercy. The whole point of offering, or sacrifice, is to put Krishna at the center of our lives, our homes and business. Since in reality Krishna is the proprietor of the business, the results should be offered to Him. The leaf, fruit, flower, and water are simply a means to awaken and evoke our dormant love and devotion for God. Ultimately, in full Krishna consciousness, we will offer everything, as Krishna recommends next.

"O son of Kunti, all that you do, all that you eat, all that you offer and give away, as well as all austerities that you may perform, should be done as an offering unto Me. In this way, you will be freed from all reactions to good and evil deeds, and by this principle of renunciation, you will be liberated and come to Me." (9.27-28) Real liberation is not found by merging into the impersonal Brahman or becoming zero or void. Liberation means becoming free from the reactions of activity. In this material world, everyone is forced to act, to perform some activity, good or bad, and to suffer the good or bad results. But by offering everything to Krishna, we can be liberated from this vicious cycle of action and reaction, birth and death.

Rupa Goswami has said that real renunciation is not to be found in the artificial negation of things but in their proper utilization, by engaging them in Krishna's service. "One is said to be situated in the fully renounced order of life if he lives in accordance with Krishna consciousness. He should be without attachment for sense gratification and should accept for himself only what is necessary for the upkeep of the body. On the other hand, one who renounces things which could be used in the service of Krishna, under the pretext that such things are material, does not practice complete renunciation." (*Bhakti-rasamrta-sindhu*, 1.2.255)

There are some *sadhus* and holymen who will not touch money when it is offered to them. They will even pull back their hands in disgust, thinking that the money will defile them. Srila Prabhupada has said, "We are not like that. If someone comes forward to offer money, we will take it enthusiastically and spend it for Krishna." There is no limit to the employment of money in Lord Krishna's service. For serving Krishna, we can print books, build temples and Krishna conscious communities, and spread the message of *Bhagavad-gita* all over the world. This cannot be done by a pauper. Money is required for any endeavor. Our motto should be, "Millions for Krishna, but not one penny for sense gratification." This is real renunciation and proper use of money.

"I envy no one, nor am I partial to anyone," Krishna says. "I am equal to all. But whoever renders service unto Me in devotion is a friend, is in Me, and I am also a friend to him." (9.29) Although Krishna sometimes acts like an enemy, we shouldn't think that He becomes inimical to anyone. When Vishnu took the side of the demigods, He was accused of partiality, but this was not the case (See *Srimad-Bhagavatam*, 7.1). Krishna also fought and destroyed many demons—Kamsa, Putana, Aghasura, Kesi—but this doesn't mean that He was their actual enemy. Krishna is simply fulfilling everyone's desire. When one wants to become a demon for his sense gratification, he indirectly chooses to make Krishna his enemy, and therefore Krishna fulfills his desire and acts like an enemy. Because the devotee wants to have Krishna as a friend, Krishna reciprocates. When we desire to surrender to Krishna, Krishna reciprocates in one way, and when we desire to rebel, He reciprocates in another. It is not that everyone gets the same reward. If we buy a ticket to Montreal, we cannot expect to arrive in New York. Krishna reciprocates according to our desire. "All of them—as they surrender unto Me—I reward accordingly." (4.11)

Krishna is sometimes compared to a desire tree, which yields whatever fruit we want. The Lord says that He is a friend to one who renders service to Him. Krishna is impartial until we take that first step toward Him. When we surrender unto Him, He becomes our friend and therefore partial, protecting what we have and personally bringing what we lack. It is our desire that determines this result. Those who want to go to the demigods go there; those who want to go to Krishna go to Him. This is impartiality. Since Krishna is the Father of all living entities, how can He be partial? He has given us independence and informed us of the results of our actions. Krishna is the wish-fulfilling tree satisfying all desires, and we can choose to pick either sweet or bitter fruit. The Lord does not interfere with our minute independence, but He encourages us over and over, "Choose Me. Surrender unto Me. Disregard everything else. Just make Me your ultimate goal." He wants us to love Him in full freedom.

Lord Krishna continues: "Even if one commits the most abominable actions, if he is engaged in devotional service, he is to be considered saintly because he is properly situated. He quickly becomes righteous and attains lasting peace. O son of Kunti, declare it boldly that My devotee never perishes." (9.30-31) This is a very astonishing statement. Even if a devotee makes a mistake and acts contrary to mundane social morality, committing acts that are considered abominable, he should still be considered a *sadhu* or saint because of his determination to become Krishna conscious. Due to some past bad habits, a devotee may fall down, but this is not his real desire. His innermost desire is to become a devotee. This is the desire we must cultivate, making certain that we have given up all others. Since Krishna is fulfilling everyone's desire, He will quickly remove all material impediments from the path of the devotee who truly wants Him to be his Lord and master. Imperfections will be rectified, and the determined devotee will quickly become righteous and attain lasting peace. He will never perish. This is the Lord's promise.

It is especially significant that the Lord tells Arjuna to announce this promise to the world. "Declare it boldly." Krishna wanted the promise to be declared by Arjuna because Krishna Himself has been known to break His promise. For instance, Krishna had promised not to participate in the battle at Kurukshetra, but when Arjuna faced death at the hands of the valiant Bhismadev, Krishna broke His promise to save His friend. Krishna did this not only to save Arjuna but also to fulfill the promise of His great devotee Bhismadev. Bhisma had been accused by Duryodhona of being partial to the Pandavas; therefore Bhisma promised to fight so heroically on the next day that he would either kill Arjuna or make Krishna break His promise. Thus it was also to fulfill the promise of His devotee, Bhisma, that Lord Krishna broke His own word. Krishna's telling Arjuna to "declare it boldly" is a way of making the promise doubly binding. All else may fail, but Krishna's devotee will never fail.

"O son of Pritha," Krishna continues, "those who take shelter in Me, though they be of lower birth—women, *vaisyas* [farmers and merchants], as well as *sudras* [workers]—can approach the supreme destination." (9.32) Here again, Krishna expresses His impartiality. There is equal opportunity for everyone, regardless of birth. Anyone can take shelter of Krishna, learn the process of devotional service by approaching a bona fide spiritual master, and become perfect. In *Srimad-Bhagavatam*, it is stated that even the *chandalas*, the dog-eaters, who are lower than the *sudra* caste, can become pure devotees of the Lord by the grace of the Lord's pure devotee. However, to attain perfection, the candidate must surrender to the instructions of the spiritual master. That is the only requirement. Just as base metal can be turned to gold by alchemy, a fallen person can be turned into a Vaishnava (pure devotee) by the expert guidance of the bona fide spiritual master.

Lord Krishna continues: "How much greater then are the *brahmanas*, the righteous, the devotees and saints who in this temporary, miserable world engage in loving service unto Me." (9.33) Here, Krishna speaks of those born with great natural advantage. It is not that they are inherently better, but their opportunity is better. It is up to them, however, to make use of it. To whom much is given, much is required. Because their opportunity is great, there are great expectations and responsibilities. In any case, the door of perfection is open to everyone, regardless of birth.

In conclusion, Lord Krishna summarizes the process of perfection: "Engage your mind always in thinking of Me, offer obeisances and worship Me. Being completely absorbed in Me, surely you will come to Me." (9.34) Standing before Arjuna on the battlefield, Krishna is telling him to think of Him, to worship Him, and surrender unto Him only. When Arjuna understands Him perfectly, he will say, "My dear Krishna, O infallible one, my illusion is now gone. I have regained my memory by Your mercy, and I am now firm and free from doubt and am prepared to act according to Your instructions." (18.73) This is Arjuna's final understanding, and it must also be ours.

Unfortunate people do not understand as Arjuna did; therefore they remain in illusion, saying that it is not to Krishna that we must surrender, but to some impersonal spirit speaking through Krishna. This means that they do not understand Krishna at all. There is no difference between Krishna's inside and outside, between His self and His body. Krishna is Absolute, and when He says, "Surrender unto Me," He wants us to surrender unto Him personally. Otherwise, why does He say, *Mam namaskuru* ("Worship Me."), or *Mam ekam saranam vraja* ("Surrender unto Me.")? The word *mam* means "Me." Are we to assume that Krishna doesn't know grammar, that He can't speak properly? Because Krishna wants us to meditate on Him personally, He uses the word *mam* six times in this final *sloka*. This is the most confidential knowledge of devotional service unto Krishna. By worshipping Krishna, bowing down to Krishna, thinking of Krishna, and becoming completely absorbed in Krishna, we ultimately go to Krishna's abode in the spiritual sky.

This is not a complicated process, but a change of heart is required. We must abandon our desire to lord it over material nature for our own selfish gratification, and we must engage everything in Krishna's service. In this way, we can easily remember Krishna, and return to Krishna at the end of this very life. "Surely you will come to Me." There is no doubt about it. This is Krishna's promise: "My devotee never perishes." Hare Krishna!

Know that all beautiful, glorious, and mighty creations spring from but a spark of My splendor. But what need is there, Arjuna, for all this detailed knowledge? With a single fragment of Myself I pervade and support this entire universe. (Bg. 10.41-42)

CHAPTER TEN

The Opulence of The Absolute

"My dear friend, mighty-armed Arjuna, listen again to my supreme word, which I shall impart to you for your benefit and which will give you great joy." (10.1)

Lord Krishna's words are spoken for the benefit of all living entities. In the preceding chapter, He proclaimed Himself "the most dear friend," (9.18) and "equal to all." (9.29) Since Lord Krishna is everyone's best friend, He alone can do good for everyone. He is everyone's "well-wisher," (5.29) the supreme welfare worker.

To be effective, welfare work must be rooted in knowledge. One may have good sentiments, intending to do good to others, but if there is no knowledge, one may unwittingly do harm. Lord Krishna, however, is always perfect in knowledge. Being complete in Himself, He is nonenvious, and as the Supreme Father, He is always benefiting everyone. Whatever advice He gives is for our good.

Sometimes neophyte devotees, due to a lingering attachment to sense gratification, cannot understand how Krishna consciousness can be joyful. As long as we are in the diseased condition, identifying ourselves with the material body, we may feel some inconvenience rendering devotional service. In the beginning, some difficulty may be perceived in *tapasya*, renunciation, but we should understand that we are only renouncing maya, that which is false. On the spiritual platform, the soul is constitutionally joyful in the Lord's service, for that is his natural function. Since Lord Krishna's words are the essence of devotional service, they are intended to give us great joy.

"Neither the hosts of the demigods nor the great sages know

149

My origin, for, in every respect, I am the source of the demigods and the sages. He who knows Me as the unborn, as the beginningless, as the Supreme Lord of all the worlds—he, undeluded among men, is freed from all sins." (10.2-3) From time to time, Krishna comes into the material world to give us knowledge of Himself and to reestablish our path back home, back to Godhead. Without knowledge of Krishna, we cannot take to Krishna consciousness. To attract us back to our eternal home, the Kingdom of God, Krishna reveals Himself and the eternal pastimes of His spiritual abode. Otherwise, how could we possibly know anything of that realm? "He who knows in truth this glory and power of Mine engages in unalloyed devotional service. Of this, there is no doubt." (10.7) We cannot be attracted to Krishna's service unless we know something of the wonderful opulences of Krishna: His power, knowledge, fame, beauty, wealth, and renunciation.

Even in the material world, people render service to the great and opulent. By his powerful position, the president of a country attracts many people into his service. Of course, people serve him thinking of their own sense gratification: "Oh, I will be helped by serving this powerful man." Similarly, if a person is very knowledgeable, famous, beautiful, wealthy, or renounced, he will also attract others, because people want to emulate and associate with greatness

Although a devotee may be attracted to Lord Krishna's service because of the Lord's limitless opulence, the devotee does not want anything in return for his service. In this way, spiritual service differs from material service. In the material world, no one will serve without the promise of sense gratification, but a devotee serves Krishna without desiring anything other than the transcendental service itself. Therefore, Lord Chaitanya prayed, "My dear Lord, I have no desire to accumulate wealth, nor do I desire beautiful women, nor do I want any number of followers. I want only Your causeless devotional service, birth after birth." (*Shikshashtaka, 4*) The pure devotee neither desires sense gratification nor hates material existence. Both attraction and repulsion are causes of bondage. But here, Lord Chaitanya says that He does not care even for liberation. As long as He can engage in devotional service, He is willing to stay in the material world "birth after birth." Indeed, the great Vaishnava saint Bilvamangala Thakur has said, "If I am engaged in devotional service unto You, my dear Lord, then I can very easily perceive Your presence everywhere. And as far as liberation is concerned, I think liberation stands at my door with folded hands, waiting to serve me." The pure devotee, therefore, is not interested in liberation from material existence, nor in any recompense for his devotional service.

Lord Krishna continues: "I am the source of all spiritual and material worlds. Everything emanates from Me. The wise who know this perfectly engage in My devotional service and worship Me with all their hearts." (10.8) This is the first of the four nutshell verses of *Bhagavad-gita*. Just as Krishna summarized the *Srimad-Bhagavatam* in four verses to Brahma, He now summarizes *Bhagavad-gita* to His disciple Arjuna. Whatever we see in the material or spiritual world emanates from Krishna. In every sense, Krishna is the origin of all things. He is both creator and destroyer of all the universes. Most philosophical men want to know about their origin and future. That is only natural, for man is more than beast. Vedic literatures inform mankind about the whole cosmic situation. By the Lord's will, this creation takes place and is maintained for a certain time, then is annihilated. In all circumstances, the supreme will is the ultimate controller. Of course, there are so-called educated men who do not believe in the supreme controller, but such disbelief is due to insufficient knowledge. "The fool hath said in his heart, There is no God." After a great expenditure of money and brainpower, scientists may succeed in putting small satellites into space, but the supreme scientist, Lord Sri Krishna, can float huge planets and stars in space, just by His will. Lord Krishna is the primeval Lord, the greatest; no one can equal Him, and no one can surpass Him. Knowing perfectly Lord Krishna's qualities, the devotee renders unalloyed devotional service to Him.

"The thoughts of My pure devotees dwell in Me, their lives are surrendered to Me, and they derive great satisfaction and bliss enlightening one another and conversing about Me." (10.9) A devotee needs nothing apart from Krishna. He is not in the least interested in mundane things. Since all his thoughts repose in Krishna's transcendental qualities, Krishna is his sole subject of conversation. He doesn't want to talk about anything but Krishna. Nor does he want to eat anything but Krishna *prasadam*, which is also Krishna. Since everything in his life is Krishna, he experiences constant and complete bliss, knowing that whatever pleasure he experiences comes from Lord Krishna, the reservoir of all pleasure. Not knowing that everything comes from Krishna, the materialist cannot experience the joy of Krishna consciousness, but the devotee, being full in the knowledge that Krishna is the origin of all, relishes unlimited pleasure. "Oh, this is coming from Krishna," he thinks at every moment of his life. Therefore he is completely satisfied in Krishna, and never wants anything else.

"To those who are constantly devoted and worship Me with love, I give the understanding by which they can come to Me." (10.10) The Supreme Personality of Godhead cannot be known by mental speculation or human endeavor, but only by His own sweet will. He is known only when He agrees to reveal Himself to His devotee. Although Krishna is everywhere, He is concealed from those with material vision. Transcendental knowledge is a gift from Krishna, which He is willing to bestow on anyone who loves Him and becomes His unalloyed devotee. In the words of *Brahma-samhita*:

> *premāñjana-cchurita-bhakti-vilocanena*
> *santaḥ sadaiva hṛdayeṣu vilokayanti*
> *yaṁ śyāmasundaram acintya-guṇa-svarūpaṁ*
> *govindam ādi-puruṣaṁ tam ahaṁ bhajāmi*

"I worship the primeval Lord, Govinda, who is always seen by the devotee whose eyes are anointed with the pulp of love. He is seen in His eternal form of Syamasundara situated within the heart of the devotee." (*Brahma-samhita*, 5.38)

This is the qualification: our eyes must be smeared with the ointment of love of God. Then Lord Krishna bestows the gift of transcendental knowledge, by which He can be seen. The price is dear: we must become His unalloyed devotees.

"Out of compassion for them, I, dwelling in their hearts, destroy with the shining lamp of knowledge the darkness born of ignorance." (10.11) In this material world, our natural condition is one of darkness and ignorance. As soon as we take birth, we are covered by ignorance. Material life has often been likened to imprisonment in a dungeon. It was Socrates who compared the human condition to life in an underground cave, where men see only the shadows that the fire throws on the opposite wall. Actually, our cave life begins with conception in the mother's womb. It continues as long as we accept this temporary material illusion as all in all and fail to surrender to Krishna, the supreme reality. *Srimad-Bhagavatam* tells how the soul, in his painful, confined condition within the mother's womb, turns in desperation to Lord Krishna and calls out, "Krishna, please deliver me. I will become Your devotee." Unfortunately, soon after taking birth, he forgets this promise to the Lord. Bewildered by the phenomenal world, he tries to enjoy sense objects, again forgetting his eternal well-wisher, Lord Krishna. But if one keeps his promise to become a devotee, Lord Krishna, dwelling as Paramatma (Supersoul) within the heart, grants the transcendental knowledge by which ignorance and darkness are dispelled.

This all comes about through the devotee's sincere desire to surrender unto Krishna. "I am seated in everyone's heart, and from Me come remembrance, knowledge and forgetfulness." (15.15) According to our desire, Krishna supplies either remembrance or forgetfulness. Residing as the Supersoul in the hearts of all, Lord Krishna is always ready to fulfill our desires. As soon as we take birth, we forget everything about our previous life, but the Supersoul is there to remind us. If we want to become Krishna conscious, Krishna reminds us from within as Supersoul, and from without by sending a bona fide spiritual master to impart transcendental knowledge. If we don't follow the spiritual master's instructions, however, whatever knowledge we have is taken away. To receive more knowledge, therefore, we must be careful to act on the knowledge already imparted.

At this point in the Tenth Chapter, Arjuna confirms what Lord Krishna has already declared. As the Supreme Personality of Godhead, Krishna's word is final. Yet His devotee's affirmation is very significant. Arjuna says: *Param brahma param dhama/ pavitram paramam bhavan.* "You are the Supreme Brahman, the ultimate, the supreme abode and purifier, the Absolute Truth, and the eternal divine person. You are the primal God, transcendental and original, and You are the unborn and all-pervading beauty. All the great sages such as Narada, Asita, Devala, and Vyasa proclaim this of You, and now You Yourself are declaring it to me." (10.12-13)

Krishna has declared Himself to be the source of everything, of both the material and spiritual worlds. In case there is any doubt, or any future misinterpretation, Arjuna here corroborates what the Lord has said, giving his full acclamation by accepting Sri Krishna as the Supreme Absolute Truth, the Supreme Personality of Godhead. Since Arjuna was personally present, his testimony is most important. Mental speculators may claim that "Krishna means this," or, "Krishna means that," but Arjuna herein says exactly what Krishna means, and Krishna certifies Arjuna's understanding as correct. Since Lord Krishna is the supreme spiritual master, and Arjuna is His perfect disciple, Arjuna's understanding sets the standard for everyone.

Significantly, Arjuna first proclaims that Krishna is the Supreme Brahman (*param brahma*), not that the Supreme Brahman is Krishna. "I am the basis of the impersonal Brahman," Krishna says. (14.27) It is not that Brahman is the basis of Krishna. the impersonal Brahman emanates from Krishna, who is the Supreme Brahman, the Param-brahman. Since Krishna is the origin of everything, there is nothing beyond Him. He is the ultimate, the supreme abode, our actual refuge and resting place. We may try to establish an abode apart from Krishna, but it cannot be final. Being part and parcel of Krishna, we cannot rest until we return to Him.

Arjuna then calls Krishna the supreme pure (*pavitram*) because He is able to purify everything without ever becoming contaminated. The sun can penetrate into privies without being polluted, and even stool and urine are purified when left in the sun. By associating with the Supreme Lord's name, form, and pastimes, we are purified of all contamination.

All truths in this material world are relative to and dependent on the Absolute Truth, declared here by Arjuna to be Lord Krishna. Since Krishna is the origin of all truths, we have to verify all truths by Him. Nothing can be true unless it is connected with Krishna. Arjuna also calls Krishna "the eternal divine person," (*purusam sasvatam divyam*). Krishna's personality is infinite and eternal. Our personality is partial and defective, but

His personality is perfect and complete. He has a perfect body and perfect senses. According to *Brahma-samhita*, His transcendental senses are so perfect that they are completely interchangeable; one sense can perform all the functions of any other. He can eat with His eyes, or He can impregnate by His glance. Being perfect and complete (*purnam*), Krishna's senses cannot be compared to our limited, defective senses.

Sometimes impersonalists say that God has no senses—no eyes, no hands, no ears, no mouth, etc. Being envious of the Lord, they try to make God blind, deaf, and mute. This is their way of saying that they are greater than God. Although living entities are imperfect, they all have senses. Even the lower creatures—cats and dogs—have senses. How is it that God, the all perfect, the supreme living entity, has no senses? If God is the origin of everything, He is the origin of the senses. Whatever we find in the creation can be found in God in its perfection. Lord Krishna is the supremely complete Personality of Godhead with supremely complete senses. By denying His transcendental form and senses, the impersonalists become the greatest offenders.

Lord Krishna is the primal God, original and transcendental, as well as supremely beautiful. "You are the unborn and all-pervading beauty," Arjuna says. God is not formless. How can something without form be beautiful? Beauty implies form; beauty is the expression of form. That transcendental form of Krishna is the origin of all beauty. Whatever beauty exists in this material world is beautiful only because it emanates from Krishna.

Arjuna does not praise Krishna in this way just because Krishna is his friend, nor does he present his own personal opinion by itself, although he is a most elevated personality. In support of his own statements, Arjuna mentions the conclusions of other great souls: "All the great sages such as Narada, Asita, Devala, and Vyasa proclaim this of You, and You Yourself are declaring it to me." He cites the testimonies of four great sages: Narada, who is called "the sage amongst the demigods;" Asita and Devala, who are great Vedic authorities; and Vyasa, the incarnation of Krishna who wrote down all the Vedic literatures. And significantly, Arjuna concludes with the supreme testimony—that of Sri Krishna Himself.

In this way, Arjuna proclaims Krishna to be the Supreme Personality of Godhead, worthy of everyone's worship and surrender. Arjuna teaches us by his example: "O Krishna, I totally accept as truth all that You have told me. Neither the gods nor demons, O Lord, know Your personality. You alone know Yourself by Your own potencies, O origin of all, Lord of all beings, God of gods, O Supreme Person, Lord of the universe!" (10.14-15) Krishna reveals Himself to His pure devotee out of love and affection. No one can know Krishna except a pure devotee. Because Arjuna was Krishna's friend and did not envy Him, he could understand Krishna as He is. Of course, being a pure devotee, Arjuna understood Lord Krishna's actual position. He did not need any further proof. It is, therefore, for our benefit that he requests a specific description of the Lord's opulences. "Please tell me in detail of Your divine powers by which You pervade all these worlds and abide in them. How should I meditate on You? In what various forms are You to be contemplated?" (10.16-17)

Lord Krishna replies: "Yes, I will tell you of My splendorous manifestations, but only of those which are prominent, O Arjuna, for My opulence is limitless. I am the Self, O Gudakesa, seated in the hearts of all creatures. I am the beginning, the middle, and the end of all beings. Of the Adityas, I am Vishnu; of lights, I am the radiant sun; I am Marici of the Maruts, and among the stars I am the moon." (10.19-21)

Lord Krishna thus begins His account of some of His prominent opulences, pointing out that He is the greatest in every category, the epitome of creation. Of all lights in the sky, He is the sun and moon, the greatest. "Of the *Vedas*, I am the *Sama-veda*; of the demigods, I am Indra." (10.22) Indra is the king of the demigods, the lord of the heavenly planets. Being the foremost demigod, he especially represents Krishna. "Of the senses, I am the mind." (10.22) Since the mind leads and controls all other senses, it represents Krishna. Krishna then says that He is Lord Shiva; Kuvera, the lord of wealth; Agni, the god of fire; the foremost priest, Brihaspati, lord of devotion; Skanda, the lord of war; among bodies of water, the great ocean; among sacrifices, *japa*, the greatest of all; the Himalayas, greatest of mountains;

the great devotee Narada amongst the sages; the monarch among men; Ananta, of the celestial serpents; of dispensers of law, Yama, the lord of death, whom no one can escape. In the material world, a criminal may escape the police, but no one can escape the Yamadutas, Yama's agents of death. Krishna's law cannot be broken without punishment. As the Supersoul in the heart of every living entity, Krishna witnesses all our activities. Since Yamaraj dispenses justice infallibly, he represents Krishna.

Krishna continues to enumerate His opulences, saying that He is Prahlada, the great devotee born into a family of demons. "Among subduers, I am time." (10.30) Under time's influence, everything is destroyed. "Of purifiers, I am the wind... Of all creations, I am the beginning, and the end, and also the middle... Of sciences, I am the spiritual science of the Self." (10.31-32) This indicates that the spiritual science is the greatest of sciences. Although today's universities teach all kinds of sciences, they foolishly neglect the greatest science of all. Unless we understand the science of the Self, our education is like decorations on a dead body— completely useless.

"I am also inexhaustible time, and of creators, I am Brahma...and I am all-devouring death." (10.33-34) Atheists deny God's existence and control, but they cannot deny the existence and control of death. Even an atheist must succumb to the force of death. Thus death represents Krishna. Surrendering to death's force, however, is not the same as surrendering to Krishna in transcendental love. By surrendering to death, one is guaranteed rebirth, but by surrendering to Krishna in love and devotion, one immediately attains the eternal Kingdom of God beyond the reach of birth and death.

"I am also the gambling of cheats," Krishna says. (10.36) People sometimes ask how it is that gambling can represent Krishna. We should not think of Krishna as one-sided. His sides are infinite. "All states of being, be they goodness, passion, or ignorance come from Me," He says. (7.12) In one sense, Krishna is everything. For Krishna, there is neither good nor bad, nor any other duality. Whatever Krishna does is transcendentally good. When Krishna was a small child, He stole butter and distributed it to the monkeys, and even that pastime is worshipp-

ed. How is this? Whatever Krishna does is perfect. If He becomes a gambler or a thief, He is worshipable. Even the victim
of His stealing and cheating benefits by His activities and enjoys
them. That is the nature of the Absolute. Whatever He does is
absolutely perfect, although for us, because we are finite and
imperfect, such activities are harmful and would warrant punishment.

"Furthermore, O Arjuna," Krishna continues, "I am the
generating seed of all existences. There is no being—moving or
unmoving—that can exist without Me." (10.39) Krishna is the
"seed-giving father" of every living being. (14.4) The worthy son
surrenders to the father, listens carefully to His instructions, and
assists Him in His mission. In this way, there is complete cooperation and happiness for both father and son. The Lord takes
pleasure in glorifying His pure devotees, and the devotees derive
satisfaction in the glorification of the Lord. Thus there is always
transcendental competition in loving affairs between the Lord
and His pure devotees.

Lord Krishna continues: "O mighty conqueror of enemies,
there is no end to My divine manifestations. What I have spoken
to you is but a mere indication of My infinite opulences." (10.40)
No one can estimate the energies or potencies of Sri Krishna.
To give us some indication of their magnitude, Krishna comes
periodically to display them. He also explains something of His
transcendental nature, which is incomprehensible to atheists and
mental speculators. Even when Krishna was personally present
five thousand years ago, only a handful of devotees could understand Him in truth. Others considered Him a clever prince, a
great king, or a powerful yogi, but they could not begin to understand Him as the Supreme Person from whom everything
emanates. This truth is revealed only to the pure devotees.
Whether the world is aware of it or not, Krishna is always full
of infinite, inconceivable potencies.

"Know that all beautiful, glorious, and mighty creations
spring from but a spark of My splendor," He says. (10.41) If we
know this, it is easy to remember Krishna whenever we see
something beautiful or wonderful. All opulences come from
Krishna, be they material or spiritual. If a devotee sees a beautiful
flower, he immediately thinks, "Oh, Krishna is such a wonderful

artist! Who could paint such a beautiful thing?" But whenever a materialist sees something beautiful or wonderful, he immediately wants to possess it for his own sense gratification. The conditioned soul's first impulse is to utilize everything for his personal enjoyment. He is like a habitual thief who wants to steal whatever he sees, in complete defiance of the proprietor and the law. Because a devotee is surrendered to Krishna, he sees everything as Krishna's property. Therefore, upon seeing anything wonderful or beautiful, he thinks, "This is Krishna's. Krishna has made this beauty, this power, this glory. How can I use it in Krishna's service?"

"But what need is there, Arjuna, for all this detailed knowledge?" Krishna asks. "With a single fragment of Myself, I pervade and support this entire universe." (10.42)

All of Krishna's opulences are revealed to His pure devotee for his complete understanding. Since the devotee does not misuse Krishna's property, Krishna is prepared to give him everything. Krishna responds in proportion to our surrender. Prabhupada used to say, "Krishna can turn over the whole world to us in a day." At Kurukshetra, Krishna delivered the world into the hands of His devotees, the Pandavas, after an eighteen-day battle. But He can do it in one day, or one second, if He wants. Lord Krishna is just as much present today, and He is ready to deliver the world into the hands of His qualified devotees. But we must know how to use everything for Krishna's service. As long as we have any material disease left in us, as long as we want to enjoy Krishna's property for our own sense gratification, Krishna will not do it. That would be detrimental for the immature devotee. "Krishna doesn't so much notice how much you give to Him," Prabhupada once said. "But He notices how much you keep for yourself." There is no fooling Krishna; we can fool only ourselves. We should understand that if Krishna withholds anything from us, it is out of kindness. He doesn't want us to become entrapped again by the clutches of maya. As long as we have a tendency to try to enjoy material nature, we can fall down.

Krishna makes us struggle very hard to purify ourselves of all desire for sense gratification. Indeed, the struggle itself is purifying. Therefore, patience is the symptom of surrender, and a sincere devotee must persevere to the end. We must learn to forgo our own desire and accept Krishna's. Krishna consciousness is both the means and the end of purification. By chanting Hare Krishna, we become purified of all the dirty things in the heart. *Ceto-darpana-marjanam*, Lord Chaitanya says. Just by chanting Hare Krishna, the Lord's holy names, we can cleanse away all the dirty things that have accumulated in the heart for many, many births. That is the means of purification. And the end? When purified, we will want nothing more than chanting Hare Krishna, the holy name—but offenselessly.

That offenseless chanting is the nectar for which the devotee longs. When we are pure, we can chant and relish the transcendental pleasure of Krishna's name. The Lord's opulences are described in this chapter so that we may understand His greatness, surrender to Him, and become His pure, unalloyed devotees. Hare Krishna.

Arjuna saw in that universal form unlimited mouths and unlimited eyes. It was all wondrous. The form was decorated with divine, dazzling ornaments and arrayed in many garbs. He was garlanded gloriously, and there were many scents smeared over His body. All was magnificent, all-expanding, unlimited. This was seen by Arjuna. *(Bg. 11.10-11)*

CHAPTER ELEVEN

The Universal Form

Arjuna says, "If You think that I am able to behold Your cosmic form, O my Lord, O master of all mystic power, then kindly show me that universal self." (11.4)

Although Arjuna is a great and fearless warrior, he approaches Lord Krishna with a humble and submissive attitude. He does not challenge Krishna, or demand to see that form by which the Lord enters into the cosmic manifestation. He says, "if You think that I am able," *(manyase yadi tac chakyam)*, indicating that he has surrendered his will unto the Lord. Since we are Krishna's servants, we must surrender our finite will to the Lord's perfect will, and thereby come to know Him in full. That is the first qualification for seeing God: surrender of our will in all humility. The second qualification is bestowed by the Lord Himself: the divine eye by which He can be seen. "Whatever you wish to see can be seen all at once in this body," Krishna says. "This universal form can show you all that you now desire, as well as whatever you may desire in the future. Everything is here completely. But you cannot see Me with your present eyes. Therefore I give to you divine eyes by which you can behold My mystic opulence." (11.7-8) No one can see Krishna unless blessed by Krishna with divine eyes. Actually, Krishna is everywhere. He is before us at the present moment, but without spiritual vision, we cannot see Him. *Brahma-samhita* states that when the eyes are smeared with the ointment of love, they can see God everywhere in His wonderful form of Shyamasundara, the beautiful two-armed form praised by Lord Brahma:

> *premāñjana-cchurita-bhakti-vilocanena*
> *santaḥ sadaiva hṛdayeṣu vilokayanti*
> *yaṁ śyāmasundaram acintya-guṇa-svarūpaṁ*
> *govindam ādi-puruṣaṁ tam ahaṁ bhajāmi*

"I worship the primeval Lord, Govinda, who is always seen by the devotee whose eyes are annointed with the pulp of love. He is seen in His eternal form of Shyamasundara, situated within the heart of the devotee." (*Brahma-samhita*,5.38) Srila Prabhupada further describes how the ideal yogi concentrates his mind on Krishna in this form of Shyamasundara, "who is as beautifully colored as a cloud, whose lotus-like face is as effulgent as the sun, whose dress is brilliant with jewels, and whose body is flower-garlanded. Illuminating all sides, is his gorgeous luster, which is called the *brahmajyoti*. He incarnates in different forms such as Rama, Nrsimha, Varaha, and Krishna, the Supreme Personality of Godhead, and He descends like a human being, as the son of Mother Yasoda, and He is known as Krishna, Govinda, and Vasudeva. He is the perfect child, husband, friend, and master, and He is full with all opulences and transcendental qualities. If one remains fully conscious of these features of the Lord, he is called the highest yogi." (*Bhagavad-gita As It Is*, 6.47, Purport)

This is not imagination. God is all-pervading, and by His mercy He can be seen by those who have surrendered unto Him in transcendental love and affection.

Verses nine through thirty in this chapter describe God's mighty power and opulence, as manifested in the cosmic creation. "Arjuna saw in that universal form unlimited mouths and unlimited eyes. It was all wondrous. The form was decorated with divine, dazzling ornaments and arrayed in many garbs. He was garlanded gloriously, and there were many scents smeared over His body. All was magnificent, all-expanding, unlimited. If hundreds of thousands of suns rose up at once into the sky, they might resemble the effulgence of the Supreme Person in that universal form. At that time, Arjuna could see in the universal form of the Lord the unlimited expansions of the universe situated in one place, although divided into many, many thousands." (11.11-13)

When the devotee is blessed by the Lord, he can see the Lord in any one of His transcendental forms. However, this particular universal form (*virata-rupa*) is not often sought by pure devotees. It is a very opulent, unlimited form expanded everywhere, manifested particularly to astound the materialists, who are always challenging God. Being a pure devotee, Arjuna was not very interested in seeing this form. Since he is eternally related to Krishna as His friend, Arjuna preferred to see the Lord in His two-armed form as Krishna. But because Krishna was declaring Himself to be the Supreme Personality of Godhead, Arjuna wanted to establish Krishna's transcendental position beyond a doubt for posterity. He did not want people to think, "Oh, Krishna is claiming to be God, and Arjuna is agreeing because he is His friend." Arjuna wanted to establish Krishna's supremacy in such a way that even gross materialists could not logically challenge Him. After hearing Arjuna's description of the universal form, any sane man must agree, "Yes, this is God. Only God can do that." This universal form is presented so that all mankind will know definitely that Krishna is the Supreme Personality of Godhead.

Arjuna was also well aware that in the future many fools and rascals would claim to be incarnations of God. He did not want them to cheat the innocent public, nor cheapen the idea of God, nor blaspheme Lord Krishna's transcendental position. By revealing the universal form, Lord Krishna set forth a criterion by which we can judge the authenticity of an incarnation. If some fool says, "I am God," we can challenge him by saying, "Then show us your universal form." Since the next incarnation of God (Kalki-avatara) is not scheduled to appear until the end of Kali-yuga, over 400,000 years from now, our challenge may go unanswered for some time.

This universal form is terrifying and fearful to behold, unlimited in scope and expanded in all directions. Even Arjuna, Krishna's personal friend, was frightened upon seeing this form. "O mighty-armed one," he says, "all the planets with their demigods are disturbed at seeing Your many faces, eyes, arms, bellies, and legs, and Your terrible teeth, and as they are disturbed, so am I. O all-pervading Vishnu, I can no longer maintain my equilibrium. Seeing Your radiant colors fill the skies, and beholding Your eyes and mouths, I am afraid." (11.23- 24) This is certainly a very wonderful form, but not a very lovable one. Krishna's pure devotees are attached to the cowherd boy of Vrindaban, Krishna's personal two-armed form, which delighted His childhood friends and intimate associates like mother

Yasoda, Nanda Maharaj, the cowherd boys and girls (*gopas* and *gopis*) and even the animals. Those original, loving pastimes are relished by devotees much more than the opulent and terrifying universal form.

Arjuna, who always knew Krishna in His two-armed form, is certainly perplexed by the universal form: "O Lord of lords, so fierce of form, please tell me who You are. I offer my obeisances unto You. Please be gracious to me. I do not know what Your mission is, and I desire to hear of it." (11.31) Like Arjuna, we should try to understand everything about Lord Krishna, including His identity and His mission. Mental speculation cannot answer these questions; we must ask the Lord Himself, or His representative, the bona fide spiritual master. We have to inquire submissively about His form and His mission in the material world. Krishna has already told Arjuna that in every millennium He comes "to deliver the pious, and to annihilate the miscreants, as well as to reestablish the principles of religion." (4.8) In this universal form, Krishna especially displays his horrific feature whereby all the miscreants are destroyed. "Time I am," He says, "destroyer of the worlds, and I have come to engage all people. With the exception of you [the Pandavas], all the soldiers here on both sides will be slain." (11.32) Arjuna sees all the soldiers, including the valiant generals and many of his kinsmen, rushing into the fiery mouths of Krishna's universal form and being crushed by His teeth. In this way, Krishna comes to destroy the miscreants who refuse to surrender to Him or to abide by His laws. Krishna has already pointed out that this material nature, working under His direction, is correcting the rebellious souls. Until we surrender unto Krishna, we will have to suffer material miseries. As soon as surrender comes, Krishna relieves us from sinful reactions. Even though the Lord's universal form is frightening, His mission remains the same: to reclaim all fallen souls.

"I have come to engage all people," Krishna says, but we should know that everyone is not engaged in the same way. Krishna gave free choice to Dhritarashtra, Duryodhana, Arjuna, and all others on the battlefield. He begged them not to fight. He wanted to settle their disputes peacefully, but they refused to follow His advice. He then gave them a choice. To one side

He would give His army, and to the other side He would give Himself. Because they were materialistic, Dhritarashtra and Duryodhana chose the army, thinking that in any engagement, an army is more valuable than the help of one man. Because the Pandavas were Krishna's devotees, however, they chose the Lord. "I want only You," Arjuna said. Thus everyone gets a chance to be engaged, as either Krishna's friend, or His enemy. The choice is ours. We all have independence. When we hear Krishna's message, we can choose to surrender or not, to render devotional service, or continue in our attempt to enjoy material nature for sense gratification. In any case, we are engaged by Krishna's energies, either material or spiritual. Those engaged by Krishna's material energy are ultimately destroyed by Time and death. Those engaged by His spiritual energy, in transcendental loving service, go to Krishna's eternal abode to associate with Him eternally.

"Therefore get up and prepare to fight," Krishna tells Arjuna. "After conquering your enemies, you will enjoy a flourishing kingdom. They are already put to death by My arrangement, and you, O Savyasacin, can be but an instrument in the fight." (11.33)

From the very beginning, Krishna has been telling Arjuna to get up and fight. Krishna is speaking *Bhagavad-gita* specifically to encourage His friend to surrender to Him and do his duty. Similarly, after hearing from the spiritual master, it is our duty to surrender and prepare to serve the spiritual master in whatever way he desires. We have to engage all our talents in Krishna's service: cooking, cleaning, working, fighting, teaching, writing, or whatever. Everyone has been given some special ability to be used in Krishna's service, according to Krishna's desire, which is also the spiritual master's desire. Between Krishna and His pure devotee, there is perfect oneness of desire. This is not the artificial oneness of the impersonalists, but the real oneness of two united in love by a common interest.

"O Hrsikesa," Arjuna says, "the world becomes joyful upon hearing Your name, and thus everyone becomes attached to You. Although the perfected beings offer You their respectful homage, the demons are afraid, and they flee here and there. All this is rightly done." (11.36) The living entities are given the independence to engage themselves under the superior or inferior energy. Those engaged in Krishna's service, always chanting His names, become joyful; the demons, who rebel against the Lord, become fearful and flee in terror. "Time I am, destroyer of worlds." No one, neither devotee nor demon, can escape Krishna's control. But Krishna gives us the choice between Himself and maya. Arjuna concludes that "all this is rightly done," because he sees that Krishna is equal to everyone. He doesn't force anyone to become a demon or a devotee. Although He fulfills everyone's desire, He also gives instructions on proper and improper desire. He tells us, "Just surrender unto Me, and I will give you all protection." This is His desire, and our desire should agree. We must trust Him. He is our dearmost friend, our eternal Father, the Supersoul within, accompanying us through all bodily changes, fulfilling our desires, and giving us the intelligence to remember Him, or forget Him. We may choose to accept Him or reject Him. Whatever the consequences, "all this is rightly done."

"You are the original Personality, the Godhead," Arjuna continues. "You are the only sanctuary of this manifested cosmic world. You know everything, and You are all that is knowable. You are above the material modes, O limitless form! This whole cosmic manifestation is pervaded by You!" (11.38)

This is a description of the Lord's all-pervasive aspect. Krishna is everything everywhere. He is the root of all existence, and whatever we perceive is an expansion of His energy. If we were in pure, Krishna consciousness, we would see Krishna at all times. Our constitutional position is to be always Krishna conscious. Therefore, throughout *Bhagavad-gita*, Lord Krishna tells us to always think of Him, become His devotee, bow down to Him, and surrender to Him. Somehow or other, this must be done.

To remind us, Krishna comes in every millennium, sends His pure devotee, or manifests as *archa-vigraha*, the temple Deity form, which enables us to serve Him, think of Him, and meditate on Him. In all ways, Lord Krishna bestows His infinite mercy on His devotees by always manifesting Himself in one or another of His varied forms.

After beholding the infinite magnitude of the Universal

Being, Arjuna feels ashamed that, due to friendship, he sometimes forgot Lord Krishna's supreme position: "I have in the past addressed You as 'O Krishna,' 'O Yadava,' 'O my friend,' without knowing Your glories. Please forgive whatever I may have done in madness or in love. I have dishonored You many times while relaxing, or while lying on the same bed, or eating together, sometimes alone and sometimes in front of many friends. Please excuse me for all my offenses. You are the Supreme Lord, to be worshipped by every living being. Thus I fall down to offer You my respects and ask Your mercy. Please tolerate the wrongs that I may have done to You, and bear with me as a father with his son, or a friend with his friend, or a lover with his beloved." (11.41-42, 44)

In the wonderful universal form, Arjuna sees Krishna as the Supreme Personality of Godhead, although Krishna is in fact his eternal friend. Therefore Arjuna fears having committed some offense during their many informal dealings arising out of friendship. Factually, Krishna does not derive the highest pleasure from worship born out of fear, awe, or reverence. Indeed, the highest relationship one can have with Krishna is that of unalloyed love. On that platform, there is no thought of Krishna as the Supreme Personality of Godhead. In Vrindaban, for example, the cowherd boys and girls and all the other Vrindaban residents do not think of Krishna as God. They think of Him as the most wonderful boy in Vrindaban—that's all. They simply love Krishna with pure, unalloyed, unmotivated, nonspeculative, totally surrendered, spontaneous love. That is the perfectional stage of existence.

That perfectional love sometimes manifests in orders given to the Lord by His friends and lovers: "Oh Krishna, You must do this, You must do that." Sometimes, with His beloved *gopis* and wives, He enjoys acting just like a henpecked husband. When Krishna's dearmost consort, Radharani, left the *rasa* dance, it is said that Krishna, unable to enjoy Himself, left the dance to search for Her. This is the nature of transcendental loving reciprocation. The Lord and His pure devotee can never be separated, although there may be some play of separation for love's sake.

In all circumstances, however, Lord Krishna remains the

Supreme Lord of all the universes. After beholding the universal form, Arjuna says: "Seeing this universal form, which I have never seen before, I am gladdened, but at the same time my mind is disturbed with fear. Therefore please bestow Your grace upon me and reveal again Your form as the Personality of Godhead, O Lord of lords, O abode of the universe." (11.45)

The universal form certainly evokes reverence, but rarely transcendental love. Lovers of God, therefore, do not care to see Him as the all-powerful *virata-rupa*, for the vision of that form is tinged with fear. In pure love, there is no fear. Therefore Arjuna requests Krishna to display again His forms as the Personality of Godhead: first, His four-armed form as Narayana, with "helmeted head, and with club, wheel, conch, and lotus flower in Your [four] hands," (11.46), and then His two-armed form of Krishna, his eternal friend.

Arjuna is asking to see these forms so that we can know Lord Krishna as the origin of all forms. We should also understand that these forms are very difficult for ordinary mortals to see. Referring to the universal form, Krishna tells Arjuna that "no one before you has ever seen this unlimited and glaringly effulgent form." (11.47) "Your mind has been perturbed upon seeing this horrible feature of Mine," Krishna adds. "With a peaceful mind, you can now see the form you desire." (11.49) Krishna then displays His four-armed form, and at last returns to His two-armed, original form. Upon seeing Krishna once again in His original form, Arjuna says, "Seeing this humanlike form, so very beautiful, my mind is now pacified, and I am restored to my original nature." (11.51) Lord Krishna replies, "My dear Arjuna, the [two-armed] form which you are now seeing is very difficult to behold. Even the demigods are ever seeking the opportunity to see this form, which is so dear." (11.52)

This original transcendental form of Krishna can never be seen through mental speculation or fruitive activity, but only through surrender in loving devotional service. "The [two-armed] form, which you are seeing with your transcendental eyes, cannot be understood simply by studying the *Vedas*, nor by undergoing serious penances, nor by charity, nor by worship. It is not by these means that one can see Me as I am. My dear Arjuna, only by undivided devotional service can I be understood as I am, standing before you, and can thus be seen directly. Only in this way can you enter into the mysteries of My understanding." (11.53-54)

God can be seen in various aspects, for He is infinite. By mental speculation, we can eventually understand Brahman, God's impersonal feature. Such knowledge allows us to differentiate between matter and spirit. By meditation, we can understand that the Lord dwells as the Supersoul within the heart of every living being (Paramatma realization). But the supreme realization of Krishna as He is cannot be attained by any method other than devotional service. Moreover, Krishna clearly states that this devotional service must be "undivided" (*ananyaya*), not tinged by fruitive activity or mental speculation. Real devotional service, like real love, cannot be divided. Bhismadeva has defined love as "reposing all affections in one person." Actually, such love can be directed only to the Supreme Personality of Godhead, Sri Krishna, for He alone possesses all lovable features. Only Krishna can attract the whole creation because only He has all opulences in full: complete beauty, strength, knowledge, wealth, fame, and renunciation. Whatever lovable features are found in this material world should be seen as perverted reflections of the qualities existing fully in Krishna.

When Lord Krishna was personally present in Vrindaban, He clearly taught that devotional service should be rendered exclusively to Him. When only a small child, He stopped the worship of Indra because there is no need to worship anyone but Himself. Therefore Krishna says, "Only by undivided devotional service can I be understood as I am, standing before you." He does not speak of the Lord in the heart, nor of the impersonal Brahman. He speaks as Arjuna's friend, standing before him in His two-armed form of Krishna. "Thus I can be seen directly." (11.54)

Krishna should never be considered a manifestation of Vishnu, nor of the impersonal Brahman. If we have the proper qualification, we can see Him directly as Krishna, as Arjuna saw Him five thousand years ago. *Bhagavad-gita* cannot be understood by any amount of hard labor, mental speculation, or Sanskrit scholarship. It is a great mystery incomprehensible to all but those who render Lord Krishna undivided, loving devotional service.

Lord Krishna thus concludes this chapter: "My dear Arjuna, one who is engaged in My pure devotional service, free from the contaminations of previous activities and from mental speculation, who is friendly to every living entity, certainly comes to Me." (11.55) It is pure devotional service, without tinges of *karma-yoga*, *jnana-yoga*, or any other yoga, that Krishna demands. This is the same message found in every other chapter: "And of all yogis, he who always abides in Me with great faith, worshipping Me in transcendental loving service, is most intimately united with Me in yoga and is the highest of all." (6.47) "Engage your mind always in thinking of Me, offer obeisances and worship Me. Being completely absorbed in Me, surely you will come to Me." (9.34) "Abandon all varieties of religion and just surrender unto Me." (18.66) The song of God is a song of surrender to Krishna.

Lord Chaitanya Mahaprabhu has appeared in the present age to teach us how to perform this undivided, unalloyed devotional service through the chanting of Hare Krishna, Hare Krishna, Krishna Krishna, Hare Hare, Hare Rama, Hare Rama, Rama Rama, Hare Hare. We should not consider these names to be on the same level as the names of demigods or mundane persons. Krishna's names are nondifferent from Krishna Himself. His names and He Himself are unequalled and unsurpassed. As the Supreme Personality of Godhead, Krishna is the source of everything. When we know this in truth, we surrender only to Krishna, chant His name only, and render unmotivated service to Him alone. By this, we become friends to all living entities.

Krishna's pure devotees want to take everyone back home, back to Godhead. Therefore pure devotees serve Krishna by spreading the glories of His holy names, not only for their own salvation, and that of their families or countrymen, but for all living entities. This is universal compassion, not limited to mundane philanthropy. In this mood, Lord Chaitanya's great devotee, Vasudeva datta Thakur, prayed, "Dear Lord, please save everyone. If You think that they are too sinful, then just let me suffer for their sins. Let me go to hell. But please save everyone." This is Vaishnava compassion, in accordance with the Lord's desire. If we also wish to become pure devotees, we have to be fixed in our determination to render undivided, unalloyed, transcendental loving service to Lord Krishna by propagating this *sankirtan* movement for the welfare of all. Hare Krishna.

The Blessed Lord said: He whose mind is fixed on My personal form, always engaged in worshipping Me with great and transcendental faith, is considered by Me to be most perfect. *(Bg. 12.2)*

CHAPTER TWELVE

Devotional Service

Arjuna inquires, "Which is considered to be more perfect: those who are properly engaged in your devotional service, or those who worship the impersonal Brahman, the unmanifested?" (12.1)

The real subject matter of *Bhagavad-gita*, from beginning to end, is devotional service. Using many different approaches and arguments, Lord Krishna tells Arjuna that surrendering unto Him is life's ultimate goal. In this chapter, however, devotional service is exclusively and directly discussed. In the first seven verses, Lord Krishna establishes the supremacy of personal worship over impersonal; in verses eight through twelve, He discusses how different classes of men can perform devotional service; and in the remaining verses, He glorifies the qualities of His pure devotees.

As pointed out before, Arjuna is an eternal associate and devotee of Lord Krishna, but for the sake of assisting the Lord, he has been put into a bewildered condition. Although Arjuna is always Krishna's devotee, for our sake he wants to firmly establish the correctness of this position. Arjuna's dilemma is really ours, and we should understand that his confusion is created so that *Bhagavad-gita* might be spoken for our benefit. Arjuna has heard much about both Krishna's impersonal feature (Brahman) and His personal form, the object of devotional service. Now he wants a decisive answer from Krishna to determine the best mode of worship.

Lord Krishna replies, "He whose mind is fixed on My personal form, always engaged in worshipping Me with great and transcendental faith, is considered by Me to be most perfect." (12.2) This direct statement, confirming devotional service as the best method for approaching the Supreme, echoes the last verse in the Sixth Chapter: "And of all yogis, he who always abides in Me with great faith, worshipping Me in transcendental loving service, is most intimately united with Me in yoga and is highest of all." (6.47) To attain the highest perfection, the devotee should always worship the person Krishna, with firm, transcendental faith, for the person Krishna is the source and goal of everything.

Lord Krishna continues: "But those who fully worship the unmanifested, that which lies beyond the perception of the senses, the all-pervading, inconceivable, fixed, and immovable—the impersonal conception of the Absolute Truth—by controlling the various senses and being equally disposed to everyone, such persons, engaged in the welfare of all, at last achieve Me." (12.3-4) One who follows the impersonalist path finally comes to the same position, but his progress is neither swift nor easy. This verse brings to mind Krishna's previous statement: "After many births and deaths, he who is actually in knowledge surrenders unto Me, knowing Me to be the cause of all causes and all that is. Such a great soul is very rare." (7.19)

After many births of following the troublesome path of impersonalism, one finally understands that Krishna is everything and surrenders unto Him. Of course, this is the personalist conclusion, but the impersonal method of meditating on the impersonal Brahman is especially difficult in this age of Kali, when the duration of life is short, and men are not very philosophically inclined. Since we have no experience of what lies beyond our senses, the impersonal conception, the unmanifest, is practically impossible to comprehend. In our daily lives, we have no experience of the unmanifested, unembodied condition. "For those whose minds are attached to the unmanifested, impersonal feature of the Supreme, advancement is very troublesome. To make progress in that discipline is always difficult for those who are embodied." (12.5) This is a direct warning: the impersonalist path is fraught with danger.

Even the most stalwart of the impersonalists, Sripad Shankaracharya, toward the end of his life acknowledged the supremacy of the personal feature, Krishna, or Govinda:

> *bhaja govindaṁ bhaja govindaṁ*
> *bhaja govindaṁ mūḍha-mate*

samprāpte sannihite kāle
na hi na hi rakṣati ḍukṛñ-karaṇe

"Worship Govinda, worship Govinda. Your philosophical speculation and grammatical word jugglery will not save you at the moment of death." Actually, Shankaracharya's impersonalist philosophy was meant to trick the atheistic Buddhists into accepting Vedic knowledge and authority. Lord Buddha had decried the *Vedas* because under the pretext of making Vedic sacrifices, people were killing animals just to satisfy their palates. To stop this unnecessary animal killing, Lord Buddha rejected the *Vedas* and adopted the philosophy of *ahimsa*, or nonviolence. Shankaracharya, an incarnation of Lord Shiva, appeared to reestablish the Vedic authority by preaching a kind of disguised Buddhism in the form of impersonalist Vedanta philosophy. Indirectly, Shankaracharya paved the way for Lord Chaitanya's correct presentation of Vedic knowledge, the philosophy of *acintya-bheda-bheda-tattva:* God is simultaneously one with and different from His creation.

Factually, all the great *acharyas* of India—Vyasadeva, Madhvacharya, Shankaracharya, Ramanuja, and Lord Chaitanya—agree that Krishna is the Supreme Personality of Godhead, and that His worship, in love and devotion, is the safe, direct process of self-realization, as this Twelfth Chapter confirms.

Arjuna, who is a great devotee, is certainly relieved to hear this verdict. To avoid deviating from spiritual life altogether, impersonalists should take heed: the impersonalist path is both difficult and dangerous. If we want to go from New York to Los Angeles, why go by way of northern Canada? Why go so far out of our way, through possibly dangerous territory? We may die before ever reaching our destination. It is better to travel the natural, easy route, following in the footsteps of the Lord's pure devotees. Guided by the bona fide spiritual master, we can make easy progress to the Supreme Person. We should not consider ourselves too intelligent to take the easy way. There is no guarantee that we will live past this very hour. In Kali-yuga, the maximum duration of human life is seventy or eighty years. We should heed Lord Krishna's warning, always thinking that death may come today, and forego struggling down a long and difficult path. The process of direct Krishna consciousness is so potent that it can immediately purify us of all material contamination.

Under the direction of a bona fide spiritual master, we can render devotional service at once, and thus attain perfection in yoga. Lord Krishna continues: "For one who worships Me, giving up all his activities unto Me and being devoted to Me without deviation, engaged in devotional service and always meditating upon Me, who has fixed his mind upon Me, O son of Pritha, for him I am the swift deliverer from the ocean of birth and death." (12.6-7) The contrast should be noted: the impersonalist path is difficult and dangerous, whereas there is a friend and savior on the path of devotion. Krishna is there, waiting for us to turn to Him in loving devotional service, our minds fixed on Him alone. For such a devotee, He is "the swift deliverer from the ocean of birth and death." This is His promise. We should immediately take to His devotional service and perform all our actions for His satisfaction. Whatever we do in the realm of business or religion should be directed to Him and performed for His satisfaction. "Just fix your mind on Me, the Supreme Personality of Godhead," Krishna says, "and engage all your intelligence in Me. Thus you will live in Me always, without a doubt." (12.8) What a gift! What a boon!

Our intelligence should not be misused to increase our sense gratification, but used wisely to serve Krishna and see how to become Krishna conscious immediately, and make others Krishna conscious. If human society can be trained to use intelligence in this way, our planet can be transformed from its present hellish condition to Vaikuntha, the Kingdom of God. Krishna has provided everything necessary for our well-being on earth. All that is lacking is Krishna consciousness. *Om purnam adah purnam idam/ purnat purnam udacyate. (Isopanishad)* Lord Krishna is *purnam*, the complete whole, and this world is also *purnam*, complete in itself, but this can be realized only by Krishna consciousness.

But if we fail to take advantage of these facilities so kindly provided by the Lord, or if we misuse them, we cannot expect a perfect and complete result. For instance, Lord Krishna has provided land and cows, rain and sunshine. By His mercy, man can live peacefully in Krishna consciousness and be happy. But if man slaughters the cows, and rapes the earth by exploiting her resources for his temporary sense gratification, he creates hell on earth. Unfortunately, our so-called leaders do not know how to protect the earth and its inhabitants. Formerly, great Krishna conscious kings like Maharaj Yudhisthira and Maharaj Pariksit ruled so expertly that the earth was jolly. There were never natural catastrophes like floods and famines, nor even excessive heat or cold. Under their rule, all living entities were carefully protected and given the maximum opportunity to advance in Krishna consciousness.

Such saintly kings were always prepared to chastise ungodly offenders. Maharaj Pariksit once met a *sudra*, disguised as a king, who was beating a cow. The great Maharaj Pariksit was prepared to kill the *sudra* at once, but the *sudra* pleaded for his life. Since the *sudra* surrendered, the compassionate Maharaj Pariksit agreed to protect him. Because the *sudra* was actually the personality of Kali, who lacks all good qualities, he was not allowed to live wherever he pleased in the kingdom. According to the king's order, he was restricted to four places: wherever there is meat eating, illicit sex, intoxication, and gambling. In this way, Maharaj Pariksit protected his kingdom from invasion by the evil influences of Kali.

Now, however, Kali-yuga has progressed five thousand years, and such godly rulers cannot be found. Today, for the sake of sense gratification, men are abusing the earth, themselves, the animals, the land, the waters, even the sky. All of man's intelligence is being directed to acquiring wealth for sense gratification. This is futile, for our sense gratification is already allotted. According to our karma, our pleasures and pains are predestined, and frustration awaits us by misusing our intelligence to increase pleasure and decrease pain. Just as suffering comes without our striving for it, pleasure also comes of its own accord. Therefore *Srimad-Bhagavatam* advises us not to waste our valuable human life attempting to increase sense gratification but to concentrate our intelligence on realizing the Supreme Personality of Godhead. "Just fix your mind on Me," Krishna says, indicating the proper use of intelligence. This is the advice He gives above all.

But due to our degraded condition, we are not always willing to follow Krishna's sound advice. Therefore Lord Krishna, out of compassion, begins to cite alternatives. "My dear Arjuna," He says, "if you cannot fix your mind upon Me without deviation, then follow the regulated principles of *bhakti-yoga*. In this way you will develop a desire to attain to Me." (12.9) If we cannot immediately come to the perfectional stage of Krishna consciousness by fixing the mind on Krishna at all times, then we can attempt to follow the regulative principles of *bhakti-yoga* under the guidance of a bona fide spiritual master. This is known as the process of *sadhana-bhakti*, regulated devotional service. Under the spiritual master's orders, the devotee rises early in the morning, takes a cold bath, attends *mangal-aratik*, chants sixteen rounds of the Hare Krishna *maha-mantra*, maintains purity within and without by observing the four basic rules (prohibiting meat eating, illicit sex, intoxication, and gambling), eats only Krishna *prasadam*, and marks his body with *tilak* to signify that it is the temple of Lord Krishna. A serious disciple follows these injunctions meticulously. The *tilak* markings, the *kanthi* beads, the dress, the shaved head, and the *sika* are all marks of a Vaishnava that help the disciple remember Krishna and also remind others of Krishna. Just as a policeman wears his uniform to remind people that he is a law enforcer, the devotee also dresses to remind all people of their constitutional position as servants of God.

It is most essential to follow the orders of the spiritual master because he knows the science of Krishna, having heard the truth in disciplic succession. He does not concoct the *sadhana* process himself. The bona fide spiritual master follows in the *parampara* beginning with Arjuna on the battlefield. He imparts the same knowledge given to Arjuna, without any personal interpretation. The potency of his teachings depends on his transmitting the spiritual vibration without change. This transmission does not depend on mundane knowledge. The spiritual master does not even have to know the disciple's language. The disciple need only hear the transcendental vibration of Hare Krishna and follow the rules and regulations. Then the process will fructify.

Lord Krishna continues: "If you cannot practice the regulations of *bhakti-yoga*, then just try to work for Me, because by working for Me, you will come to the perfect stage. If, however, you are unable to work in this consciousness, then try to give up all results of your work, and try to be self-situated." (12.10-11) If the disciple can't follow all the rules imparted by the spiritual master, he should at least try to give up the results of his work for the sake of Krishna consciousness. In this way, he can become detached from fruitive activity. If one advances only one percent in Krishna consciousness, that is a permanent asset. In his next life, he can begin at two percent and make further progress. Of course, it is advisable to complete the process in this lifetime, and this is possible if we accept the special mercy of Lord Chaitanya Mahaprabhu, who is so munificent that He can deliver the most fallen persons to the highest position, pure love of God, by the mercy of the holy name.

Lord Krishna continues: "If you cannot take to this practice, then engage yourself in the cultivation of knowledge. Better than knowledge, however, is meditation, and better than meditation is renunciation of the fruits of action, for by such renunciation one can 'attain peace of mind." (12.12)

Renunciation must be there, regardless of the process. Krishna consciousness means renunciation. If we cannot take to advanced renunciation, we should at least cultivate knowledge, beginning with the understanding that we are not the temporary material body but the spirit soul within. The first step in the cultivation of knowledge is to realize *aham brahmasmi*, "I am Brahman, not matter." The eternal individual soul is part and parcel of Parambrahman, the Supreme Soul. This is the beginning of knowledge.

By cultivating knowledge, we can eventually attain the platform of meditation on the Lord in the heart. Then we can gradually learn that God is great and is the source of everything. Understanding this, we can begin to take to renunciation, recognizing that "nothing is mine; everything is God's." By such renunciation, we can attain peace of mind. In this way, Krishna consciousness is a step by step process.

In the remaining verses of this chapter, Lord Krishna describes and glorifies the qualities of His pure devotees.

"One who is not envious but who is a kind friend to all living entities, who does not think himself a proprietor, who is free from false ego and equal in both happiness and distress, who is always satisfied and engaged in devotional service with determination, and whose mind and intelligence are in agreement with Me—he is very dear to Me." (12.13-14)

The pure devotee is always even-minded, equipoised in any condition, because he sees and agrees with Krishna in all respects. This kind of oneness with Krishna is a very wonderful stage, not to be confused with the oneness of the impersonalists who want to lose their identity by merging into the impersonal Brahman. Such oneness is hellish to a devotee because it excludes a loving relationship with the Lord. Therefore the impersonalist's oneness is called spiritual suicide. The oneness of the pure devotee is that of transcendental love, wherein the devotee, seeing the spiritual nature of everything, surrenders to Krishna and acts on His behalf. In both happiness and distress, he sees Krishna. He is equipoised and happy. "Happy is the man who likes what he gets," it is said. If something pleasant or favorable comes his way, he thinks, "Oh, Krishna is so kind to have sent me this." And if distress comes, he thinks, "Oh, Krishna is so kind that He is reminding me that I cannot enjoy material nature because my real happiness is on the spiritual platform in relationship with Him." The pure devotee never blames Krishna for anything. When suffering comes, he welcomes it, thinking, "I have committed so many sins in the past that now Krishna is giving me just a little taste of my sinful reactions so that I will never forget Him and commit such sins again. Actually, I deserve much worse." Since the devotee thinks in this way, there is perfect agreement and harmony between him and Krishna.

Lord Krishna continues: "He for whom no one is put into difficulty, and who is not disturbed by anxiety, who is steady in happiness and distress, is very dear to Me." (12.15) The pure devotee never causes anyone anxiety or distress. Rather, he is always ready to relieve the anxiety of others. In this material world, everyone is full of anxiety; therefore this world is called *kuntha*, the place of anxiety. The spiritual world is called *Vaikuntha*, the place without anxiety, because everyone there is in full Krishna consciousness. Only when we surrender to Krishna can we be freed from anxiety and enjoy complete peace of mind. Being totally surrendered, the pure devotees are always in Vaikuntha, even though serving Krishna in this material world.

They try to relieve everyone else of anxiety by preaching the gospel of surrender to Krishna, and in this way try to bring everyone into the blissful atmosphere of Krishna consciousness.

There are many examples of the great compassion of pure devotees. Prahlad Maharaj, who survived many attempts by his demonic father to kill him, said, "I am not concerned about my own future. Whether I go to heaven or hell, I can always think of Krishna, but I am concerned for those poor fools and rascals who have created this anxiety-filled, humbug civilization." (*Bhag.* 7.9.43)

As in Prahlad's day, we are confronted by a civilization manufactured and controlled by atheistic materialists. Prahlad's materialistic father, Hiranyakasipu, was certainly advanced materially, but being a great demon, he created a hellish atmosphere. Today, the world is controlled by demons totally devoid of Krishna consciousness, and, as demons will, they are trying to make everyone happy by promoting sense gratification. Of course, this is not possible; instead, everyone becomes more and more enslaved, frustrated, and unhappy. As the material miseries increase due to sinful activity, anxiety also increases. In such an atmosphere, there can be neither peace nor happiness. Until the Lord's devotees spread Krishna consciousness throughout the world, there will be no peace.

"A devotee, who is not dependent on the ordinary course of activities, who is pure, expert, without cares, free from all pains, and who does not strive for some result, is very dear to Me." (12.16) Relying completely on the Lord, a devotee does not depend on the ordinary course of activities. Ordinarily, a person depends on his own hard work, and the world is revolving on the basis of the hard struggle for existence. If a man doesn't work hard at his job, he cannot enjoy sense gratification. Everyone is working and struggling very hard to squeeze some enjoyment from material nature. The devotee, on the other hand, accepts whatever Krishna sends as his allotment, and sees it as Krishna's mercy. He does not depend on anyone or anything. He has taken Lord Krishna at His word: "Those who worship Me with devotion, meditating on My transcendental form—to them I carry what they lack and preserve what they have." (9.22) Lord Krishna always protects His devotee. "Declare it boldly,

My devotee never perishes." (9.31) In full Krishna consciousness, a devotee never hankers or laments under any circumstances. He does not strive for any material result; he is always happy in his service to Krishna, and therefore he is very dear to Krishna.

Lord Krishna continues: "One who grasps neither pleasure or grief, who neither laments nor desires, and who renounces both auspicious and inauspicious things, is very dear to Me." (12.17)

Krishna's pure devotee is always free from the dualities of material existence. In the material world, everyone is subject to the dualities of heat and cold, happiness and distress, success and failure. But because the devotee does not function on the bodily platform, he is free from all this. Dualities exist for those who identify with the material body and senses, but a pure devotee knows that he is different from the body. Knowing that he is the eternal part and parcel of Krishna, the devotee is content to serve Krishna in any circumstance. He makes no demands for his own happiness. He is happy with his service, and Lord Krishna is pleased with him.

"One who is equal to friends and enemies, who is equipoised in honor and dishonor, heat and cold, happiness and distress, fame and infamy, who is always free from contamination, always silent and satisfied with anything, who doesn't care for any residence, who is fixed in knowledge and engaged in devotional service, is very dear to Me." (12.18-19) Once we are fixed in knowledge and engaged in devotional service, we are free from all the dualities of material nature. Of course, to attain this platform, we must be firmly convinced that Krishna is the Supreme Lord of all. The devotee is fixed in his realization that he can never become the Supreme, that his eternal identity is servant of the Supreme. Knowing this, he engages in devotional service without any expectation for reward. According to *Srimad-Bhagavatam* (1.2.6), devotional service must be unmotivated and uninterrupted to completely satisfy both the individual self and the Supreme Self. When one is steady and unmotivated, he is very dear to Krishna.

Lord Krishna concludes: "He who follows this imperishable path of devotional service and who completely engages himself with faith, making Me the supreme goal, is very, very dear to Me." (12.20)

The path of devotional service is imperishable. Mayavadis, or impersonalists, think that *bhakti-yoga* can be useful to arrive at a certain point, but must then be abandoned for higher realization. They say that once we realize our identity with Krishna, we will kill Krishna and merge into God. Then we don't have to serve any longer; we can become the supreme enjoyer. Because this mentality is basically envious, the impersonalists receive the same reward as the demons. When Krishna kills demons, He allows them to merge into His impersonal nature. The impersonalists meet with the same fate: they merge in the *brahmajyoti* effulgence of Lord Krishna's body.

The devotee, on the other hand, realizes that happiness lies in rendering uninterrupted and unmotivated devotional service to the Lord. Just as a fish cannot be happy out of water, we cannot be happy without transcendental loving service. We are not material objects; we are eternal spirit soul, but being infinitesimal particles of the Supreme Spirit, we are eternally subordinate to Him. Krishna clearly says that His devotees make Him the supreme goal. They do not consider themselves the supreme goal. In recognizing Krishna as their sole object and goal, as the complete whole, the devotees enjoy perfect transcendental happiness, *sat-cit-ananda*, eternal being, knowledge, and bliss in connection with Him. All this comes with complete surrender to Krishna.

This is, of course, Krishna's purpose in speaking *Bhagavad-gita*: to get Arjuna to surrender to His will and fight. Similarly, for our own benefit, He wants us to give up our false ego, false hopes, and false plans, and just surrender to His supreme will. This is easily understandable when we chant Krishna's names, which are nondifferent from the Lord Himself. The sublime chanting of Hare Krishna can immediately place us in this divine consciousness and establish us in full surrender at the Lord's lotus feet. Hare Krishna.

Yet in this body there is another, a transcendental enjoyer who is the Lord, the supreme proprietor, who exists as the overseer and permitter, and who is known as the Supersoul. *(Bg. 13.23)*

CHAPTER THIRTEEN

Nature, the Enjoyer, and Consciousness

In the first six chapters of *Bhagavad-gita*, Lord Krishna explained the nature of the living entity, his constitutional position, action in renunciation, methods of advancement in *bhakti-yoga*, and the way to become a perfect yogi by worshipping Him with transcendental faith. In the second six chapters, the Lord described His own position as the Supreme Personality of Godhead, the means for entrance into devotional service, and the ultimate goal of pure devotion. Now, in this chapter, the Lord explains the fall of the living entity into material consciousness, the position of nature and the living entity, and the Supersoul.

"O my dear Krishna," Arjuna says, "I wish to know about *prakriti* [nature], Purusha [the enjoyer], and the field and the knower of the field, and of knowledge and the end of knowledge." (13.1) Lord Krishna replies, "This body, O son of Kunti, is called the field, and one who knows this body is called the knower of the field." (13.2)

In material consciousness, it is not possible to understand the difference between the field (the body) and the knower of the field (the soul). Transcendental knowledge begins with the awareness that the body and soul are different. This is not very difficult to understand. If we have an accident and lose an arm, our consciousness is not diminished. The severed arm is thrown away, but the soul and its symptom, consciousness, remain as complete as ever, although a part of the body is lost. We may even say, "Well, I lost an arm, but I'm still here, thank God." Similarly, we may lose both arms, both legs, the head, and the rest of the body without the soul's being touched or diminished. In the course of a lifetime, the body undergoes transformations from childhood, to youth, to adulthood, to old age, and the unchanged knower within the body can recall all these changes. In transcendental knowledge, one can distinguish between the body and its knower.

Lord Krishna continues: "O scion of Bharata, you should understand that I am also the knower in all bodies, and to understand this body and its owner is called knowledge. That is My opinion." (13.3) Besides knowing the difference between the body and the knower of the body, we must understand that there is a supreme knower who knows all bodies. The body, consisting of senses, is our instrument for acquiring knowledge, but these senses do not belong to us. They are the property of Hrishikesha, Krishna, the proprietor of all senses. As part and parcel of the Supreme, the senses of any particular body are meant to render service to the Supreme. One who knows this engages in Krishna's transcendental loving service.

Lord Krishna says: "Now please hear My brief description of this field of activity and how it is constituted, what its changes are, whence it is produced, who that knower of the field of activities is, and what his influences are. This knowledge of the field of activities and its knower is described by various sages in Vedic writings—especially the *Vedanta-sutra*—and is presented with all reasoning as to cause and effect." (13.4-5) Later, Lord Krishna says, "I am the compiler of Vedanta, and I am the knower of the *Veda*." (15.15) From Lord Krishna, we should understand the proper way to present knowledge of the Absolute. Perfect knowledge is never presented as one's own creation or speculation. Of course, being the Supreme Personality of Godhead, Lord Krishna can present what He wants, but when He comes to this world, He Himself accepts a spiritual master and cites Vedic authorities when speaking *Bhagavad-gita*. Being the greatest authority, His conclusion is final. Still, He refers to the authority of the Vedic writings. From this, we should learn to avoid theorizing on the basis of our limited brainpower and imperfect senses. Everything should be accepted according to the bona fide system of *parampara*, an unbroken disciplic succession from the Supreme Lord Himself.

This is the only way to know Absolute Truth. Not even Brahma, the creator of this universe, can manufacture Vedic knowledge. According to *Srimad-Bhagavatam:* "Real religious principles are enacted by the Supreme Personality of Godhead. Although fully situated in the mode of goodness, even the great *rishis* who occupy the topmost planets cannot ascertain the real religious principles, nor can the demigods, nor the leaders of Siddhaloka, to say nothing of the *asuras,* ordinary human beings, Vidyadharas, and Caranas." (6.3.19) Brahma also has to hear from Krishna. Therefore, *Srimad-Bhagavatam* says, *Tene brahma hrda:* (1.1.1) Brahma heard the truth from within his heart. Brahma imparted that knowledge to Narada, Narada gave it to Vyasadeva, and Vyasadeva has presented it in written form for the benefit of all mankind. This is the only process for transmitting spiritual knowledge.

Lord Krishna next explains the field of the body according to the system of Sankhya philosophy, which presents material nature analytically. "The five great elements, false ego, intelligence, the unmanifested, the ten senses, the mind, the five sense objects, desire, hatred, happiness, distress, the aggregate, the life symptoms, and convictions—all these are considered, in summary, to be the field of activities and its interactions." (13.6-7) The ultimate purpose of *Sankhya-yoga* is to understand the distinctions between the body, the knower of the body, and the supreme knower of all bodies. Thus establishing the components of the field of the body, Lord Krishna enumerates the various components of knowledge.

"Humility, pridelessness, nonviolence, tolerance, simplicity, approaching a bona fide spiritual master, cleanliness, steadiness and self-control; renunciation of the objects of sense gratification, absence of false ego, the perception of the evil of birth, death, old age, and disease; nonattachment to children, wife, home, and the rest, and evenmindedness amid pleasant and unpleasant events; constant and unalloyed devotion to Me, resorting to solitary places, detachment from the general mass of people; accepting the importance of self-realization, and philosophical search for the Absolute Truth— all these I thus declare to be knowledge, and what is contrary to these is ignorance." (13.8-12)

Interestingly, Lord Krishna enunciates the components of knowledge, not ignorance. Whatever is contrary to these, He says, is ignorance. Ignorance is negative; Krishna is positive. There is no nescience in Him. Whatever lacks Krishna consciousness, or is separate from Krishna, is ignorance. The material world, a covered portion of the Lord's creation, is a place of ignorance. One section of the spiritual sky is covered by a cloud, and beneath that cloud the Supreme Personality of Godhead is not visible. This is the place of darkness and ignorance, where Krishna consciousness is lacking. Srila Prabhupada used to quote his spiritual master, Srila Bhaktisiddhanta Saraswati: "I see nothing lacking in the whole world except Krishna consciousness." Krishna consciousness will solve all problems, including the problems of eating, sleeping, mating, and defending. In the highest sense, there is no difference between the material and spiritual worlds for one in pure Krishna consciousness. For him, everything is filled with the perfect light of Krishna consciousness. Therefore the most important component of knowledge mentioned here is constant and unalloyed devotion to Krishna. To achieve this, one must follow the second most important item: approaching a bona fide spiritual master, under whose guidance all good qualities—humility, pridelessness, nonviolence, tolerance, etc.—will automatically develop.

Lord Krishna continues: "I shall now explain the knowable, knowing which you will taste the eternal. This is beginningless, and it is subordinate to Me. It is called Brahman, the spirit, and it lies beyond the cause and effect of this material world." (13.13) The knowable is the individual soul and the Supersoul. Within every individual body reside the individual soul (jiva-atma) and Krishna's expansion, the Supersoul (Paramatma). The soul, or spirit, is called Brahman, and here Lord Krishna says that this Brahman is subordinate to Him. The term Brahman is often used to denote the impersonal aspect of the Supreme, the effulgence of Lord Krishna's body, but here the term Brahman is used more generally to describe the spiritual nature of the soul and everything else. For instance, in the Vedanta-sutra, it is stated: athato brahma-jijnasa. "Now, in this human form of life, one should enquire about Brahman." Brahman is the underlying spiritual essence of everything. And Krishna is the basis of that Brahman.

In reality, Brahman is not impersonal or void. It is, however, realized in three aspects: prakriti (nature), the jiva-soul, and

Parambrahman, the controller of everything. In the material world, Krishna is present as *prakriti*, the field of all activity. The *jiva*, the individual soul, is also part and parcel of Krishna, and is subordinate to Him. Parambrahman, the supreme Brahman, is also Lord Krishna, but Lord Krishna in His personal form is superior to that Parambrahman. As the Lord of Vaikuntha, Lord Krishna is the ultimate controller. He is also the origin of all Vaikuntha forms, and all other Vishnu expansions, including the Mahavishnu. This Mahavishnu, also called Karanodakasayi Vishnu, is the first *purusha* incarnation, and from the pores of His skin all the universes are generated. In each universe He expands again as Garbhodakasayi Vishnu and lies down on the waters of His own perspiration. From the navel of Garbhodakasayi Vishnu, Lord Brahma is born, and he in turn acts as the engineer of material creation. From Garbhodakasayi Vishnu there is yet another expansion, Ksirodakasayi Vishnu, the collective Supersoul of every living being. He is also called Hari, and all the incarnations within the material world expand from Him. Factually, all incarnations are expansions of Krishna. Krishna is not an incarnation of Vishnu, as some people maintain. As confirmed in *Srimad-Bhagavatam: krsnas tu bhagavan svayam.* "All the above mentioned incarnations are either plenary portions or portions of the plenary portions of the Lord, but Lord Sri Krishna is the original Personality of Godhead. All of them appear on planets whenever there is a disturbance created by the atheists. The Lord incarnates to protect the theists." (1.3.28) Thus everything is subordinate to Krishna. This is the ultimate goal of knowledge: to know Krishna as the Supreme Lord of all that be.

Lord Krishna continues: "Everywhere are His hands and legs, His eyes and faces, and He hears everything. In this way, the Supersoul exists." (13.14) We are limited in our perception. No one can claim that his hands and legs are everywhere, or that he sees and hears everything. Although our functions are limited, the Supersoul dwelling within everyone is unlimited. "The Supersoul is the original source of all senses," Krishna continues, "yet He is without senses. He is unattached, although He is the maintainer of all living beings. He transcends the modes of nature, and at the same time He is the master of all modes

of material nature." (13.15) Krishna has already pointed out that
the material nature is working under His direction (*mayadhyaksena
prakrtih*) (9.10). As the Supersoul present within and between
every atom, He is the original source of everything in the material
world. No one can see anything unless the Supersoul sees it
first; therefore He says that He is the source of the senses, although He is without senses. "Without senses" does not imply
that He cannot see, hear, taste, etc. "Without senses" means
that His senses are not covered, contaminated, or limited. In the
material world, everything is covered by the *maha-tattva*, the
material elements. Our senses are limited, covered by matter in
the form of the material body. No man can claim to have unlimited perception. The Supersoul, however, is never covered
by material nature. He is material nature's transcendental master.
Therefore He has no material, limited senses as we have; rather,
with His inconceivable, transcendental senses, He sees everything, hears everything, knows everything.

"The Supreme Truth exists both internally and externally,
in the moving and nonmoving. He is beyond the power of the
material senses to see or to know. Although far, far away, He
is also near to all." (13.16) In *Srimad-Bhagavatam* (1.1.1), it is also
stated that the Supreme Personality of Godhead knows everything directly and indirectly. He is present within and without,
internally and externally, within and between every atom, in
the heart of every living being, infinitely beyond the reach and
knowledge of the material senses.

Although Krishna cannot be known by the blunt material
senses, He can be known by surrender. "Only by pure devotional
service can I be known as I am." (11.54) Krishna is always veiled
by His creative potency of *yoga-maya*, but surrender removes
that veil. He does not have to reveal Himself to everyone, but
He reveals Himself to His friends and devotees. In this way only
can He be known as He is.

"Although the Supersoul appears to be divided, He is never
divided. He is situated as one. Although He is the maintainer
of every living entity, it is to be understood that He devours
and develops all." (13.17) To clarify this verse, Srila Prabhupada
used the example of the sun. The sun is one, but at noon a man
in New York will think that the sun is shining over his head,

and people in Washington, Atlanta, Detroit and other cities will also think that the sun is shining over their heads. Although the sun is situated as one, it is perceived from different angles of vision. Similarly, the Supersoul is perceived in everyone's heart, but the Supersoul is not divided. He is one. He maintains all living entities, and He is not dependent on anyone for His own maintenance. When there is creation, everything develops under His direction, and when there is annihilation, everything is wound up under His direction.

"He is the source of light in all luminous objects. He is beyond the darkness of matter and is unmanifested. He is knowledge, He is the object of knowledge, and He is the goal of knowledge. He is situated in everyone's heart. Thus the field of activities [the body], knowledge, and the knowable have been summarily described by Me. Only My devotees can understand this thoroughly and thus attain to My nature." (13.18-19)

This knowledge cannot be acquired through any amount of study. One cannot hope to understand *Bhagavad-gita* simply by becoming a famous scholar. Srila Prabhupada used to point out that although one very famous scholar wrote about and studied *Bhagavad-gita* throughout his life, he did not understand Lord Krishna at all. When Lord Krishna said, "Always think of Me, bow down to Me, worship Me, become My devotee," the big scholar commented, "It is not to the person Krishna that we have to surrender, but to the unmanifested, unborn within Krishna." Thus this highly decorated scholar, baffled by the material energy, could not understand Krishna as He is.

Lord Krishna is Absolute. There is no difference between His inside and outside. He exists both internally and externally. Although He is all-pervading, He never loses His identity. He is the source of all light. *Brahma-samhita* states that the *brahmajyoti*, the glaring effulgence of the spiritual sky, is the light emanating from the transcendental body of the Supreme Personality of Godhead. As described in the Tenth Chapter of *Bhagavad-gita,* Krishna is the source of all energies perceived in both the phenomenal and noumenal worlds. Whatever we perceive is but a fragment of His divine energy. Only His devotees can factually understand that He is the source of everything, for only by surrendering to Him and pleasing Him can we receive the mercy of transcendental knowledge. Being the reservoir of all knowledge, Krishna can both impart and withold knowledge. As the cause of all causes, He is the controller of everything.

"Material nature and the living entities should be under-stood to be beginningless. Their transformations and the modes of matter are products of material nature." (13.20) Throughout *Bhagavad-gita*, there are five basic subjects: the Lord, the living entity, time, material nature, and karma. Of these, only karma is not eternal. The others are all beginningless and endless. Of course, any particular material manifestation is temporary, but the process of material nature is eternal. Before this creation, the living entities and material nature existed. During this manifesta-tion, changes take place: we are born, we grow, we remain for some time, produce some by-products, dwindle, and vanish. Everything in this material world undergoes these transforma-tions, but the soul and the Supersoul do not.

Since Krishna has given us minute independence for eter-nity, the material nature, *prakriti*, which coexists with the misuse of our fragmental independence, is also eternal. Material nature gives us a chance to correct ourselves in order to go back home, back to Godhead. Similarly, although it may appear 'fleeting, time is also eternal. But when time is seen as the supreme power over all that exists, we can understand how its control is another feature of the supreme controller, the supreme eternal Lord.

Karma alone is not eternal. If the results of our past activities were eternal, there would be no escaping them. Indeed, it is on this point that Krishna conscious philosophy differs radically from that of contemporary Christians, who maintain that a man may be sentenced to hell eternally due to his sinful activities. God is not so cruel. Even a human father, whose compassion is certainly limited, would not be so unkind. How can God, whose love and compassion are unlimited, condemn a man to suffer unlimitedly for the sins of one limited lifetime? No. The effects of karma may last a long time, but they are not eternal.

Lord Krishna continues: "Nature is said to be the cause of all material activities and effects, whereas the living entity is the cause of the various sufferings and enjoyments in this world." (13.21) Pleasure and pain arise from sense perception. One man's pleasure is another's pain; one man's nectar is another's poison.

According to his desire for sense gratification, the living entity creates his own pleasure and pain. Material nature, under the Lord's direction, simply provides the facilities by which the living entity can fulfill his desires. When he attains transcendental knowledge, however, and, understanding himself to be distinct from the material body, abandons his desire for sense gratification, he rises above these dualities of material life. In knowledge, he gives up both suffering and enjoyment and comes to the spiritual platform of *sat-cit-ananda*—eternity, knowledge, and bliss.

"The living entity in material nature thus follows the ways of life, enjoying the three modes of nature. This is due to his association with that material nature. Thus he meets with good and evil amongst various species." (13.22) This process is more elaborately described in the Fifteenth Chapter, where Krishna explains that "the living entity in the material world carries his different conceptions of life from one body to another as the air carries aromas.... Thus taking another gross body, he obtains a certain type of ear, eye, tongue, nose, and sense of touch, which are grouped about the mind....[He thus] enjoys a particular set of sense objects." (15.8-9) Material nature supplies a specific body according to one's desires. Due to his identification with that body, the living entity enjoys or suffers in contact with it. This is all caused by desire. As soon as all desires are turned to the Supreme Personality of Godhead, the living entity becomes transcendental to good and evil, pleasure and pain, and all the other dualities of material life. "Yet in this body there is another, a transcendental enjoyer, who is the Lord, the supreme proprietor, who exists as the overseer and permitter, and who is known as the Supersoul." (13.23) Although the Lord is always transcendental to the pleasures and pains of the living entity, He accompanies the living being through all these bodily changes just to give him direction and sanction. Therefore He is called the overseer and permitter. The *Mundaka Upanishad* speaks of two birds sitting on the same tree (the material body). One bird, the living entity, is enjoying the tree's fruits (the sense objects), while the other bird, the Supersoul, is simply watching. The Supreme Lord has no need to enjoy this material nature. Being *atma-rama*, complete in Himself, He does not come here for sense gratification. The individual soul, however, due to his foolish desire to enjoy separately from the Lord, comes into this material world to exploit the senses. As long as he tries to enjoy the fruits of the body, he stays in the material world to enjoy and suffer. Although the Lord permits this, He Himself is never entangled; He simply sanctions and witnesses the living entity's licit and illicit activities, remaining always in the transcendental position, forever aloof.

"One who understands this philosophy concerning material nature, the living entity, and the interaction of the modes of nature, is sure to attain liberation. He will not take birth again, regardless of his present position." (13.24) Repetition of birth and death occur because the living entity wants to enjoy the material senses. When he gives up this desire and surrenders unto the Lord, agreeing to work for the Lord's enjoyment, there is no more rebirth.

Lord Krishna continues: "That Supersoul is perceived by some through meditation, by some through the cultivation of knowledge, and by others through working without fruitive desire. Again, there are those who, although not conversant in spiritual knowledge, begin to worship the Supreme Person upon hearing about Him from others. Because of their tendency to hear from authorities, they also transcend the path of birth and death." (13.25-26)

Lord Chaitanya Mahaprabhu has especially recommended this process of hearing from authorities. In this age of Kali, meditation and mental speculation are never recommended. For Kali-yuga, the recommended method is chanting the holy names and hearing from bona fide authorities. The transcendental sound of the Hare Krishna *maha-mantra* should be received from the bona fide spiritual master, Lord Krishna's pure devotee. Then it will quickly act, and one can transcend repeated birth and death.

"O chief of the Bharatas, whatever you see in existence, both moving and unmoving, is only the combination of the field of activities and the knower of the field." (13.27) All creations in this material world result from the combination of the living force with material nature. Everything, both moving and non-moving, is a combination of spirit and matter.

"One who sees the Supersoul accompanying the individual soul in all bodies and who understands that neither the soul nor the Supersoul is ever destroyed, actually sees." (13.28) From the very beginning of *Bhagavad-gita*, Lord Krishna has taught that for the soul, there is neither birth nor death. This is true for both the soul and Supersoul. "Never was there a time when I did not exist, nor you, nor all these kings; nor in the future shall any of us cease to be." (2.12) The separate identities of both the soul and Supersoul are eternal. The individual soul does not merge into the Supersoul and cease to exist. Krishna teaches eternal coexistence.

"One who sees the Supersoul in every living being, equal everywhere, does not degrade himself by his mind. Thus he approaches the transcendental destination." (13.29) In the Sixth Chapter, Lord Krishna said, "For one who has conquered the mind, the Supersoul is already reached, for he has attained tranquility. To such a man, happiness and distress, heat and cold, honor and dishonor are all the same." (6.7) When one sees the Supersoul everywhere, he does not allow himself to be degraded by the uncontrolled mind, which is always searching for sense gratification. In an agitated condition, one cannot perceive the Supersoul, nor can he enjoy equal vision. A degraded man identifies himself with matter and is forced by material nature to accept one body after another in the evolutionary cycle of 8,400,000 species. This is certainly an embarrassment and falldown for the soul, whose actual nature is *sat-cit-ananda*, eternal, and full of knowledge and bliss. By contrast, the material body is temporary, and full of nescience and suffering. It is a degradation for the soul to become involved in such a temporary and miserable condition.

There is no limit to this degradation. According to the *Puranas*, Indra, the king of heaven, once displeased his spiritual master and was cursed to become a hog. As a hog, Indra had a wife and many piglets. He and his hog family lived very happily together, wallowing in slime and eating stool. Back at the heavenly kingdom, however, there were some disturbances due to Indra's absence, and Lord Brahma himself came to fetch Indra. But when Brahma approached Indra, who was enjoying himself as a hog, and requested him to return to heaven, Indra replied,

"I cannot go. Who will take care of my wife and children? Besides, I'm enjoying myself." How cruel maya is! Even though the King of heaven was condemned to inhabit the body of a hog and eat stool in a filthy place, he still thought he was enjoying life. He was even thinking that the farmer who brought him slop to eat was his good friend, not realizing that the farmer was fattening him for the kill. Indeed, despite all of Brahma's pleas, Indra would not go with him until Brahma himself killed Indra's pig family and forced Indra to recognize his degraded condition. We shouldn't laugh at Indra, for we are all in that position in the material world. Material life is a most degraded condition for the soul, forcing us to wallow in filth, and suffer the miseries of birth, old age, disease, and death.

To avoid this, the living entity must first control his mind by engaging all the senses in Krishna's service. Krishna, the master of the senses, asked Arjuna to engage all his senses in fighting for Him. As soon as Arjuna agreed to fight, he became a perfect yogi. His mind was fixed in transcendental consciousness, and he was gifted with transcendental vision.

"One who can see that all activities are performed by the body, which is created of material nature, and sees that the self does nothing, actually sees." (13.30) Krishna is the only doer, and He alone is fulfilling the desires of every living being. Man proposes, and God disposes. We cannot do anything without the sanction of Krishna. If the sun doesn't rise in the morning, what can we do? In all situations, we are dependent on Krishna's potencies to fulfill our desires.

"When a sensible man ceases to see different identities, which are due to different material bodies, he attains to the Brahman conception. Thus he sees that beings are expanded everywhere. Those with the vision of eternity can see that the soul is transcendental, eternal, and beyond the modes of nature. Despite contact with the material body, O Arjuna, the soul neither does anything nor is entangled." (13.31-32)

Srila Rupa Goswami has pointed out that when we engage in devotional service, we are liberated, even though still within the material body. As soon as our senses are completely engaged in Krishna's service, we are on the transcendental platform and no longer subject to the material conditions.

Lord Krishna continues: "The sky, due to its subtle nature, does not mix with anything, although it is all-pervading. Similarly, the soul, situated in Brahman vision, does not mix with the body, though situated in that body." (13.33) A driver certainly does not identify with his automobile, although he uses it to get to his destination. The devotee may be using the material body, but he does not identify with it. He sees it as an instrument for rendering devotional service to Krishna, and the greatest service is to instruct others in the science of Krishna. Therefore pure devotees are always chanting the glories of the Lord and explaining them to others. They have no other business.

"O son of Bharata, as the sun alone illuminates all this universe, so does the living entity, one within the body, illuminate the entire body by consciousness." (13.34) Consciousness is the symptom of the spirit soul's presence. Due to the presence of the soul within the heart, consciousness is spread all over the material body. As soon as the soul leaves, consciousness ceases. The body is then dead.

"One who knowingly sees the difference between the body and the owner of the body and can understand the process of liberation from this bondage, also attains to the supreme goal." (13.35) Liberation awaits one who understands that he is different from the material body. Material bondage has no other cause than misidentification with the body for the purpose of sense gratification. Once we understand that we are spirit soul, we will naturally give up the desire for sense gratification and proceed straight on the path of liberation. Hare Krishna.

When you see that there is nothing beyond these modes of nature (goodness, passion and ignorance) in all activities and that the Supreme Lord is transcendental to all these modes, then you can know My spiritual nature. *(Bg. 14.19)*

CHAPTER FOURTEEN

The Three Modes of Material Nature

Lord Krishna says, "Again I shall declare to you this supreme wisdom, the best of all knowledge, knowing which all the sages have attained to supreme perfection." (14.1) In this chapter, Lord Krishna discusses the three modes of material nature in more detail. Earlier, He said, "This divine energy of Mine, consisting of the three modes of material nature, is difficult to overcome, but those who have surrendered unto Me can easily cross beyond it." (7.14) No one can attain the supreme perfection of transcendental knowledge, Krishna consciousness, without overcoming the three modes—goodness, passion, and ignorance. As long as the living entity is conditioned by these modes, he is doomed to birth and death repeatedly.

"By becoming fixed in this knowledge," Krishna says, "one can attain to the transcendental nature, which is like My own nature. Thus established, one is not born at the time of creation nor disturbed at the time of dissolution." (14.2) A devotee who becomes fully Krishna conscious attains a nature like Krishna's in quality, not quantity. That nature is called Brahman, or spirit. Like Krishna, we are Brahman, but we are not the Supreme Brahman. *Achintya-bheda-abheda-tattva.* Lord Chaitanya taught that the living entity is simultaneously, inconceivably one with and different from the Supreme Lord. He is one in quality, but different in quantity. He is one in the spiritual quality of Brahman, and he is different in magnitude: he is an infinitesimal part, and Krishna is the complete whole.

To realize our spiritual constitution and transcend the three modes of nature, we have to become fixed in Krishna consciousness, which culminates in pure devotional service. Under the sway of the three modes, the living entity behaves like a madman under a witch's spell. As long as he is under this spell, he acts according to the particular body awarded by material nature for his past activities.

Lord Krishna continues: "The total material substance, called Brahman, is the source of birth, and it is that Brahman that I impregnate, making possible the births of all living beings, O son of Bharata." (14.3) Here again, Brahman refers to three distinct categories: *prakriti* (material nature), *jiva* (the individual soul), and the Supreme Personality of Godhead. Krishna impregnates *prakriti* with the individual spirit soul, a particle of Himself. All living beings exist within the material world by virtue of this combination of spirit and matter. Krishna says, "It should be understood that all species of life, O son of Kunti, are made possible by birth in this material nature, and that I am the seed-giving father." (14.4) The living entities are originally spiritual, but due to their desire for sense gratification, they are temporarily covered with the material energy and are called conditioned souls. When the conditioned souls, by Lord Krishna's grace and mercy, are relieved of this spell of maya, they become liberated. It is up to us to qualify for His mercy by placing ourselves under the control of His superior energy through devotional service.

"Material nature consists of the three modes—goodness, passion, and ignorance. When the living entity comes in contact with nature, he becomes conditioned by these modes." (14.5) Just by associating with material nature, the living entity comes under the spell of goodness, passion, and ignorance. Although he is spiritual, he is infinitesimal—*anu*, or atomic. Since he is constitutionally very small, he is easily allured by material nature and captured. Then he acts under the sway of one of the modes. According to his desires, he is given a body, with which he mistakenly identifies, and performs activities that cause him to enjoy and suffer repeatedly, thereby perpetuating his material existence.

Lord Krishna continues: "O sinless one, the mode of goodness, being purer than the others, is illuminating, and it frees one from all sinful reactions. Those situated in that mode develop knowledge, but they become conditioned by the concept of happiness." (14.6) Because the mode of goodness is the purest mode, one acting in goodness is called a *brahmana*. A *brahmana* is supposed to be very pure and clean. He should cultivate knowledge and be free from all sinful activity, for a *brahmana* is known by his qualities, not his birthright. If one continues to commit sins, he cannot be considered a *brahmana*, nor can he cultivate knowledge. But even the pure *brahmana* is not free from all reactions. That is, he becomes conditioned by the concept of material well-being in the mode of goodness. If there is no liberation for those in the mode of goodness, there is certainly less chance for those in passion and ignorance.

"The mode of passion is born of unlimited desires and longings, O son of Kunti, and because of this, one is bound to material fruitive activities." (14.7) This mode is characterized by the affection between the sexes, and it is based on the desire to enjoy sense gratification. Due to the desire to lord it over the material creation, one develops unlimited hankerings for this and that. The mode of passion is typified by hankering and lamentation. When a person wants something very much, he strives for it with great endeavor. When he does not get it, or when he gets it and then loses it, he laments. Therefore, in the mode of passion, one is always miserable and distressed, for one is always hankering and lamenting. In passion, there is no question of happiness.

"O son of Bharata, the mode of ignorance causes the delusion of all living entities. The result of this mode is madness, indolence, and sleep, which bind the conditioned soul." (14.8) One who is bereft of knowledge is said to be in the mode of ignorance. Such a person does not understand that he is spirit soul, nor does he know anything about the Supreme Personality of Godhead. All his activities are centered around the body. Since he is more or less in animal consciousness, he sleeps as much as possible. Of course, the material body requires rest, but six hours a day should be sufficient. Those who want to sleep ten or twelve hours or more a day are like dogs. As soon as a dog gets a chance, he lies down and goes to sleep. Man should not waste his developed consciousness in this way. Human consciousness is meant for contemplating and understanding the supreme consciousness. In ignorance, a man wants to forget everything by intoxication and sleep. One who dies in this mode sinks into lower species of life, or takes birth in the lower planetary systems.

"The mode of goodness conditions one to happiness, passion conditions him to the fruits of action, and ignorance to madness. Sometimes the mode of passion becomes prominent, defeating the mode of goodness, O son of Bharata. And sometimes the mode of goodness defeats passion, and at other times the mode of ignorance defeats goodness and passion. In this way, there is always competition for supremacy." (14.9-10) These three modes compete against one another to dominate the living entity. Generally, one is not exclusively under the control of any one mode but a combination. People often have a mixture of good and passionate qualities. And sometimes we see ignorant people with some good qualities. Thus there is a struggle for dominance. When the mode of goodness predominates, the modes of passion and ignorance are automatically subdued. Similarly, when the mode of ignorance predominates, the qualities of goodness, and even those of passion, are lost. The living entity can control the modes only by following the regulative principles of freedom, as described in the Second Chapter. By determination to renounce sinful activity and redirect all desires to Krishna, one can attain the mode of pure goodness, *suddha-sattva*, the transcendental position of Krishna consciousness.

"The manifestations of the mode of goodness can be experienced when all the gates of the body are illuminated by knowledge." (14.11) The body has nine gates: two eyes, two ears, two nostrils, a mouth, an anus, and the genitals. When these are illuminated by knowledge, one knows that God is the body's proprietor and therefore renders service to Him. Whatever goes into or comes out of the body should be transcendentally pure. Whatever we speak should be truthful, beneficial, and pure, and we should see with purified vision. It is essential for one in purified goodness to make sure that the gates of the body remain pure.

"O chief of the Bharatas," Krishna continues, "when there is an increase in the mode of passion, the symptoms of great attachment, uncontrollable desire, hankering, and intense endeavor develop." (14.12) When one is controlled by passion, he hankers for more and more. Since there is no end to the desire for sense gratification, he is never satisfied. The senses have been compared to serpents, which are always envious and never satisfied. They are also said to burn like fire, and trying to gratify them is compared to pouring gasoline on this fire. Instead of being extinguished, the fire blazes more and more violently. Until we surrender the senses to the master of the senses, Hrishikesha, Krishna, they are always raging out of control.

The senses are also compared to wild horses. Horses are certainly a great help in travelling to one's destination, but wild horses, running out of control, are sure to lead us to destruction. Therefore, devotees pray each day: "This material body is a network of ignorance, and the senses are one's deadly enemies, for they throw the soul into this ocean of material sense enjoyment. Among those senses, the tongue is the most voracious and uncontrollable. It is very difficult to conquer the tongue in this world. Being very merciful, Lord Krishna has given us the remnants of His food (*prasadam*) just to control the tongue. Now please accept that nectarean Krishna-*prasadam* and sing the glories of Their Lordships Sri Sri Radha and Krishna, and in love call out for Lord Chaitanya and Nityananda to save us." (*Gitavali*, Bhaktivinoda Thakura) In this attitude, one can always be protected from the dangers of uncontrolled senses.

Lord Krishna continues: "O son of Kuru, when there is an increase in the mode of ignorance, madness, illusion, inertia, and darkness are manifested." (14.13) In ignorance, a person acts whimsically for his own immediate gratification. Although there is consciousness, it has no proper direction. Such a person may be active, but his activities serve no useful purpose. Human life is meant for God realization; apart from this, it has no particular value. Human beings are not as strong as animals, and they can neither eat as much, nor enjoy sex as often as some, but human life is unique in that it can be directed toward God realization. If a person engages the body in self-realization, he is in the mode of goodness. If he engages it for sense gratification, he is in the mode of passion. And if he does not engage it at all, or if he acts whimsically, to no purpose, he is in the mode of ignorance.

"When one dies in the mode of goodness, he attains the

pure higher planets." (14.14) Godly beings reside on planets like
Brahmaloka and Janaloka, and one can attain such planets by
cultivating the mode of goodness. "When one dies in the mode
of passion, he takes birth among those engaged in fruitive activities; and 'when he dies in the mode of ignorance, he takes
birth in the animal kingdom." (14.15) Many people think that
once they attain the human form, it is not possible to sink again
into the animal species, but Lord Krishna rejects this. Those who
are attached to the fruits of their labor remain on earth as humans,
and those in ignorance are reborn as animals. By neglecting the
prime duty of human life, we always degrade ourselves. Just as
we elevate ourselves by cultivating godly qualities, we degrade
ourselves by cultivating bestial qualities. All animals are absorbed
in four basic activities: eating, sleeping, defending, and mating.
Animals have no other business. We never find an animal chanting Hare Krishna, worshipping in the temple, or studying scripture. So-called humans who are simply eating, sleeping, defending, and mating are surely developing animal bodies for their
next life.

"By acting in the mode of goodness, one becomes purified.
Works done in the mode of passion result in distress, and actions
peformed in the mode of ignorance result in foolishness." (14.16)
Unaware of the functions of the modes, people become more
and more entangled. By acting in goodness, one can be relatively
happy in this material world. But even if, through goodness,
one is elevated to Brahmaloka, the highest material planet, he
will still find repetition of birth and death. In the mode of passion,
one is always distressed. Generally, people in passion engage
in animal killing, not knowing that the law of karma dictates
that they will be killed in their next life. This is a just retribution.
When we break the laws of the state, we are punished by the
agents of the state, and when we break the laws of God, we are
punished by the agents of God. Ignorance is no excuse; the law
acts. If we kill, we will be killed. If we inflict pain on others,
that pain will return to us. We may escape the police, but there
is no escaping the stringent laws of material nature. In this regard, Srila Prabhupada has pointed out that cow slaughter is
the most heinous of acts committed in grossest ignorance. *Namo
brahmanya-devaya go brahmana-hitaya ca*. Lord Krishna is the well-

wisher of all, but especially to the cows and the *brahmanas*. Brahminical culture is meant for self-realization, and the cow provides the foundation for the proper functioning of brahminical society. *Go-mata*, mother cow, is Lord Krishna's special gift to man. Just by eating grass, the gentle cow provides milk, a miracle food that provides fine brain tissues for understanding God, and the bull tills the soil to provide us with life's necessities. When these animals are butchered, society must pay according to the law of karma. As long as people kill cows, men will be killed, either by warfare or natural calamities. That is the law of nature. Peace cannot exist in an animal-killing society.

Lord Krishna continues: "From the mode of goodness, real knowledge develops; from the mode of passion, grief develops; and from the mode of ignorance, foolishness, madness, and illusion develop." (14.17) If we want to cultivate the mode of goodness, we must take to the principles of Krishna consciousness, which can elevate us from the inferior modes of passion and ignorance to the mode of pure goodness. From goodness, we can understand our real position as spirit soul, eternal servant of God. Ultimately, we must transcend all the modes of material existence to be established in the Lord's transcendental devotional service. It is very difficult to understand that the self is different from the body if we are in the modes of passion and ignorance. Unless we hear about our true spiritual nature from a qualified *brahmana* and elevate ourselves to the mode of goodness, we will hardly understand transcendental knowledge.

Lord Krishna continues: "Those situated in the mode of goodness gradually go upward to the higher planets. Those in the mode of passion live on the earthly planets; and those in the mode of ignorance go down to the hellish worlds. When you see that there is nothing beyond these modes of nature in all activities and that the Supreme Lord is transcendental to all these modes, then you can know My spiritual nature." (14.18-19) Since Lord Krishna is the supreme spiritual master, His instructions on the transcendental nature of the soul are supremely authoritative. The Krishna conscious man regards his body as the instrument of the Lord, and in this consciousness, he transcends the three modes and lives happily even while in this material world.

"When the embodied being is able to transcend these three modes, he can become free from birth, death, old age, and their distresses, and can enjoy nectar even in this life." (14.20) This is confirmed by Srila Rupa Goswami, who said that the Krishna conscious man is already on the transcendental platform while in the material body. Even a neophyte, though not fully purified, is considered liberated from the three modes if he engages in pure devotional service under the guidance of a bona fide spiritual master. "Even if one commits the most abominable actions, if he is engaged in devotional service, he is to be considered saintly because he is properly situated." (9.30)

Arjuna asks, "By what symptoms is one known who is transcendental to those modes? What is his behavior? And how does he transcend the modes of nature?" (14.21)

Lord Krishna replies, "He who does not hate illumination, attachment, and delusion when they are present, nor longs for them when they disappear; who is seated like one unconcerned, being situated beyond these material reactions of the modes of nature; who remains firm, knowing that the modes alone are active; who regards alike pleasure and pain, and looks on a clod, a stone, and a piece of gold with an equal eye; who is wise and holds praise and blame to be the same; who is unchanged in honor and dishonor; who treats friend and foe alike; who has abandoned all fruitive undertakings—such a man is said to have transcended the modes of nature." (14.22-25)

Once a man is freed from the modes of nature, he does not hanker for anything. He is fully satisfied in all circumstances. How is this possible? When a devotee fully surrenders to the Lord, he directly perceives that Krishna has taken charge of his life, and that whatever comes is sent personally by Krishna for his welfare. He is satisfied simply by the knowledge that Krishna is his dearmost friend and that his only obligation is to serve the Lord unconditionally, without desiring any reward. In this way, the devotee is always aloof from whatever the material body experiences. His mind is always absorbed in thinking of Krishna and serving Him without profit. He is not affected by honor or dishonor, for he is content in his service to Krishna. He sees everything equally, whether it be dung or gold. Of course, this does not mean that he will not accept gold for

Krishna's service. Indeed, he is obligated to use everything in Krishna's service. A stone can be used to build a temple for Krishna, and gold can be used to buy items for the Deities. But nothing should be used for sense gratification. Everything is Krishna's property, to be used exclusively for serving Krishna; therefore the devotee sees everything equally.

Lord Krishna continues: "One who engages in full devotional service, who does not fall down in any circumstance, at once transcends the modes of material nature and thus comes to the level of Brahman." (14.26) Here, Brahman refers to the platform of spirit soul. This is Brahman realization. When we have attained such determination and faith in Krishna, we are never deviated by the illusory material energy. On this spiritual platform, we see Krishna everywhere. Individuality is not lost, however, for the identity of servitor and served is never lost. Krishna is served eternally by His eternal servant, the devotee, and devotional service is the devotee's eternal activity. This is the sum and substance of self-realization.

Lord Krishna concludes: "And I am the basis of the impersonal Brahman, which is the constitutional position of ultimate happiness, and which is immortal, imperishable, and eternal." (14.27) The Mayavadi impersonalists claim that the impersonal Brahman is the source of all incarnations, including Krishna, but here, Lord Krishna emphatically rejects this. Krishna does not emanate from anything else; everything emanates from Krishna. In fact, Brahman, the *brahmajyoti*, is nothing but the effulgence of His transcendental body. Because the impersonalists cannot penetrate beyond this effulgence, they take it to be the ultimate source of everything. This is due to their poor fund of knowledge. Therefore the devotee prays:

> *hiranmayena pātrena*
> *satyasyāpihitam mukham*
> *tat tvam pūsann apāvrnu*
> *satya-dharmāya drstaye*

"O my Lord, sustainer of all that lives, Your real face is covered by Your dazzling effulgence. Kindly remove that covering, and exhibit Yourself to Your pure devotee." (*Isopanishad*, 15)

The devotee wants to see the Lord as He is. In full Krishna

consciousness, he realizes the Supreme Personality of Godhead in three stages—Brahman, Paramatma, and Bhagavan. Once established in this perfect knowledge, the devotee never falls again into the material whirlpool. This, then, is the constitutional position of ultimate happiness. We are Lord Krishna's eternal servants, and our devotional service is immortal, imperishable, and eternal. Even in the spiritual world, our service to Lord Krishna will continue. When we engage in this service while in the material world, we are guaranteed passage back home, back to Godhead. Hare Krishna.

The Blessed Lord said: There is a banyan tree which has its roots upward and its branches down and whose leaves are the Vedic hymns. One who knows this tree is the knower of the Vedas. (Bg. 15.1)

CHAPTER FIFTEEN

The Yoga of the Supreme Person

Earlier, in the Twelfth Chapter, Lord Krishna advised Arjuna to realize Him in His personal feature by always thinking of Him in the form of Krishna. Once again, in this chapter, Krishna emphasizes that according to the *Vedas*, God is to be ultimately realized as the Supreme Person. God is Absolute, and Absolute realization must include His personal feature. Yoga, therefore, means yoking or linking up with God as the Supreme Person. Impersonal realization is not really yoga at all. We do not link up with a blank wall, or a candle, or a picture on the wall, unless the picture is of the Supreme Person, who is nondifferent from His picture. It is again clearly proved in this chapter that the culmination of all Vedic knowledge is worship of the Supreme Personality of Godhead.

Lord Krishna says, "There is a banyan tree which has its roots upward and its branches down and whose leaves are the Vedic hymns. One who knows this tree is the knower of the *Vedas.*" (15.1) The *Vedas* impart knowledge of God beyond the range of the material senses, culminating in Krishna consciousness. The banyan tree spoken of here is different from an ordinary banyan tree. In this material world, the only way to see a banyan tree with its roots upward and branches downward is to look into the water and see the reflection of a tree on the banks. That tree, pervertedly reflected, is compared to the material world, where everything is upside down because it is only a reflection of the spiritual world.

Lord Krishna continues: "The branches of this tree extend downward and upward, nourished by the three modes of material nature. The twigs are the objects of the senses. This tree also has roots going down, and these are bound to the fruitive actions

213

of human society." (15.2) A huge banyan tree sends its roots out in every direction, and they quickly form a complex, entangling labyrinth. Similarly, when the conditioned soul enters this material world, his fruitive activities reach out in all directions, and he becomes increasingly bound up and entangled in the actions and reactions of material existence.

Lord Krishna continues: "The real form of this tree cannot be perceived in this world. No one can understand where it ends, where it begins, or where its foundation is. But with determination, one must cut down this tree with the weapon of detachment. So doing, one must seek that place from which, having once gone, one never returns, and there surrender to that Supreme Personality of Godhead from whom everything has begun and in whom everything is abiding since time immemorial." (15.3-4) In the Fourth Chapter, Krishna also speaks of cutting with a weapon: "Therefore the doubts which have arisen in your heart out of ignorance should be slashed by the weapon of knowledge." (4.42) The weapon of detachment and the weapon of knowledge are one and the same, for transcendental knowledge brings detachment from this material world. Detachment is never possible for one who identifies with the body instead of the spirit soul. Realization of oneself as spirit soul is the beginning of transcendental knowledge. For further advancement, we must be determined to pursue spiritual knowledge under the guidance of a bona fide spiritual master. When we hear submissively and regularly from the Lord's pure devotee, we can trace out the origin of our material entanglement. This is not possible by mental speculation or mundane research work. Only by hearing from proper authorities can we locate the root of material existence, and, with proper understanding, cut down this perverted tree of material life.

It should be understood that everything about this tree is inverted, for only its reflection is seen. In material consciousness, everything is seen backwards, compared to spiritual consciousness. For instance, in the Second Chapter, it was stated, "What is night for all beings is the time of awakening for the self-controlled; and the time of awakening for all beings is night for the introspective sage." (2.69) When Srila Prabhupada first began teaching in America, he wrote a little pamphlet entitled "Who is Crazy?" The materialists say that the transcendentalists, or devotees, are crazy, and vice versa. So, who will decide? What is the criterion for judging sanity? The English word "sane" is derived from the Latin *sanus*, meaning "healthy." The word sane generally refers to someone who is mentally healthy, or capable of judging things properly, and insane refers to someone who cannot perceive or judge in terms of reality. The insane live in an unreal world. This may be the world of second childhood for a senile grandmother, or the nightmare world of a schizophrenic. Sometimes people say that the devotees are trying to escape reality. But we should understand what "reality" means in this material world. Birth is reality, old age is reality, disease is reality, and death is reality. To ignore these realities is certainly insanity, and to solve them is sanity.

To accept the body as the self is also insanity, because the body is temporary, and the self is eternal. Neglecting self-realization, an insane man throws away the precious gift of human life by pursuing temporary sense gratification, which any animal can enjoy. Because he is crazy, a materialist sees everything topsy-turvy. He lives in a perverted world, for he is seeing only reflections of reality. By speaking of a reflection, however, we necessarily posit the existence of a reality: the spiritual world. The sage, by virtue of surrender to the Supreme Personality of Godhead, sees things as they are, because he beholds Krishna, the Supreme Reality, in everything at every moment. Without this loving surrender to God, the reality of spiritual existence can never be seen.

Through surrender, the devotee develops causeless knowledge and detachment automatically. By *bhakti-yoga*, loving devotional service to Krishna, he can easily cut down the great banyan tree of material life. *Bhakti-yoga* is all that is needed, for it automatically brings the real basis of detachment, and full knowledge of everything material and spiritual.

Lord Krishna continues: "One who is free from illusion, false prestige, and false association, who understands the eternal, who is done with material lust and is freed from the duality of happiness and distress, and who knows how to surrender unto the Supreme Person, attains to that eternal kingdom." (15.5) The step by step process of surrender is concisely described here.

One who is under the illusion of material life, thinking the reflection of the banyan tree to be the real tree, develops false prestige, or pride. "Pride goeth before destruction," *Proverbs* warns, "and an haughty spirit before a fall." Due to being puffed up with pride, one thinks himself to be something he is not. We are just tiny particles of Krishna, but in illusion we think ourselves to be independently great, wonderful, and powerful. Factually, the living entity is controlled at every moment. Birth, old age, disease, and death are miseries meant to impress upon him the fact that he is the controlled, not the controller, but due to pride and illusion, he foolishly thinks otherwise, despite these material miseries. Therefore the living entity struggles to create and maintain many false associations—family, friends, society, country, etc.—for greater bodily sense gratification, and thereby increases his entanglement. Thus, like a silkworm, he encases himself in a cocoon of his own creation.

How strange it is that people become puffed up because of the material body! Whether the body is white, black, red, brown, or yellow, male, or female, it is basically a bag of pus, blood, bile, urine, and stool, destined to grow old and die. No one should be proud of associating with the material body. Rather, one should try his best to understand that he is distinct from it. When one understands himself to be spirit soul, he naturally wants to associate with others on a spiritual basis. The International Society for Krishna Consciousness offers everyone an opportunity to understand his eternal relationship with Lord Krishna in the association of devotees. This benefits all, both now and in the future, whereas material association for sense gratification is temporary and degrading.

The understanding of the eternal should be pursued directly and indirectly. By the *neti neti* process, one can analyze all material things and understand their temporary nature. For instance, a man is naturally attracted to a beautiful woman, but when he sees this beauty as temporary and understands that the woman will soon change and become ugly, he can control his lust. He soberly reflects that the eternal beauty, for which everyone is truly hankering, cannot be found here. To understand the eternal directly, we must understand the eternal beauty of the Supreme Lord Sri Krishna. When we see His supreme beauty, we automatically become detached from all inferior beauty. Of this, Srila Rupa Goswami wrote: "My dear friend, if you still have any desire to enjoy the company of your friends within this material world, then don't look upon the form of Krishna, who is standing on the bank of Kesi-ghata. He is known as Govinda, and His eyes are very enchanting. He is playing upon His flute, and on his head there is a peacock feather. And His whole body is illuminated by the moonlight in the sky." Who would fail to be attracted by the incomparable beauty of the Supreme Personality of Godhead, Lord Krishna?

In the surrendering process, after one has understood the eternal, he becomes free from lust and the duality of happiness and distress. In the Second Chapter, Krishna explained that lust has its origin in the contemplation of sense objects, which are related to the duality of happiness and distress, pleasure and pain. One is attracted to whatever gives pleasure and repelled by whatever gives pain. But one who understands himself to be eternal does not identify with the senses or sense objects; therefore he is free from all duality.

By knowing perfectly the process of surrender and the Supreme Person to whom we surrender, a devotee makes steady progress on the path back home, back to Krishna's supreme abode, which is described in the next verse.

"That abode of Mine is not illumined by the sun or moon, nor by electricity. One who reaches it never returns to this material world." (15.6) By surrender and devotional service, one attains the eternal, spiritual kingdom of God. That supreme abode is not defective in any way. No artificial light is needed because all the spiritual planets are self-luminous, being the personal residence of the Supreme Personality of Godhead. The entire spiritual sky is illumined by the *brahmajyoti* effulgence emanating from His transcendental body. By contrast, the material world is always defective. Here, everything depends on something else. For light, the sun, moon, and electricity are needed, and they, in turn, are dependent on something else. In the Kingdom of God, however, everything is complete, being of the same spiritual essence as God Himself.

Lord Krishna continues: "The living entities in this conditioned world are My eternal, fragmental parts. Due to conditioned life, they are struggling very hard with the six senses, which include the mind." (15.7) The Mayavadi impersonalists claim that due to maya, we think that we are fragmental parts of Krishna. After liberation, they say, we will again merge into the Supreme and become one. But here Krishna says that we are fragmental parts eternally (*jiva-bhutah sanatanah*). It is not that at some point the Lord is fragmented into countless *jiva*-souls, and then at another point He merges everything into Himself and becomes one. The word *sanatana* (eternal) contradicts this. In the Second Chapter, it is stated that "the soul can never be cut into pieces by any weapon." (2.23) Since the Supreme Personality of Godhead is pure spirit, He cannot be cut (*nainam chindanti*), nor divided in any way. The living entities are by nature the Lord's eternal parts, just as arms and legs are parts of a body, and are never severed from Him.

The Lord has many energies. In the spiritual world, He expands Himself by personal expansions known as *Vishnu-tattva*. He also expands Himself as apparently separated parts and parcels known as *jiva-atma*, the living entities. The eternal function (*sanatana-dharma*) of these living entities is to render transcendental loving service to the whole. In knowledge, we know God as He is and ourselves as His eternal parts and parcels, and in this knowledge we surrender to Him and render loving service. In conditional life, the living entity forgets this constitutional servitorship; therefore he struggles very hard to satisfy the material senses, including the mind. Satisfaction, of course, is not possible, because the mind's desires are illusory and insatiable. To be completely satisfied, we have to wake up to Krishna consciousness.

"The living entity in the material world carries his different conceptions from one body to another, as the air carries aromas." (15.8) In the spiritual world, all the living entities are fully Krishna conscious and serve the Lord eternally. In the material world, due to the desire to lord it over material nature, the living entity transmigrates from one body to another. This change of body does not take place in the spiritual world, where there is no difference between the body and the soul. Transmigration was elaborately explained in the Eighth Chapter, wherein it is said, "Whatever state of being one remembers when he quits his body, that state he will attain without fail." (8.6) Maharaja Bharata, being attached to a deer, thought of a deer at the time of death and so was obliged to take birth as a deer. Therefore a devotee trains himself to always think of Krishna. Especially at moments of distress, the devotee calls out to Krishna because he knows no shelter other than the Lord. Remembering Krishna everyday by chanting His holy names—at least sixteen rounds on *japa*-beads—the devotee will surely remember Krishna at the time of death, and call out loudly: Hare Krishna, Hare Krishna, Krishna Krishna, Hare Hare, Hare Rama, Hare Rama, Rama Rama, Hare Hare. Chanting in this way, the devotee will go to Krishna without fail.

Lord Krishna continues: "The living entity, thus taking another gross body, obtains a certain type of ear, eye, tongue, nose, and sense of touch, which are grouped about the mind. He thus enjoys a particular set of sense objects." (15.9) The consciousness of the living being develops around a particular kind of body due to his desire. Consciousness is originally pure, but when it is agitated by the desire for sense gratification, it becomes impure, like muddied water. When the pure consciousness is agitated by the mode of goodness, it stays relatively pure, but becomes conditioned by a material sense of happiness. When it is agitated by the mode of passion, it becomes distressed. And when agitated by the mode of ignorance, it becomes mad. In this way, the living being in the material world is always being contaminated by one or more of the three modes of material nature, and his pure consciousness is always muddied. Pure consciousness is Krishna consciousness, and as soon as one turns his consciousness again to Krishna, giving up the desire to be lord, enjoyer, controller, or proprietor, he regains his pure state.

Lord Krishna continues: "The foolish cannot understand how a living entity can quit his body, nor can they understand what sort of body he enjoys under the spell of the modes of nature. But one whose eyes are trained in knowledge can see all this." (15.10) Unless one sees through the eyes of *shastra* (scripture), or the eyes of the spiritual master, he cannot see things as they are. Not knowing how to approach the Supreme Lord or His representatives, the foolish do not understand the process of transmigration, nor do they know how to stop it. But those who are trained in spiritual knowledge are never confused, for they know how to remember the Supreme Personality of Godhead and return to Him.

"The endeavoring transcendentalist, who is situated in self-realization, can see all this clearly. But those who are not situated in self-realization cannot see what is taking place, though they may try to." (15.11) The real yogi is never confused. At the conclusion of the Sixth Chapter, Krishna said, "And of all yogis, he who always abides in Me with great faith, worshipping Me in transcendental loving service, is most intimately united with Me in yoga and is the highest of all." (6.47) We must understand the science of *bhakti-yoga* and realize our relationship with the Supreme Lord. By understanding this relationship, and the workings of *prakriti*, or material nature, we can establish ourselves in devotional service and stop the repetition of birth and death.

Lord Krishna continues: "The splendor of the sun, which dissipates the darkness of this whole world, comes from Me. And the splendor of the moon and the splendor of fire are also from Me." (15.12) Here, Lord Krishna explains how a devotee can always think of Him. We cannot live without the sun, nor would life be very tolerable without fire. The moon gives light and beauty to the night. By seeing Krishna in these things, we can begin to understand His importance in our daily lives.

"I enter into each planet, and by My energy they stay in orbit. I become the moon and thereby supply the juice of life to all vegetables." (15.13) Due to Lord Krishna's presence, planets are able to float in space in perfect order. Modern astronomers try to describe this phenomenon by calling it gravity or whatever, but the miracle of the sun and planets remains just as astonishing. They are floating in space perfectly, and all that is holding them up is Krishna's mystic power. The scientists are certainly not holding them up. Scientists may name and describe the universe, but they cannot create, maintain, or destroy it. Clearly, just by studying the wonders of the universe with humility, we can remember Krishna.

"I am the fire of digestion in every living body, and I am the air of life, outgoing and incoming, by which I digest the four kinds of foodstuff." (15.14) We cannot even digest our food without Krishna's help. From the moment of our birth till the moment of death, air is going in and out of our lungs. In *Genesis,* it is said that God breathed into man's nostrils the breath of life. And according to *Srimad-Bhagavatam,* as Mahavishnu breathes, all the universes emanate from the pores of His transcendental body. How great is the power of God's breath! Krishna is the very air of life. If we can just meditate on this fact, we will be Krishna conscious at every breath we take.

"I am seated in everyone's heart, and from Me come remembrance, knowledge, and forgetfulness. By all the *Vedas* am I to be known; indeed, I am the compiler of Vedanta, and I am the knower of the *Vedas.*" (15.15) As soon as we change bodies, we forget everything, but the Lord, as the Supersoul in our hearts, knows everything—past, present, and future. He is always present to remind us of our past desires, saying, "You have gotten this particular body because you wanted to enjoy in this way. Now act like a dog (or a man, or a demigod)." And as Krishna gives us remembrance according to our desires, He also gives us forgetfulness. If we want to forget the purpose of human life and live like animals, Krishna will help us forget. If we so choose, we can continue forgetting Krishna birth after birth. Nature will award us a body suitable to our forgetfulness. Material nature awards bodies according to the living entity's predominant mode—goodness, passion, or ignorance. Thus the living entity is given a demigod, human, or animal body, according to his quality of action.

Krishna is fulfilling everyone's desire. If we want knowledge, we should turn to Him, for He is the compiler of Vedanta and the original speaker of the *Vedas.* Who can know a thing better than its author? All knowledge, both material and transcendental, comes from Krishna.

Lord Krishna continues: "There are two classes of beings, the fallible and the infallible. In the material world, every entity is fallible, and in the spiritual world, every entity is called infallible." (15.16) Under the influence of time, everyone has to change his body and forget everything. As soon as one changes his body, he forgets his previous life. Being forgetful, the living entity is fallible. In the spiritual world, however, there is no change of body, and no forgetfulness. The soul is eternal, and in the spiritual world, the spiritual body is one in quality with the Lord—*sat-cit-ananda*, eternal, full of knowledge and bliss. However, Krishna's supreme spiritual body is infinite in quality and quantity. He is the supreme infinite, and we are infinitesimal.

"Because I am transcendental, beyond both the fallible and the infallible, and because I am the greatest, I am celebrated both in the world and in the *Vedas* as that Supreme Person." (15.18) Lord Krishna and the living entities are both persons, but Krishna is the Supreme Person. *Nityo nityanam cetanas cetananam. (Katha Upanishad,* 2.2.13) Because He maintains all the finite eternal beings, the Lord is the chief eternal living entity. As the omnipotent, omniscient Lord, He knows and controls everyone and everything.

"Whoever knows Me as the Supreme Personality of Godhead, without doubting, is to be understood as the knower of everything, and he therefore engages himself in full devotional service, O son of Bharata." (15.19) When one agrees to surrender to the Lord and render devotional service, he can attain transcendental knowledge, for he knows his position in respect to the Lord. The Lord is everything, within everything, and beyond everything. Since the Lord is everything, and the devotee knows the Lord, the devotee is the knower of everything. As confirmed in *Svetasvatara Upanishad* (6.23), "Only unto those great souls who have implicit faith in both the Lord and the spiritual master are all the imports of Vedic knowledge automatically revealed." The Lord directly gives His pure devotee full knowledge by which he can engage in transcendental loving pastimes with the Lord eternally, either here or in the Kingdom of God.

Lord Krishna concludes: "This is the most confidential part of the Vedic scriptures, O sinless one, and it is disclosed now by Me. Whoever understands this will become wise, and his endeavors will know perfection." (15.20) The Ninth Chapter also deals with the most confidential knowledge, and here Lord Krishna discusses the same subject, devotional service, the king of knowledge and education. Devotional service brings the highest perfection, but its knowledge is imparted only to those who have become nonenvious, or sinless. One becomes sinless when he no longer desires to compete with the Lord by trying to lord it over material nature for sense gratification. Pure devotional service is rendered by those who have surrendered unto the Lord in complete faith, agreeing to become His eternal servants.

The Hare Krishna movement spreads knowledge of Krishna through the chanting of the Hare Krishna *maha-mantra:* Hare Krishna, Hare Krishna, Krishna Krishna, Hare Hare, Hare Rama, Hare Rama, Rama Rama, Hare Hare. Whether we live inside or outside a temple, our duty is to tell everyone about the glories of Lord Krishna and His holy name. The material world is a place of suffering, and the only remedy is Krishna consciousness. We must give it to others, that they may also benefit. Hare Krishna.

The transcendental qualities are conducive to liberation, whereas the demonic qualities make for bondage. Do not worry, O son of Pandu, for you are born with the divine qualities. *(Bg. 16.5)*

CHAPTER SIXTEEN

The Divine and Demoniac Natures

Although the divine and demoniac natures are often easily perceived, they are not so easily understood. How do they arise? Where do they come from? Can they be changed? These are some of the questions considered here.

Sometimes people refer to a person as being good, or bad, or coming from good seed or bad seed. Indeed, one school of traditional thought maintains that character is largely determined by heredity, or genetics, while another likens a child to a blank slate *(tabula rasa)*, on which society and the environment write. But what does Lord Krishna, the supreme and ultimate Authority, have to say about these questions?

Lord Krishna does not agree that the divine and demoniac natures result from birth. Rather, He describes them by qualities cultivated in this life, or in previous lifetimes. Similarly, in the Fourth Chapter, Lord Krishna described the four castes *(brahmana, kshatriya, vaishya, and sudra)* according to qualities *(guna-karma-vibhagasah)*, not birthright. In modern India, the caste system has become a rigid order of social stratification based on birth. If one is born into a *brahmana* family, he is accepted as a *brahmana;* if he is born into a *kshatriya* or a *sudra* family, he is accepted as a *kshatriya* or *sudra.* But this is not the way Lord Krishna defines the social classes *(catur-varnyam)* in *Bhagavad-gita.* Nor does He define the divine and demoniac natures in this way. Rather, He describes the qualities of those guided by the divine and demoniac natures. Therefore, anyone can elevate himself to Krishna consciousness simply by changing his activities. If he purifies his existence by developing the godly qualities, he should be regarded as godly, even though born into a demoniac family. But without the godly qualities, one should

225

be considered demoniac, even though his outward dress be that of a *brahmana* or *sannyasi*. By his fruits a man is known.

Lord Krishna says, "Fearlessness, purification of one's existence, cultivation of spiritual knowledge, charity, self-control, performance of sacrifice, study of the Vedas, austerity, and simplicity; nonviolence, truthfulness, freedom from anger; renunciation, tranquility, aversion to fault-finding; compassion, and freedom from covetousness; gentleness, modesty, and steady determination; vigor, forgiveness, fortitude, and cleanliness; freedom from envy and the passion for honor—these transcendental qualities, O son of Bharata, belong to godly men endowed with divine nature." (16.1-3)

In the Thirteenth Chapter, Lord Krishna enumerated similar qualities leading to knowledge: "Humility, pridelessness, nonviolence, tolerance, simplicity, approaching a bona fide spiritual master, cleanliness, steadiness, and self-control; renunciation of the objects of sense gratification, absence of false ego, the perception of the evil of birth, death, old age, and disease; non-attachment to children, wife, home, and the rest, and evenmindedness amid pleasant and unpleasant events; constant and unalloyed devotion to Me, resorting to solitary places, detachment from the general mass of people; accepting the importance of self-realization, and philosophical search for the Absolute Truth—all these I thus declare to be knowledge, and what is contrary to these is ignorance." (13.8-12)

By comparing these lists, we can see that they are similar. When one develops the godly qualities of the divine nature, he also develops knowledge as a by-product. Those who are of the divine nature want to cultivate knowledge of the Supreme, while the demoniac do not. Why? Because their desires are different. "I am seated in everyone's heart," Krishna says, "and from Me come remembrance, knowledge, and forgetfulness." (15.15) When the living entity wants to become lord of everything, he has to forget the real Lord. In the presence of Krishna, no one can claim to be God. When Arjuna saw the universal form of God, he became very fearful, although he was a great courageous warrior. He immediately bowed down, thinking, "Oh, maybe I have committed some offense. Let me pray for forgiveness." God is so great and powerful that any sane man would automatically bow down in His presence. Before Him, no one would dare stand up and say, "I am God." But when the living entity wants to be the supreme enjoyer, or equal to God, the Supreme Lord gives him a chance to fulfill his desire.

Thus the living entity is placed in ignorance. In illusion, he thinks, "I am as good as God." When one acts like this, he is certainly ignorant of God's greatness. A knower and lover of God could not possibly think himself equal to God or greater than God. There is only this one basic difference between the demons and the devotees: the demons rebel against God and refuse to follow His laws, and the devotees surrender to God and render loving devotional service. Otherwise, they are equal, for all are part and parcel of God.

We are all children of God, expansions of His own nature. Lord Krishna declares that He is the seed-giving Father of everyone. (14.4) He also says, "I envy no one, nor am I partial to anyone. I am equal to all. But whoever renders service unto Me in devotion is a friend, is in Me, and I am also a friend to him." (9.29) Although God is impartial, He does not give the same facility to devotees and demons. Those who want to rebel against God are put into this material world where they can fulfill their desires as demons. And those who want to surrender unto Him are invited back home, back to Godhead, where they can render personal loving service unto the Lord. God is equal to all, but all desires are not equal.

Throughout *Bhagavad-gita*, Lord Krishna has described the qualities of those cultivating the divine nature. In this chapter, He focuses on the demoniac qualities. "Arrogance, pride, anger, conceit, harshness, and ignorance—these qualities belong to those of demoniac nature, O son of Pritha." (16.4) Although demons have nothing to be proud of, they take pride in their family, bodily beauty, and accumulated material possessions, not knowing that these are all awarded by material nature according to past activities, or karma. Just as they are awarded by higher powers, they will also be taken away by higher powers. Although he is only enjoying them temporarily, the proud demon claims, "These are mine." Since his pride has no real basis, it is called "false pride."

Thus illusioned, he thinks these temporary things to be all

in all, although Lord Krishna has defined the real as that which never ceases to be. (2.16) This material existence is a changing phenomenon and therefore unreal. By "unreal," we mean "temporary." Reality is eternal, but due to illusion, the demoniac consider this temporary manifestation of God's energy to be all in all and falsely claim it as their own. Under the grip of illusion, they try to lord it over the material resources for their sense gratification, but ultimately they themselves are destroyed by material nature. "Time I am," Krishna says, "destroyer of the worlds." (11.32) In time, every demon is destroyed and forced to take birth again according to his karma. Although the demoniac man arrogantly thinks, "I am the greatest," he is forced at death to take another body, according to the dictates of higher powers. At death, he cannot say, "Oh, give me the body of a demigod." No. He has already chosen his next body by his life. Although he has rebelled against the laws of God, he cannot escape them. "Though the mills of God grind slowly, yet they grind exceeding small." The law of karma (action and reaction) will take effect, even though the transgressor claims ignorance, disbelief, or whatever.

Lord Krishna continues: "O son of Pritha, in this world there are two kinds of created beings. One is called the divine and the other demoniac. I have already explained to you at length the divine qualities. Now hear from Me of the demoniac." (16.6) Generally, people don't like to hear the truth about demons, or heaven and hell. Sometimes artists portray demons as very ugly creatures with horns and pitchforks, but actually demons more often wear beautiful clothes, ride in luxurious cars, attend the best schools, and present themselves as cultured ladies and gentlemen. Since the demoniac strive hard to usurp God's property for sense gratification, they often possess the opulences of this world—wealth, fame, beauty, strength, etc.— but they have stolen them all. The demoniac are thieves dressed in stolen garments, and, like all thieves, they are eventually caught and punished by the laws of material nature. They may flourish for a season, but their chastisement is certain. The devotees, on the other hand, may seem poor externally because they try to use everything for God's service, but within they are spiritually rich with love for Krishna. Taking joy in His service, they know peace of mind and heart.

"Those who are demoniac do not know what is to be done and what is not to be done. Neither cleanliness nor proper behavior nor truth is found in them." (16.7) In a rebellious spirit, forgetting that Krishna is the lord and proprietor of everything, the demoniac cannot understand the proper course of action. Krishna is the source of everything, the maintainer of everything, and the destroyer of everything. Since the demoniac cannot understand this, they are constantly frustrated and angry. They do not know what to do, nor what to leave undone. They may appear very clean externally, but their hearts are dirty. Real cleanliness is a matter of the heart. When one thinks that he is God, or can become God, or is equal to God, or is the proprietor of God's property, he is untruthful and unclean in heart and mind. In truth, Krishna is the Supreme Personality of Godhead, and everything belongs to Him. Since the demoniac deny this, they are liars and thieves.

Lord Krishna continues: "They say that this world is unreal, that there is no foundation, and that there is no God in control. It is produced of sex desire, and has no cause other than lust." (16.8) This is a very common demoniac philosophy. Some years ago, the famous French writer Albert Camus proposed, like many others before him, that life is absurd and meaningless. Of course, since everything is unreal and absurd, the only worthwhile way to live is to eat, drink, and be merry as long as possible. Sex invariably takes the place of God for such atheists, because sex is the epitome of mundane pleasure. But we should understand that such "enjoyment" cannot continue indefinitely. We are all forced to grow old, suffer disease and distress, and ultimately die. Incidently, Camus, the philosopher of the absurd, was awarded an absurd death when his sportscar overturned. As we approach Krishna, so He awards us. Such demons may think that the world is absurd, but it is they who are absurd, because they have forgotten Krishna, the cause of all causes. Therefore they come to an absurd end.

"Following such conclusions, the demoniac, who are lost to themselves and who have no intelligence, engage in unbeneficial, horrible works meant to destroy the world." (16.9) Puffed up from thinking themselves intelligent, such demons claim to bring great advancement to civilization, but in actuality they are destroying the world by exploiting the earth's resources for sense gratification. In this century, man is especially proud of his scientific achievements. He has discovered the existence of atomic energy, and although he claims that this will benefit the world, to date it has simply wrought destruction. Today, all mankind is threatened by the horrible works of the demons. They create hellish factories to manufacture useless goods for sense gratification. They pump oil out of the earth, burn it for sense gratification, and pollute the atmosphere. Even scientists are admitting that man is quickly polluting himself into extinction. Already, millions of species of plants and animals have vanished from this earth. Factually, the atmosphere has become so polluted by demoniac smoke that the weather is radically changing for the worse. As nations stockpile weapons of destruction to defend their false claim of proprietorship, the earth's resources are drained and depleted. Because of this, demons claim that nature is not providing sufficiently for earth's increasing population. Now they propose to murder the future generation before it can even leave the womb.

Om purnam adah purnam idam. Because the Supreme Personality of Godhead is all-perfect and complete, His creation is perfect and complete. But when demons reject God's plan and try to improve on His work, rejecting His divine laws, they wreak havoc. Possessed of the demoniac mentality of enjoying more and more sense gratification, they succeed only in bringing more misery to themselves and others.

"The demoniac, taking shelter of insatiable lust, pride, and false prestige, and being thus illusioned, are always sworn to unclean work, attracted by the impermanent." (16.10) The demoniac cannot understand that all the fruits of their labor will eventually be lost. Spurred on by insatiable lust, they work like asses for the sake of the material body, not considering that their work has no permanent value. When the mind is filled with lust, that lust burns like fire and cannot be extinguished by any amount of indulgence. The demons, then, are doomed to suffer in the fire of their own lust.

"They believe that to gratify the senses unto the end of life is the prime necessity of human civilization. Thus there is no end to their anxiety. Being bound by hundreds and thousands of desires, by lust and anger, they secure money by illegal means for sense gratification." (16.11-12) Considering sense enjoyment to be life's ultimate goal, the demons chase the illusory energy until their dying day. Even on their death beds, old men try to flirt with their nurses. Demons are so blinded by lust that they undergo any danger to gratify their desires. No one should attempt to enjoy sex life up to death's door. According to Vedic culture, one is first trained as a *brahmachari* (celibate student). When he knows how to control his senses, he is allowed to marry and enjoy restricted sense gratification. But in the *vanaprastha ashrama* (retired life), he must again take up the principle of renunciation of sex life. Finally, in the last stage of life, *sannyasa*, one is expected to perfect his renunciation and preach Krishna consciousness. Vedic culture thus proposes control of the sex drive because unrestrained lust is the very cause of our conditioning. For the sake of spiritual life, sex life must be renounced, except for producing Krishna conscious children.

Demons, of course, do not want to renounce anything. They are prepared to enjoy this life up to the last moment. Sacrifice for a higher purpose is unknown to them, and they resent even hearing of it. Politicians are so lusty for power that they remain in office up to the age of seventy or eighty, or until death forces them out. But this is not the Vedic way. A follower of the *Vedas* voluntarily retires from material life to cultivate Krishna consciousness before death overtakes him. No one should leave this life like the cats and dogs. Being the only animal capable of knowing that he has to die, man should prepare for the next life.

Lord Krishna continues: "The demoniac person thinks: 'So much wealth do I have today, and I will gain more according to my schemes. So much is mine now, and it will increase in the future, more and more. He is my enemy, and I have killed him; and my other enemy will also be killed. I am the lord of everything, I am the enjoyer, I am perfect, powerful, and happy. I am the richest man, surrounded by aristocratic relatives. There is none so powerful and happy as I am. I shall perform sacrifices, I shall give some charity, and thus I shall rejoice.' In this way,

such persons are deluded by ignorance. Thus perplexed by various anxieties and bound by a network of illusions, one becomes
too strongly attached to sense enjoyment, and falls down into
hell." (16.13-16)

This description of the demoniac man, given by Lord
Krishna Himself, is as true today as it was five thousand years
ago. The demoniac mentality never changes. *Bhagavad-gita* is the
enunciation of eternal truths, and when Lord Krishna defines
the demon, He defines him absolutely. Knowing all things, even
the demon's most secret thoughts, Lord Krishna is the supreme
psychologist. The demoniac man always thinks of getting more
and more sense gratification, and he uses any means to this end.
Thinking in this way, he becomes increasingly bound by the
modes (*gunas*) of material nature. Another meaning of *guna* is
"rope." Bound by the ropes of goodness, passion, and ignorance,
the demons glide into hell.

"Self-complacent and always impudent, deluded by wealth
and false prestige, they sometimes perform sacrifices in name
only without following any rules or regulations." (16.17) To as-
suage their bad conscience, demons sometimes perform sacrifices and make charitable contributions, but they do so whimsically. Real religion is practiced according to specific rules and
regulations, not according to one's personal desires. It is not
sufficient to perform a ritual and then ignore the rules and regulations. For success in spiritual life, the rules of scripture must
be followed. Of course, the demoniac man likes to invent his
own rules. He thinks, "Why should I obey scripture? Why listen
to the laws of God? That is old-fashioned and very troublesome.
Since I am great and powerful, I'll perform sacrifices in my own
way." Being thus illusioned, the demon performs sacrifices in
name only, without beneficial results.

"Bewildered by false ego, strength, pride, lust, and anger,
the demon becomes envious of the Supreme Personality of
Godhead, who is situated in his own body and in the bodies of
others, and blasphemes against the real religion." (16.18) Real
religion means surrendering to the Supreme Lord and rendering
transcendental loving service to Him. But the demon laughs at
this, thinking, "Why should I surrender to God? I am as good
as God." Thus he blasphemes the Supreme Personality of

Godhead residing in his own body. *Sri Isopanishad* describes such demons as *atma-hanah*, killers of their own souls and the souls of others.

Of course, the soul cannot be killed—"For the soul there is never birth nor death." (2.20)—but the demons are killing the soul's chance for self-realization while in the human form. Human life is an opportunity for the soul to come to his real position of eternity, knowledge, and bliss. Since the demon is killing that opportunity, he will be punished. According to nature's law, those who perform impious activities are degraded to lower species, wherein their chance for liberation is lost. Therefore they are known as *atma-hanah*, killers of the soul.

Lord Krishna continues: "Those who are envious and mischievous, who are the lowest among men, are cast by Me into the ocean of material existence, into various demoniac species of life." (16.19) Here, Krishna directly states that He is the controller of everyone's fate. The demoniac species are the animal species, because animals cannot become self-realized. It is out of mercy that the Lord puts the demoniac into the lower species, for in this way they cannot blaspheme Him life after life. By the evolutionary process through 8,400,000 species, they can gradually attain the human form and get another opportunity to become Krishna conscious. In all spheres, God's mercy is working. By His mercy, He gives Himself to His devotee. And by His mercy, the demon is thrown back into the ocean of material existence.

"Attaining repeated birth amongst the species of demoniac life, such persons can never approach Me. Gradually they sink down to the most abominable type of existence. There are three gates leading to this hell—lust, anger, and greed. Every sane man should give these up, for they lead to the degradation of the soul." (16.20-21)

In the Second Chapter, Lord Krishna said, "While contemplating the objects of the senses, a person develops attachment for them, and from such attachment lust develops, and from lust anger arises. From anger, delusion arises, and from delusion, bewilderment of memory. When memory is bewildered, intelligence is lost, and when intelligence is lost, one falls down again into the material pool." (2.62-63) It should be noted that this process begins in the mind, with the contemplation of sense objects. We can conquer lust, anger, and greed only through controlling the mind from the very beginning by surrendering to Krishna and chanting His holy names—Hare Krishna, Hare Krishna, Krishna Krishna, Hare Hare, Hare Rama, Hare Rama, Rama Rama, Hare Hare. If lust is not curbed from the very beginning, we will surely enter the gates of hell.

"The man who has escaped these three gates of hell, O son of Kunti, performs acts conducive to self-realization and thus gradually attains the supreme destination." (16.22) A man is either elevated or degraded in the modes of nature according to his activities. By performing pious activities, one can understand the Supreme Lord and surrender to Him. By impious activities, one enters further into the hellish condition and destroys his chances for self-realization.

"But he who discards scriptural injunctions and acts according to his own whims, attains neither perfection, nor happiness, nor the supreme destination." (16.23) Here, Krishna emphasizes the necessity for everyone to act under superior authority. Such authority comes from the Lord as guru (the spiritual master), sadhu (the whole disciplic succession of saintly teachers starting from Lord Krishna), and shastra (scripture spoken by or about Lord Krishna). Without such guidance, one cannot attain happiness, perfection, or the abode of Krishna. Therefore the intelligent will search out a bona fide spiritual master and learn this science of Krishna consciousness by submissive aural reception.

Lord Krishna concludes: "One should understand what is duty and what is not duty by the regulations of the scriptures. Knowing such rules and regulations, one should act so that he may gradually be elevated." (16.24) Not only should we learn the truth, but we must act on the basis of that knowledge. This means following the instructions of guru, sadhu, and shastra. First, we must hear from proven authority, then we must chant, or repeat what we have heard. The holy names of Krishna and the rules for chanting them are imparted by the spiritual master to the sincere disciple so that he may quickly attain the desired result—love of Krishna. It is the disciple's duty to follow the rules and constantly chant the Lord's holy names. By so doing, he can progress in Krishna consciousness, go back home, back to Godhead, and live eternally with Krishna in His transcendental abode. Hare Krishna.

The Absolute Truth is the objective of devotional sacrifice, and it is indicated by the word sat. These works of sacrifice, of penance and of charity, true to the absolute nature, are performed to please the Supreme Person, O son of Prtha. Bg. 17.26-27)

CHAPTER SEVENTEEN

The Divisions of Faith

Arjuna inquires, "O Krishna, what is the situation of one who does not follow the principles of scripture but worships according to his own imagination?" (17.1)

Lord Krishna replies, "According to the modes of nature acquired by the embodied soul, one's faith can be of three kinds: goodness, passion, or ignorance. Now hear about these." (17.2) According to the particular religious authority consulted, worship is conducted under a particular mode. If we consult the Supreme Personality of Godhead, or His representative, the bona fide spiritual master, we worship in the mode of purified goodness. If, desiring to attain some material goal, we consult an ordinary human being, we worship in passion, and if we consult whimsically or foolishly, out of ignorance, we worship in darkness. Blind faith cannot help us. For perfection in life, we must consult the person who has realized the Absolute Truth, the Supreme Personality of Godhead.

"Those who undergo severe austerities and penances not recommended in the scriptures, performing them out of pride, egotism, lust, and attachment, who are impelled by passion, and who torture their bodily organs as well as the Supersoul dwelling within, are to be known as demons." (17.5-6)

In this verse, severe austerities are condemned. In the Middle Ages, monks used to flagellate themselves to atone for their sins. In India, when a yogi wants popular adulation, he may starve himself for some months, or lie on a bed of nails. Others, giving notice to the press, have themselves buried, remain underground for some days by suspending their breath, then have themselves dug up, to the amazement of the innocent public. All these showbottle tricks are performed out of spiritual pride, material lust, desire for name and fame, or attachment to some mundane goal. Such activities are clearly condemned as demoniac.

Lord Krishna continues: "Even food of which all partake is of three kinds, according to the three modes of material nature. The same is true of sacrifices, austerities, and charity. Listen, and I shall tell you of the distinctions of these. Foods in the mode of goodness increase the duration of life, purify one's existence, and give strength, health, happiness, and satisfaction. Such nourishing foods are sweet, juicy, fattening, and palatable. Foods that are too bitter, too sour, salty, pungent, dry, and hot, are liked by people in the mode of passion. Such foods cause pain, distress, and disease. Food cooked more than three hours before being eaten, which is tasteless, stale, putrid, decomposed, and unclean, is food liked by people in the mode of ignorance." (17.7-10)

Krishna is so kind that He has given us nice fruits, vegetables, grains, milk, and milk products by which we can make hundreds and thousands of wonderful preparations in the mode of goodness. Such nutritious and satisfying dishes can be offered to the Lord in sacrifice. Lord Krishna says, "If one offers Me with love and devotion a leaf, a flower, fruit or water, I will accept it." (9.26) These are available in all parts of the world. Even the poorest man can pick a leaf or flower, or find some fruit and water, offer them to the Lord with love and devotion, and thereby advance in Krishna consciousness. Such food that has been offered to the Lord is called *prasadam*, or the Lord's mercy, for it feeds the soul as well as the body. Sometimes impersonalists and neophyte spiritualists, thinking that a devotee should not eat palatable dishes, concoct so-called spiritual diets of bland, tasteless foods. But this is not the teaching of the scriptures, nor of the *acharyas*, who emphasize preparing foods with love and devotion for Krishna. For the Lord, we can make countless delicious preparations. The *Chaitanya-caritamrita* contains an elaborate account of the hundreds of sumptuous dishes prepared for Lord Chaitanya by a devotee named Raghava. The Lord accepted all of these offerings due to the intense love Raghava put into their preparation.

Food for offering need not be cooked Indian style. One may

offer any pure foods (not contaminated by animal slaughter or disease) by preparing them in a clean manner, using plenty of water to wash them on the outside, and constantly chanting Hare Krishna to purify oneself on the inside. When the foods are offered to Krishna with love and devotion, they become completely transcendental, sustain good health, and purify the soul. Any food not carefully prepared and offered to Lord Krishna is in the modes of passion and ignorance, and will certainly lead to distress and disease. "The devotees of the Lord are released from all kinds of sins because they eat food which is offered first for sacrifice. Others, who prepare food for personal sense enjoyment, verily eat only sin." (3.13) The illusion of sense gratification is so strong that people reject the beautiful, simple, rewarding path of Krishna conscious living for a life of sin and suffering and a promise of momentary pleasure. *Prasadam* is beautiful to the sight, delicious to the taste, and beneficial for the soul. Foods in the modes of passion and ignorance are offensive to the sight, putrid to the taste, and degrading to the soul. Who would consider a slice of bloody meat, hacked from a slaughtered animal, beautiful to behold? Before consumption, meat is generally two or three weeks old, and in an advanced state of decay. Many of the latest scientific studies confirm that meat eaters are more susceptible to cancer, heart disease, and numerous other ailments. There is also a correlation between meat eating and the consumption of alcohol, for which Americans alone spend five million dollars an hour, according to 1983 statistics (CBS News). The insensitivity and cruelty of meat eaters and alcoholics, resulting from animal slaughter and the abuse of their own bodies, cannot be denied. For their own personal sense gratification, they are prepared to act in any abominable way.

But the illusory material energy is more clever than alcoholics and meat eaters, and crueler as well. Even though they try hard to enjoy themselves, they can't, for they reap only hangovers and disease. Although people in passion and ignorance want to enjoy palatable foods, they factually fill their bellies with stale, canned, commercial, plastic junk-foods that neither satisfy the taste nor promote health.

We should treat ourselves more kindly. If we really want

to enjoy good food, we should visit the nearest Hare Krishna temple and relish the food offered to the Lord *(prasadam)*. In this way, everyone will be satisfied. "Be happy," Srila Prabhupada used to say. "Take Krishna *prasadam* and be happy."

Lord Krishna continues: "Of sacrifices, that sacrifice performed according to duty and to scriptural rules, and with no expectation of reward, is of the nature of goodness. But that sacrifice performed for some material end or benefit, or performed ostentatiously, out of pride, is of the nature of passion, O chief of the Bharatas. And that sacrifice performed in defiance of scriptural injunctions, in which no spiritual food is distributed, no hymns are chanted, and no remunerations are made to the priests, and which is faithless—that sacrifice is of the nature of ignorance." (17.11-13)

In previous ages, especially in the Treta-yuga, animal sacrifices were recommended. The *brahmanas* conducting such sacrifices were so expert that by means of mantras, they could revive the sacrificed animal in a new body, or even in a human body. Since such powerful *brahmanas* are not found in Kali-yuga, animal sacrifice is forbidden in this age. Even today, sometimes in Kali temples throughout India, goats are sacrificed on the night of the dark moon. These sacrifices, however, are performed only to give meat-eaters some facility, not to satisfy the Supreme Personality of Godhead. It is a kind of restriction. Rather than open a meat-packing business, persons addicted to eating flesh are permitted to slaughter a useless animal, like a chicken or goat, before the goddess Kali. In the course of the sacrifice, mantras are chanted to the effect that in a future life, the roles will be reversed, and the sacrificial animal will kill the person now sacrificing it. In addition to restricting sacrifices to once monthly, this process should make an intelligent person think, "Why am I risking my future and inflicting so much pain just to eat a little flesh?" Thus the whole process is intended to discourage animal slaughter and meat eating altogether.

Lord Buddha, however, would not tolerate even this concession. Out of compassion for the poor animals, Lord Buddha preached *ahimsa* (nonviolence), and specifically condemned animal sacrifice by denying the whole Vedic system of sacrifice and rejecting the *Vedas* as well. Although we accept Lord Buddha as an incarnation of God, we consider His teachings atheistic. He came specifically to stop animal killing and to delude the rebellious atheists by convincing them to worship Him and thereby surrender to God indirectly.

Clearly, in this age, people are so fallen that they must avoid animal sacrifices altogether. Since they are neither expert in chanting the proper hymns, nor capable of assuring the animal a higher birth, they conduct sacrifices in name only. Such sacrifices are not much superior to slaughter, and should be avoided by anyone wanting to progress in Krishna consciousness. If sacrifices are made in the wrong way, we cannot expect the desired results. If we want proper results, we must follow the instructions of *guru-sadhu-shastra*.

The sacrifice specifically recommended for this age is *sankirtan-yajna*, the chanting of Hare Krishna, Hare Krishna, Krishna Krishna, Hare Hare, Hare Rama, Hare Rama, Rama Rama, Hare Hare. This sacrifice is everyone's duty and birthright, according to scriptural injunctions and the instructions of Lord Chaitanya Mahaprabhu. Anyone can perform it at any time. It costs no money, nor does it harm or offend any living entity. Rather, it benefits all who hear its vibration, even plants and animals. There are no hard and fast rules for chanting, but when the holy names are chanted in a humble state of mind, without expectation of any material reward, they will quickly elevate us to the perfectional platform, pure love of God.

Lord Krishna continues: "The austerity of the body consists in this: worship of the Supreme Lord, the *brahmanas*, the spiritual master, and superiors like the father and mother. Cleanliness, simplicity, celibacy, and nonviolence are also austerities of the body. Austerity of speech consists in speaking truthfully and beneficially, and in avoiding speech that offends. One should also recite the *Vedas* regularly." (17.14-15)

Perhaps it is easy to understand why we should worship the Supreme Lord, qualified *brahmanas* perfect in goodness, and the spiritual master, who represents Lord Krishna, but why should ordinary superiors like the father and mother be worshipped? According to Vedic culture, all genuine superiors are representatives of God. The king was supposed to be a *rajarsi*, a saintly king; otherwise he had no right to rule. Similarly, *Srimad-*

Bhagavatam says, "One who cannot deliver his dependents from the path of repeated birth and death should never become a spiritual master, a father, a husband, a mother, or a worshipable demigod." (5.5.18) Real authorities or superiors are pure devotees of the Lord, qualified to represent the Lord.

The austerities of the body— cleanliness, simplicity, celibacy, and nonviolence—are important for controlling the senses. Cleanliness is next to godliness, and to be brahminical, we must be very clean, both externally and internally. By following the four basic regulative principles of Krishna consciousness, we can perfect external cleanliness, and by chanting Hare Krishna we can cleanse the heart of all dirty things. This is the verdict of Lord Chaitanya, who says, *ceto-darpanam-marjanam:* "Glory to the Sri Krishna sankirtan, which cleanses the heart of all the dust accumulated for years and extinguishes the fire of conditional life, of repeated birth and death. This *sankirtan* movement is the prime benediction for humanity at large because it spreads the rays of the benediction moon. It is the life of all transcendental knowledge. It increases the ocean of transcendental bliss, and it enables us to fully taste the nectar for which we are always anxious." (Shikshashtaka,1)

Of course, one may ask, "Should we chant publicly even if others don't want to hear the *Vedas* or the chanting of Hare Krishna?" In ignorance, people do not know what is good or bad. Although a small child may not want to eat nourishing food, the loving parent tactfully and intelligently encourages him. Similarly, we must take up the responsibility of benefiting others. Recitation of the *Vedas* is never offensive, though the ignorant may think so. When the *Vedas* are recited, everyone benefits. Sometimes, devotees appear to offend others when they spread Krishna consciousness by chanting publicly and distributing books, but in reality, these activities render no offense to the souls of others. Only their ignorance is offended.

"And serenity, simplicity, gravity, self-control, and purity of thought are the austerities of the mind. This threefold austerity, practiced by men whose aim is not to benefit themselves materially but to please the Supreme, is of the nature of goodness. Those ostentatious penances and austerities performed in order to gain respect, honor, and reverence are said to be in the mode of passion. They are neither stable nor permanent." (17.16-18)

Whatever is done in the mode of passion may have some temporary result for sense gratification, but it is not stable. By its ephemeral nature, sense gratification appears pleasant today, but tomorrow its fruits are painful. In the mode of passion, people perform activities hoping to become happy by appeasing the senses, but since the senses are insatiable, the attempts to appease them never end. According to Greek tradition, Sisyphus, the king of Corinth, was condemned to Hades to perpetually roll a heavy stone up a steep hill, only to have it roll down again as it neared the top. Attempting to gratify the senses is like eternally rolling that heavy stone up the hill of desire. No sooner do we reach the top, than the stone rolls down and must be pushed up again. As soon as we give the insatiable senses what they want, they scream for more and more. Since penances and austerities for the sake of respect, honor, and reverence are passionate by nature, they cannot benefit us permanently. They are simply labors lost for illusory rewards. By satisfying the real self within, Krishna consciousness puts an end to all these laborious, frustrating endeavors.

"And those penances and austerities which are performed foolishly by means of obstinate self-torture, or to destroy or injure others, are said to be in the mode of ignorance." (17.19)

Today, nations are working hard individually and collectively to stockpile weapons and maintain enormous armed forces. Eating, sleeping, mating, and defending are animal activities provided for automatically by nature, but men, out of passion and ignorance, strive hard to amass more and more material goods for sense gratification. Sometimes men fight to acquire material resources, and what is acquired must then be defended. In either case, out of ignorance, men must labor hard, and in this struggle they waste their valuable human life. The Krishna conscious man, however, does not waste his time on sense gratification. Having realized himself to be eternal spirit soul, he solves all problems. He is not unaware of human suffering, but he knows its real cause and cure. Indeed, he sees the sufferings of others as his own. Knowing Krishna consciousness to be the only remedy for all problems, he always works for the welfare of others by telling them about Krishna.

"That gift which is given out of duty, at the proper time and place, to a worthy person, and without expectation of return, is considered to be charity in the mode of goodness. But charity performed with the expectation of some return, or with a desire for fruitive results, or in a grudging mood, is said to be charity in the mode of passion." (17.20-21)

One in the mode of goodness can actually renounce, whereas one in the mode of passion is always expecting some return. Everything done by a man in passion has some business motive. Sometimes people approach God with this business mentality, donating money to the church with the expectation of some material gain. In India, Ganesh, the god of commerce, is widely worshipped by people seeking material wealth. Foolish men are always thinking of ways to cheat God, not knowing that as the Supersoul in the hearts of all, the Supreme Lord knows our most secret thoughts and desires. Krishna says that He knows everything directly and indirectly, and He sees everything, past, present, and future. We may fool ourselves, but we can never fool God.

Lord Krishna does not consider the gift as important as the loving devotion of the giver. "If one offers Me with love and devotion a leaf, a flower, fruit, or water, I will accept it." (9.26) Of course, this is not all we should offer Krishna. This is just the beginning. "O son of Kunti, all that you do, all that you eat, all that you offer and give away, as well as all austerities that you may perform, should be done as an offering to Me." (9.27) This is transcendental charity beyond the modes of nature. Whatever we do—eating, giving, or performing austerities—becomes transcendental when Krishna is the center.

"And charity performed at an improper place and time and given to unworthy persons without respect and with contempt is charity in the mode of ignorance." (17.22)

In modern society, most charity is in the mode of ignorance. People give charity on the street to beggars who are completely unworthy. Such beggars, usually destitute and dirty because of their sinful activity, should not be given money to misuse; rather, they should be given *prasadam*, transcendental food, for their spiritual benefit. When given money, they buy intoxicants or other objects for sense gratification and thereby increase their sinful activities and concomitant suffering. Charity given to such people is given in the mode of ignorance. The so-called benefactors also have to suffer the results of the sinful activities committed by the recipients of their misdirected charity. Thus charity in the mode of ignorance sets in motion a vicious cycle of suffering for all.

Lord Krishna continues: "From the beginning of creation, the three syllables—*om tat sat*—have been used to indicate the Supreme Absolute Truth [Brahman]. They were uttered by *brahmanas* while chanting Vedic hymns and during sacrifices, for the satisfaction of the Supreme. Thus the transcendentalists undertake sacrifices, charities, and penances, beginning always with *om*, to attain the Supreme. One should perform sacrifice, penance, and charity with the word *tat*. The purpose of such transcendental activities is to get free from the material entanglement. The Absolute Truth is the objective of devotional sacrifice, and it is indicated by the word *sat*. These works of sacrifice, of penance, and of charity, true to the absolute nature, are performed to please the Supreme Person, O son of Pritha." (17.23-27)

Unless sacrifices, charities, and penances are executed from the transcendental platform, in Krishna consciousness, they cannot liberate us from the repetition of birth and death. By the utterance of *om tat sat*, indicating devotional service to the Supreme Personality of Godhead, all activities are transcendental. In other words, whatever activities are performed as devotional service to the Supreme Lord are liberating. It is not a question of simply repeating a mantra or formula. The results of all our activities must be surrendered to the Supreme Lord. This is the direct method of Krishna consciousness.

"But sacrifices, austerities, and charities performed without faith in the Supreme are nonpermanent, O son of Pritha, regardless of whatever rites are performed. They are called *asat*, and are useless both in this life and the next." (17.28) Without devotional service to Krishna, our activities are useless, be they philanthropy, welfare work, or whatever. Moreover, they are abominable because they present themselves as messengers of truth, but factually they are demons of error. Without faith and proper guidance, no one can please God. Through his faith, a devotee can actually perceive things not visible to the eye. To gain such faith, one should hear from the bona fide spiritual master who speaks the Absolute Truth as it descends by the *parampara* (disciplic succession). As one's faith matures, with patience and surrender, it is called Krishna *prema*, pure love of God.

The mode of passion is superior to the mode of ignorance, and goodness is better than passion, but Krishna consciousness is transcendental to all modes of nature. Therefore, everyone should take directly to Krishna consciousness by the recommended process of chanting Hare Krishna, Hare Krishna, Krishna Krishna, Hare Hare, Hare Rama, Hare Rama, Rama Rama, Hare Hare. That is the essential teaching of this chapter. Hare Krishna!

Arjuna said, My dear Krsna, O infallible one, my illusion is now gone. I have regained my memory by Your mercy, and I am now firm and free from doubt and am prepared to act according to Your instructions. *(Bg. 18.73)*

CHAPTER EIGHTEEN

Conclusion—The Perfection of Renunciation

A rjuna begins this final chapter with the following inquiry: "O mighty-armed one, I wish to understand the purpose of renunciation (*tyaga*) and of the renounced order of life (*sannyasa*), O killer of the Keshi demon, Hrishikesha." (18.1)

Lord Krishna replies: "To give up the results of all activities is called renunciation [*tyaga*] by the wise. And that stage is called the renounced order of life [*sannyasa*] by great learned men. Some learned men declare that all kinds of fruitive activities should be given up, but there are yet other sages who maintain that acts of sacrifice, charity, and penance should never be abandoned. All these activities should be performed without any expectation of result. They should be performed as a matter of duty, O son of Pritha. That is My final opinion. Prescribed duties should never be renounced. If, by illusion, one gives up his prescribed duties, such renunciation is said to be in the mode of ignorance." (18.2-3,6-7)

Like everything else, renunciation can be performed in the modes of goodness, passion, or ignorance. If a person thinks that he is renounced simply because he gives up something, he is probably in the mode of ignorance. One's duties must be performed according to the scriptures. That is a positive injunction. To renounce one's prescribed duty is renunciation in the mode of ignorance. Indeed, this is what Arjuna was proposing at the beginning of *Bhagavad-gita*.

Renunciation must be properly directed; otherwise, how can one know what to renounce and what not to renounce? At the beginning of the Sixth Chapter, Lord Krishna said, "One who is unattached to the fruits of his work and who works as he is obligated is in the renounced order of life, and he is the true mystic, not he who lights no fire and performs no work." (6.1) One comes to the material world to enjoy, or lord it over the material resources for personal sense gratification. The purpose of life, however, is to renounce this illusion of sense gratification and enter into the blissful reality of the Lord's transcendental service. Generally, people do not like to hear of renunciation because of their strong attachment for sense enjoyment, but when one realizes that this world of so-called sense enjoyment is unreal, illusory, and full of misery, he can easily renounce it. This is something like renouncing disease by taking the medicine of a qualified doctor. Who would not want to regain his health? To renounce disease is certainly intelligent; to reject sense enjoyment is to reject the path of death.

Lord Krishna continues: "Anyone who gives up prescribed duties as troublesome, or out of fear, is said to be in the mode of passion. Such action never leads to the elevation of renunciation. But he who performs his prescribed duty only because it ought to be done, and renounces all attachment to the fruit—his renunciation is of the nature of goodness, O Arjuna. Those who are situated in the mode of goodness, who neither hate inauspicious work nor are attached to auspicious work; have no doubts about work. It is indeed impossible for an embodied being to give up all activities. Therefore it is said that he who renounces the fruits of action is one who has truly renounced." (18.8-11)

Real renunciation is different from the superficial renunciation envisioned by the impersonalists, or monists, who think that it is sufficient to go to the forest and become void, or zero. They try vainly to negate all activities, but activity is natural for the spirit soul, whether in the liberated or conditioned state. Being constitutionally spiritual, the living entity craves spiritual activities. Real renunciation means renouncing the illusory material activities in favor of spiritual activities, which are fully transcendental and satisfying to the self. Instead of binding one to the material world, transcendental activities become the means for liberation. As long as we try to enjoy material activities, we are subjected to reactions, either auspicious, inauspicious, or mixed. But when we realize our identity as spirit soul, part and parcel of the Supreme Spirit Soul, and act spiritually, we are freed from the reactions of work.

"For one who is not renounced, the threefold fruits of action-desirable, undesirable, and mixed—accrue after death. But those who are in the renounced order of life have no such results to suffer or enjoy." (18.12)

The principal distinction between renunciation and sense gratification depends on the consciousness by which the work is performed. Everyone must work. "All men are forced to act helplessly according to the impulses born of the modes of material nature; therefore no one can refrain from doing something, not even for a moment." (3.5) The sustenance of life involves work, but how that work is performed determines whether one must suffer the results or become free. When one tries to enjoy the fruits of his actions, he either suffers or enjoys, depending on whether his acts are pious or impious. But if one engages in devotional service, and works only for Krishna's satisfaction, he renounces all results and suffers no reactions. Therefore one who wants to be free from material bondage must learn the art of performing all activities in Krishna consciousness, giving up the results for Krishna's satisfaction.

Lord Krishna continues: "O mighty-armed Arjuna, learn from Me of the five factors which bring about the accomplishment of all action. These are declared in Sankhya philosophy to be the place of action, the performer, the senses, the endeavor, and ultimately the Supersoul." (18.13-14) All of the causes of action are rooted in the activities of the Supreme Soul, Sri Krishna. Only in illusion do we think, "I am the doer," and fail to consider the supreme will, the ultimate controller. Our activities are checked by the three modes of material nature, just as the activities of a criminal are checked by the warden in a prison. The prisoners who are submissive and obedient may be transferred to first class cells, whereas those who are insubordinate and disruptive are put into solitary confinement. Such control by the modes of material nature is reflected in all our activities. An obedient prisoner may even become eligible for early parole. By elevating ourselves from the modes of ignorance and passion to goodness, we become eligible to understand transcendence and thereby gain liberation from material bondage.

From verses twenty to forty in this final chapter, Lord Krishna explains in detail the categories of knowledge, work, the worker, intelligence, understanding, determination, and happiness, according to the modes of goodness, passion, and ignorance.

Classifying knowledge in the modes, the Lord says: "That knowledge by which one undivided spiritual nature is seen in all existences, undivided in the divided, is knowledge in the mode of goodness." (18.20) This is the *achintya-bheda-abheda-tattva* philosophy of Lord Chaitanya Mahaprabhu. God is simultaneously one with and different from His creation. He is undivided in the divided. The Supreme Personality of Godhead is all-pervading by His energies, and everything is situated in Him, yet He is independent from everything, existing complete in Himself in His own abode. Knowledge by which the same spiritual nature is seen dwelling in all beings is knowledge in the mode of goodness.

"That knowledge by which a different type of living entity is seen to be dwelling in different bodies, is knowledge in the mode of passion." (18.21) This is knowledge by which one works for his personal sense gratification and for that of his bodily extensions, family, friends, and society. "And that knowledge by which one is attached to one kind of work as the all in all, without knowing the truth, and which is very meager, is said to be in the mode of darkness." (18.22) A common man who works hard like an animal just to eat, sleep, defend, and mate, is certainly on the animal platform and is therefore in the darkness of ignorance.

Lord Krishna continues: "That action [work] in accordance with duty, performed without attachment, without love or hate, by one who has renounced fruitive results, is called action in the mode of goodness. But action performed with great effort by one seeking to gratify his desires, and which is enacted from a sense of false ego, is called action in the mode of passion. And that action performed in ignorance and delusion without consideration of future bondage or consequences, which inflicts injury and is impractical, is said to be action in the mode of ignorance." (18.23-25) Here we can clearly see that workers in the mode of ignorance perform work that is unbeneficial both to themselves and others, and for this, they remain in illusion. But those who work without trying to enjoy the results, sacrificing everything for others' benefit and for the sake of the Supreme, become liberated from the reactions of work.

A man's action and the man himself can hardly be separated. Just as work is classified by the modes, so are those who perform the work. Krishna says: "The worker who is free from all material attachments and false ego, who is enthusiastic and resolute, and who is indifferent to success or failure, is a worker in the mode of goodness. But that worker who is attached to the fruits of his labor, and who passionately wants to enjoy them, who is greedy, envious, and impure, and moved by happiness and distress, is a worker in the mode of passion. And that worker who is always engaged in work against the injunctions of the scripture, who is materialistic, obstinate, cheating, and expert in insulting others, who is lazy, always morose, and procrastinating, is a worker in the mode of ignorance." (18.26-28)

It is very rare in this world to find a worker in the mode of goodness, especially in Kali-yuga. Practically everyone in this age is attached to the fruits of his labor. If the boss doesn't pay, who will work? And whatever money is earned is spent on sense gratification, either for oneself or one's bodily extensions like wife, children, society, and friends. Nothing good comes from the worker in ignorance, for he works for his own destruction and that of others.

"O son of Pritha, that understanding by which one knows what ought to be done and what ought not to be done, what is to be feared and what is not to be feared, what is binding and what is liberating, that understanding is established in the mode of goodness." (18.30) A devotee should always fear whatever makes him forget Krishna. Whatever promotes Krishna consciousness should be accepted, and whatever impedes Krishna consciousness should be feared, shunned, and rejected. When the devotee is engaged in preaching the glories of Krishna, he is fearless, because he is acting in accordance with scripture for the benefit of all, and is therefore always fully protected by the Supreme Lord.

"And that understanding which cannot distinguish between

the religious way of life and the irreligious, between action that should be done, and action that should not be done, that imperfect understanding, O son of Pritha, is in the mode of passion." (18.31) This passionate understanding is very fashionable today. People like to live by their own concocted philosophy. "Do your own thing," they say. "Be your own guru." Since they never accept a spiritual master, they follow no regulative principles, and consequently they never know the difference between the religious and irreligious. Religion cannot be concocted by our finite brains. *Srimad-Bhagavatam* states: "Real religious principles are enacted by the Supreme Personality of Godhead. Although fully situated in the mode of goodness, even the great *rishis* who occupy the topmost planets cannot ascertain the real religious principles, nor can the demigods, nor the leaders of Siddhaloka, to say nothing of the asuras, ordinary human beings, Vidyadharas, and Caranas." (6.3.19) Religion is the law handed down by God and explained by His pure devotee. Those who never follow His rules, or who never accept a bona fide spiritual master, are always confused and bewildered by the modes.

"That understanding which considers irreligion to be religion, and religion to be irreligion, under the spell of illusion and darkness, and strives always in the wrong direction, O Partha, is in the mode of ignorance." (18.32) The demoniac openly proclaim irreligion to be religion, and vice versa. Recently, one so-called guru from India was proclaimed "the sex guru" by the American press. This person has become very popular in the Western countries because he preaches realization of God through unrestricted sex. Reportedly, both he and his students engage in orgies in the name of religion. This is most misleading and abominable. *Kama*, lust, is "the all-devouring sinful enemy of this world," (3.37) and the strongest bond to material existence. If a spiritual master does not teach his disciples to break this bond by regulating the senses, he is a great cheater. Contemporary society is nothing but a society of cheaters and cheated. When the blind lead the blind, they both fall into the ditch. Such misrepresentation of the religious principles is in the mode of darkest ignorance.

Lord Krishna continues: "O son of Pritha, that determination which is unbreakable, which is sustained with steadfastness by yoga practice, and thus controls the mind, life, and the acts of the senses, is in the mode of goodness." (18.33) There is an important connection between determination and real yoga, which aims at controlling the senses. When there is proper determination, the mind is fixed on Krishna by the chanting of His holy names—Hare Krishna, Hare Krishna, Krishna Krishna, Hare Hare, Hare Rama, Hare Rama, Rama Rama, Hare Hare— and when the mind is thus fixed, the senses are easily controlled. The controlled mind and senses then cooperate together for Krishna consciousness. Without sufficient determination to control the senses, the mind cannot be controlled by any means. In the uncontrolled mind, there is no possibility of Krishna consciousness, for an uncontrolled mind soon drags the soul to hell. By *bhakti-yoga*, however, the mind is fixed on Krishna with determination; therefore *bhakti-yoga* is declared by Krishna to be the topmost yoga. But only when one is unattached to sense gratification, can he be determined in devotional service. "In the minds of those who are too attached to sense enjoyment and material opulence; and who are bewildered by such things, the resolute determination of devotional service to the Supreme Lord does not take place." (2.44) Determination is a quality of one whose mind is controlled in goodness. It is unbreakable because it is rooted in yoga, the discipline of devotional service.

"And that determination by which one holds fast to fruitive result in religion, economic development, and sense gratification, is of the nature of passion, O Arjuna." (18.34) A person who desires fruitive results in his activities, religious or otherwise, is in the mode of passion. Such determination wavers with the results, good or bad.

"And that determination which cannot go beyond dreaming, fearfulness, lamentation, moroseness, and illusion—such unintelligent determination is in the mode of darkness." (18.35) It is said that there are two kinds of fools, the lazy fool and the active fool. Of the two, the active fool is worse because he does more damage. Similarly, an ignorant man who is very determined is very dangerous.

Lord Krishna continues: "That happiness which in the beginning may be just like poison, but at the end is just like nectar, and which awakens one to self-realization is said to be happiness in the mode of goodness. That happiness which is derived from contact of the senses with their objects, and which appears like nectar at first but poison at the end, is said to be of the nature of passion. And that happiness which is blind to self-realization, which is delusion from beginning to end, and which arises from sleep, laziness and illusion, is said to be of the nature of ignorance." (18.37-39)

Happiness in the mode of ignorance is based on a kind of intoxication. Neither factual nor enduring, it ultimately leads to frustration and pain. The process leading to happiness in the mode of goodness may be very difficult or distasteful to practice in the beginning, but because it awakens one to knowledge of his eternal position as spirit soul, the happiness is real and enduring. Krishna consciousness is not based on sentiment but reality. It is not temporary but everlasting. Therefore the most intelligent men will certainly take it up. But since everyone is meant to make progress in Krishna consciousness, society should be divided into four sections, or *varnas*, by which all men can make maximum progress spiritually according to their capacity. These *varnas* are next described by Lord Krishna in more detail.

"Peacefulness, self-control, austerity, purity, tolerance, honesty, wisdom, knowledge, and religiousness—these are the qualities by which the *brahmanas* work." (18.42) We should note that Lord Krishna does not say that one becomes a *brahmana* simply by taking birth in a *brahmana* family. Being a qualified *brahmana* has nothing to do with birth. Rather, Krishna says that a *brahmana* is to be identified by his qualities. When a person manifests the brahminical qualities of goodness, he should be considered a *brahmana*, regardless of time and place.

Srila Prabhupada used to tell the story of a boy who once asked Gotama Muni, a great holyman, for initiation. In those days, since initiation was generally granted only to the caste *brahmanas*, the *muni* asked, "Who is your father?" The boy replied, "I don't know." The *muni* then said, "Go ask your mother." When the boy asked his mother, she replied, "My dear son, I must tell you that in my youth I was not very chaste. Since I knew many men, I cannot tell you who your father is." When the boy returned to the *muni*, he said, "Since my mother was a prostitute, I don't know who my father is." Gotama Muni then said, "Oh, my dear boy, you are a *brahmana*. You are very truth-ful. Now you can become my student." This story shows that a *brahmana* is known by qualification, not by birth.

Lord Krishna continues: "Heroism, power, determination, resourcefulness, courage in battle, generosity, and leadership are the qualities of work for the *kshatriyas*." (18.43) In Vedic times, there were no armchair generals. Heads of state did not sit behind guarded doors in their capitals while others risked their lives on the battlefield. If there was fighting to be done, the king himself would lead his army and personally challenge the enemy. Of course, to be a *kshatriya* is to be, more or less, in the mode of passion. But when a *kshatriya* king accepts the guid-ance of qualified *brahmanas*, his properly channelled passion also becomes a means for liberation. Unfortunately, modern civilization is not being led by qualified *kshatriyas* trained in the principles of Vedic culture. Nor are wars fought for righteous causes. The world is being led to hell by low-born men of still lower qualities. Leaders today have neither courage, heroism, nor exemplary leadership. Government has fallen into the hands of ruthless businessmen and greedy laborers who are neither properly qualified nor submissive to the qualified *brahmanas* who could counsel them. In such a society, devoid of the quality of goodness, there can be neither peace nor real prosperity.

"Farming, cow protection, and business are the qualities of work for the *vaishyas*," Krishna says, "and for the *sudras*, there is labor and service to others." (18.44) Just because there are higher and lower divisions, we should not think that one class, being higher, can exploit another. Implicit in these categories, however, is the fact that some duties are more important than others. For instance, in the human body, there are different parts: the head, the arms, the belly, and the legs. The body's head (*brahmanas*) is considered most important. When there is danger, one immediately raises his arms (*kshatriyas*) to protect his head. If the arm or leg is lost, one can survive, but if the head is lost, the body is finished. Similarly, a society lacking direction by qualified *brahmanas* is like a body without a head. It cannot endure. It is essentially a dead society, for it has no spiritual awareness.

Although these divisions certainly exist, it should be noted that every individual is equally important in the sight of God. Lord Krishna clearly says, "By following his qualities of work, every man can become perfect. By worship of the Lord, who is the source of all beings and who is all-pervading, every man can, in the performance of his own duty, attain perfection." (18.45-46) Whether one is *brahmana*, *kshatriya*, *vaishya*, or *sudra*, he becomes perfect if he performs his duty for the satisfaction of Krishna. This is the essence of *Bhagavad-gita:* to learn how to act for Krishna. Although Arjuna was a warrior, he wanted to abandon his duty, but he was convinced by Krishna to fight, not for any materialistic reason, not for himself, or for his family, or for sense gratification, but only to fulfill Krishna's desire. Such work, performed for the satisfaction of the Lord, is our very means of perfection and of liberation from the entanglement of material life. This is the divine consciousness that transforms an ordinary living being into a son of God.

Lord Krishna continues: "It is better to engage in one's own occupation, even though one may perform it imperfectly, than to accept another's occupation and perform it perfectly. Prescribed duties, according to one's nature, are never affected by sinful reactions. Every endeavor is covered by some sort of fault, just as fire is covered by smoke. Therefore one should not give up the work which is born of his nature, O son of Kunti, even if such work is full of fault." (18.47-48)

Regardless of one's occupation, he can attain perfection by surrendering to Krishna. In this material world, often called the world of duality, or relativity, we cannot expect all our daily endeavors to be perfect, even if we join the Society for Krishna Consciousness. Faults and mistakes are inherent in all activities. To err is human. The living entity in this material world is subject to four defects: he is sure to commit mistakes, he is limited by imperfect senses, he is illusioned, and he has a cheating capacity. How, then, can his endeavors be faultless? Even the most erudite scholar will make mistakes. Since he has not read or experienced everything, his knowledge is limited. Even the greatest general loses a battle from time to time. A farmer sometimes loses his crop, a merchant experiences both profit and loss, and a mechanic sometimes becomes baffled trying to repair a machine. All endeavors are covered by some kind of smoke, some kind of fault. Taking this into consideration, we should still carry on our prescribed duty in the spirit of devotion and surrender the results to Krishna. This is renunciation: giving up the tendency to enjoy and acting only for the satisfaction of the Lord. Only God is perfect. Even though our duties may not be performed perfectly, they become perfect when our only desire is to serve Him perfectly.

"One can obtain the results of renunciation simply by self-control, and by becoming unattached to material things and disregarding material enjoyments. That is the highest perfectional stage of renunciation." (18.49) This is a summation of what the Lord has so far explained about the nature of renunciation. Real renunciation means giving up the tendency to act out of a desire to gratify the senses. We should act only in the consciousness of satisfying the Lord by our actions. In this way, we will attain the perfectional stage, pure devotional service, beyond the modes of material nature. Beginning with the following verse, Lord Krishna explains how this highest platform of Krishna consciousness can be reached.

"O son of Kunti, learn from Me in brief how one can attain to the supreme perfectional stage, Brahman, by acting in the way which I shall now summarize. Being purified by his intelligence, and controlling the mind with determination, giving up the objects of sense gratification, being freed from attachment and hatred, one who lives in a secluded place, who eats little, and who controls the body and the tongue, and is always in trance, and is detached, who is without false ego, false strength, false pride, lust, anger, and who does not accept material things, such a person is certainly elevated to the position of self-realization." (18.50-53)

Here, Lord Krishna describes the wonderful characteristics of His devotee. A devotee's intelligence is purified because he no longer identifies himself with the material body. Because he has realized himself to be spirit soul and is no longer attached to sense gratification, he is able to control the mind. Fixed in devotional service, he is free from false ego, false strength, and false pride. It is not that he is free from ego, strength, and pride, but only their false aspects. Ego means identity, and identity cannot be denied. Everyone certainly has a sense of "I am." One may say, "I am an American, I am an Indian, I am a rich man, I am a poor man, I am a white man, I am a black man, etc." All these, however, are false identities arising from false ego, or identity based on the temporary material body. But false ego also implies that there is true ego, which says, "I am God's servant." The "I am" remains the same, but our conception of it changes. Our eternal, constitutional position exists. Who can deny it? Unfortunately, we have forgotten our real identity. According to Lord Chaitanya Mahaprabhu, "I am not *brahmana*, *kshatriya*, *vaishya*, or *sudra*. I am not *brahmachari*, *grihastha*, *vanaprastha*, or *sannyasi*." People generally identify themselves according to family, occupation, or social position, but all these are false, not eternal. What am I? Lord Chaitanya replies, "I am *dasa-dasa-anudasa*. I am the servant of the servant of Krishna." That is our real, eternal identity.

Just as there is false ego, there is also false strength. Every living entity is given some strength by the Lord, but when that strength is used for the wrong purpose, for the enjoyment of sense gratification, it is false. The materialist thinks, "Because of my material resources, I am strong," but the devotee realizes that since all strength comes from Krishna, it should be used to serve Him.

Similarly, false pride arises from a false sense of ownership. The materialist takes pride in "his" wife, children, home, wealth, education, worldly fame, physical strength or beauty, not considering that these are temporary manifestations of material nature, whose master is Lord Krishna. Such pride certainly precedeth a fall, for the conception of "mine" is an illusion. But if one feels proud that he, like every other living entity, is part and parcel of Krishna, that he is not of the material world but of the spiritual kingdom, that it is his duty and his right to offer devotional service to Krishna, and that Krishna is his loving father and dearmost friend, then his pride is just. In due course, this kind of pride will elevate one to the Kingdom of God.

Lord Krishna continues: "One who is thus transcendentally situated, at once realizes the Supreme Brahman. He never laments nor desires to have anything; he is equally disposed to every living entity. In that state, he attains pure devotional service unto Me." (18.54)

We may note that in these final pages of *Bhagavad-gita*, Lord Krishna speaks of *bhakti-yoga* in every verse. Essentially, only *bhakti-yoga* is taught throughout *Bhagavad-gita*, although *jnana-yoga*, *hatha-yoga*, and *karma-yoga* are also discussed. But all other yogas have been shown to mature in *bhakti-yoga*. Now we can see that Lord Krishna is zeroing in on the full flower of *bhakti-yoga*: surrender unto Him in loving, devotional service.

If we were not ourselves Brahman, we could never realize the Supreme Brahman. Upon realizing that we are an infinitesimal portion of the Supreme Brahman, we neither lament nor hanker for anything. Since we are constitutionally eternal, full of knowledge, and bliss, we have nothing to gain or lose. For the spirit soul, there is neither birth nor death (2.20). When one perceives the soul, he is equally disposed to every living entity because he sees everyone—the *brahmana*, the cow, the elephant, the dog, and the dog-eater—as part and parcel of God (5.18). Everywhere, he sees the same spiritual essence coming from Lord Krishna Himself. This is the real vision of equality attained in pure devotional service.

"One can understand the Supreme Personality as He is only by devotional service. And when one is in full consciousness of the Supreme Lord by such devotion, he can enter into the kingdom of God." (18.55) Again, Lord Krishna emphasizes that the Supreme Personality of Godhead can be realized by devotional service and by no other means. In the Eleventh Chapter, He also said, "My dear Arjuna, only by undivided devotional service can I be understood as I am, standing before you, and can thus be seen directly. Only in this way can you enter into the mysteries of My understanding." (11.54) Devotional service is the only means to understand Krishna as He is and enter into the kingdom of God. For our complete understanding, Krishna has repeated this point.

"Though engaged in all kinds of activities, My devotee, under My protection, reaches the eternal and imperishable abode by My grace." (18.56) Krishna encourages Arjuna by telling him that he can perform his duty without worrying about incurring sinful reactions and future suffering. By surrendering the results of action unto Krishna, we automatically get Krishna's protection. It is not exactly by our works that we attain the Kingdom of God, but by God's mercy, which we receive when the Lord is pleased with our devotional service. Our works, rendered in loving devotional service, are only instrumental for the reception of divine grace.

"In all activities, just depend upon Me and work always under My protection. In such devotional service, be fully conscious of Me." (18.57) No one can be fully conscious of Krishna without rendering devotional service. Devotional service, however, does not necessarily entail hard work or physical exertion. According to Prahlad Maharaj, it can be performed in nine different ways: "Hearing and chanting about the transcendental holy name, form, qualities, paraphernalia and pastimes of Lord Vishnu, remembering them, serving the lotus feet of the Lord, offering the Lord respectful worship with sixteen types of paraphernalia, offering prayers to the Lord, becoming His servant, considering the Lord one's best friend, and surrendering everything unto Him [in other words, serving Him with the body, mind and words]—these nine processes are accepted as pure devotional service. One who has dedicated his life to the service of Krishna through these nine methods should be understood to be the most learned person, for he has acquired complete knowledge." (*Srimad-Bhagavatam*, 7.5.23-24)

Factually, devotional service is *apratihata* (*Srimad-Bhagavatam*, 1.2.6), unbroken, eternal, and without any material impediment. It can be performed by old and young, rich and poor, learned and illiterate. Indeed, in any condition, we can think of Krishna and make progress in Krishna consciousness. By such devotional service, we will gradually come to understand that Krishna is the supreme doer of everything. Without God's sanction, not a blade of grass can move. Since the devotee knows that whatever he does is done by the grace of God, he never feels puffed up from false pride. Never thinking that he is the doer or enjoyer, he never becomes entangled in fruitive reactions.

Lord Krishna continues: "If you become conscious of Me, you will pass over all the obstacles of conditional life by My grace. If, however, you do not work in such consciousness but act through false ego, not hearing Me, you will be lost." (18.58) As soon as we forget that Krishna is the supreme enjoyer and supreme doer, we immediately fall into maya, thinking, "I am the doer, and everything is mine to enjoy." In such false consciousness, we suffer the reactions of work, thereby undergoing the repetition of birth and death. Therefore Krishna urges Arjuna to abandon such false ideas and surrender to Him.

"If you do not act according to My direction and do not fight, you will be falsely directed. By your nature, you will have to be engaged in warfare." (18.59) Even if we do not choose to surrender to Krishna, we have to engage in activity according to our nature. If Arjuna chooses not to fight for Krishna, he will follow his nature as a *kshatriya* and fight for some material reason. By fighting in false consciousness, however, he would be doomed to the cycle of repeated birth and death. It is not that Krishna wanted Arjuna to fight for a mundane kingdom; He wanted Arjuna to fight for His divine purpose. The activities of a devotee are transcendental because they are performed on Krishna's behalf, under the direction of Krishna or His representative, the bona fide spiritual master. By performing all activities for His satisfaction, we become free.

"Under illusion, you are now declining to act according to My direction. But, compelled by your own nature, you will act all the same, O son of Kunti." (18.60) Arjuna's reasons for not fighting were false from several angles of vision. First, he thought that if he killed his kinsmen, he could not enjoy the kingdom. Thus he had forgotten that the spirit soul is eternal and can never be killed. Also, there is no question of enjoying a kingdom because we are not enjoyers but servants. Our only position is to satisfy the Supreme Lord, who is the supreme enjoyer. Because Krishna wanted the war, it was Arjuna's duty to fight on Krishna's behalf. Always knowing what is best, Krishna knew that His devotees would have to be victorious for the world to be happy. Therefore He wanted to reestablish the rule of His devotees, the Pandavas, for the welfare of all. The Kurus, having disobeyed the Lord and usurped the throne unlawfully, were doomed by their own sinful activities. Krishna wanted Arjuna to be His instrument for their destruction. Although the Lord is the real doer, He takes more pleasure in glorifying His devotees, who act on His behalf, than in being glorified Himself.

"The Supreme Lord is situated in everyone's heart, O Arjuna, and is directing the wanderings of all living entities, who

are seated as on a machine, made of the material energy." (18.61)
We drive the material body just as a chauffeur drives a car, from
one destination to another. As soon as we take birth under the
modes of material nature, we acquire a certain nature and are
forced to act. Of course, this is all carried out by the ultimate
will of the Supreme, but in all cases He is fulfilling our desires.
We may choose to wander from Him in search of sense gratification, but out of loving kindness, He, the supreme controller,
directs our wanderings so that one day we may return to Him.
Accompanying the living entity in the form of Supersoul, the
Supreme Lord is always there to remind us of our past desires.
"Oh, you wanted to enjoy material nature. Now here is your
chance. Take this body suitable for such enjoyment." In this
way, the Lord accompanies the living being and speaks to him,
giving him a chance to enjoy the material body according to his
previous desires. Even more important, the Lord is also present
to remind us of our eternal relationship with Him as our dearmost
friend. The *Upanishads* give the example of the Lord and the
living entity sitting in the heart like two birds in a tree. As one
bird tries to enjoy the tree's fruits, the other bird witnesses. The
jiva-atma, the finite living entity, tries to enjoy the material body,
but instead, he should turn to his friend, the Supreme Witness
seated in the heart as Supersoul. As soon as we turn to the Lord,
He reminds us of our real position as spirit soul and thus en-
lightens us from within.

Lord Krishna continues: "O scion of Bharata, surrender unto
Him utterly. By His grace you will attain transcendental peace
and the supreme and eternal abode." (18.62) There is no possibility of attaining peace until we realize our identity as spirit
soul, transcendental to matter, and understand our eternal relationship with the Supreme Lord. "Thus I have explained to
you the most confidential of all knowledge. Deliberate on this
fully, and then do what you wish to do." (18.63) Again, Lord
Krishna reminds Arjuna that this supreme transcendental knowledge is higher than all theoretical learning, for it pertains to the
soul and the soul's relationship to the Supreme Soul, Lord
Krishna. Every human being has the intelligence to deliberate
fully on these instructions. We should not accept *Bhagavad-gita*
blindly, but on the basis of reason and proper inquiry. Nor

should we blindly accept a spiritual master. We should ascertain that he actually represents Krishna by always speaking according to the *parampara* system of disciplic succession coming from the Lord. If he actually represents Lord Krishna, his statements must agree with Krishna's teachings to Arjuna. These teachings should be deliberated upon fully, with all intelligence. Then, Krishna says, "do what you wish to do."

The Supreme Lord never forces us to surrender. He gives us minute independence. After hearing *Bhagavad-gita*, we can voluntarily surrender to Krishna or go our own way trying to enjoy material life more and more. We should know, however, what will be the results of our action. If we surrender to the Supreme Lord, He promises to give us all protection. This means that there will be no more birth and death and that we can go back home, back to Godhead. If, however, we choose to persist in our rebellious attitude, trying to become God and enjoy material nature for sense gratification, we will be forced to take birth in the 8,400,000 species according to our karma. This is God's law. The choice is ours, and we should be well aware of the consequences.

Lord Krishna continues: "Because you are My very dear friend, I am speaking to you the most confidential part of knowledge. Hear this from Me, for it is for your benefit." (18.64) When Lord Krishna speaks, He speaks for everyone's benefit. Being our eternal father and dearmost friend, He offers us the most confidential knowledge. But He does not interfere with our freedom to accept it or reject it. Out of friendship and compassion, Lord Krishna spoke the *Bhagavad-gita* to enlighten Arjuna. But when Lord Krishna acts, He acts on many levels simultaneously. *Bhagavad-gita* was also spoken for us and for the enlightenment of all mankind. Today, the same *Bhagavad-gita* is delivered by the bona fide representative of Krishna to relieve us of all doubt and delusion. But until we surrender to Krishna, or His representative, we cannot possibly understand it.

"Always think of Me and become My devotee. Worship Me and offer your homage unto Me. Thus you will come to Me without fail. I promise you this because you are My very dear friend." (18.65) Krishna speaks this most confidential knowledge to Arjuna because Arjuna is His friend and devotee. This summary statement reminds us of the concluding verse of the Ninth Chapter: "Engage your mind always in thinking of Me, offer obeisances and worship Me. Being completely absorbed in Me, surely you will come to Me." (9.34) Again and again, Lord Krishna tells us to become His devotee, think of Him always, worship Him with all our heart and soul, and in this way, attain Him. Lord Krishna certainly does not lie to His friend and devotee Arjuna, nor does He lie to us. Are we to think that the Supreme Lord does not fulfill His promise? No. He is telling us the exact truth. If we just surrender unto Him, all auspiciousness awaits us.

"Abandon all varieties of religion and just surrender unto Me. I shall deliver you from all sinful reaction. Do not fear." (18.66) Although Arjuna is about to engage in the most ghastly warfare, Lord Krishna assures him that He will rescue him from all sinful reaction. Significantly, He tells him to abandon all varieties of religion (*dharma*). There are many systems of yoga, and many speculative processes as well. *Artha*, *dharma*, *kama*, and *moksha*—economic development, religion, sense enjoyment, and liberation—work to elevate us in the modes of material nature, from ignorance, to passion, to goodness. But if we just surrender to Krishna, we will be immediately elevated to the topmost transcendental position. Therefore Lord Krishna advises His dear friend, "Just surrender unto Me." There is nothing to fear from surrender. Surrender to Krishna is the ultimate conclusion of all knowledge, the object and goal of knowledge, and the essence of *Bhagavad-gita*, which is the essence of all Vedic wisdom. By surrendering to Krishna, we are guaranteed success in this very lifetime.

"This confidential knowledge may not be explained to those who are not austere, or devoted, or engaged in devotional service, nor to one who is envious of Me." (18.67) In the Ninth Chapter, Lord Krishna said, "My dear Arjuna, because you are never envious of Me, I shall impart to you this most secret wisdom, knowing which you shall be relieved of the miseries of material existence." (9.1) This is the qualification for understanding *Bhagavad-gita*. It is not sufficient to understand theoretically that Krishna is the Supreme Personality of Godhead. We have to be nonenvious of Krishna, and our engagement in His devotional service will be the proof. Whatever we do, should be done for Krishna's enjoyment, not for our own personal satisfaction. Since everything is Krishna's property, our body and mind also belong to Him. Actually, we have no right to use the body for any purpose unrelated to Krishna, nor the mind to think of anything other than Krishna. Devotional service means relating all our thoughts, words, and deeds—everything—to Krishna.

"For one who explains the supreme secret to the devotees, devotional service is guaranteed, and at the end he will come to Me." (18.68) Here, Krishna clearly says that explaining this transcendental knowledge of *Bhagavad-gita* is the greatest service one can render. First we must hear *Bhagavad-gita* properly, and then explain it to others. Of the nine processes of devotional service, the foremost are *sravanam kirtanam*, hearing and chanting, or repeating. After hearing and understanding *Bhagavad-gita* from the bona fide representative of Krishna, we must repeat it for the benefit of others.

"There is no servant in this world more dear to Me than he, nor will there ever be one more dear." (18.69) To make ourselves dear to Lord Krishna, we must have compassion on other fallen souls. In this material world, everyone is suffering birth, old age, disease, and death. No one can escape the miseries inherent in material life. Lord Krishna does not want us to suffer pains caused by misuse of our minute independence. By helping Him reclaim the fallen souls, we relieve both ourselves and others of miseries, and become Krishna's dearmost friends and servants.

"And I declare that he who studies this sacred conversation worships Me by his intelligence." (18.70) Intelligence is properly used in the study of *Bhagavad-gita* and other scriptures that teach us about Krishna. Intelligence is meant for understanding our relationship with God, and it is misused when it is directed toward sense gratification. By such misuse, men lose the ability to understand the difference between matter and spirit, forget their relationship with Krishna, and sink into the most degraded type of existence.

"And one who listens with faith and without envy becomes free from sinful reaction and attains to the planets where the pious dwell." (18.71) By hearing these transcendental topics of Lord Krishna, we purify our consciousness and become qualified for entrance into the Kingdom of God, the world of Vaikuntha, a place of perfect peace.

Lord Krishna concludes: "O conqueror of wealth, Arjuna, have you heard this attentively with your mind? And are your illusions and ignorance now dispelled?" (18.72) Under illusion, Arjuna was misidentifying himself with his family and friends, and therefore declining to fight. Now Krishna is asking whether he understands that his only real friend is Lord Krishna. Has his illusion been removed? Does Arjuna realize himself to be part and parcel of Krishna, and is he ready to act on the Lord's behalf?

Arjuna replies, "My dear Krishna, O infallible one, my illusion is now gone. I have regained my memory by Your mercy, and I am now firm and free from doubt, and am prepared to act according to Your instructions." (18.73)

When our illusion and ignorance are dispelled by these transcendental teachings, we will find ourselves in the same position as Arjuna. We will understand that Krishna is our dearmost friend, Achyuta, the infallible one, who never falls down, who never forgets Himself, and who never changes His body. Even when Lord Krishna comes to this material world, He does not change His body, but appears in His original, spiritual body. His activities, also, are wholly transcendental. When we understand this, our illusion, like Arjuna's, will disappear, for we will cease to identify with the material position. We will no longer consider ourselves to belong to a particular family or country, but we will know ourselves to be eternal servants of Krishna. By remembering our eternal relationship with Krishna, we will remain firm and free from doubt, determined to act according to the Lord's instructions.

Those who are serious in realizing these instructions should follow the bona fide spiritual master whom Krishna has kindly sent us. Krishna's representative simply repeats the same message Lord Krishna delivered to Arjuna five thousand years ago at Kurukshetra. The spiritual master is great not because he has manufactured something, but because he presents the real thing without changing it. Conditioned souls want to change everything according to their latest mental speculations, but the bona fide representative of Krishna knows that Krishna and Krishna's

Bhagavad-gita are all-perfect. He therefore presents *Bhagavad-gita* without change, as it is. This, then, is the all-auspicious message of *Bhagavad-gita:* surrender to Krishna and be free from all illusion and doubt. Once we surrender, we will see that a marvelous victory is ours.

"Wherever there is Krishna, the master of all mystics, and wherever there is Arjuna, the supreme archer, there will also certainly be opulence, victory, extraordinary power, and morality. That is my opinion." (18.78)

This is the opinion of the sage Sanjaya and all other bona fide authorities as well. Krishna is the Supreme Personality of Godhead, full with six opulences. He is also the husband of the Goddess of Fortune. Furthermore, He is called Yogesvara, the master of all mystic powers. Lord Brahma is certainly a great mystic, for he creates the whole material universe, but even Brahma is bewildered by the supreme mystic power of the Lord. Finally, Lord Krishna is the father of morality and its measure as well. No one can be more moral than He. Whether He is killing demons, dancing at night with the *gopis,* or telling Arjuna to fight, He sets the absolute standard of morality. If this were not so, how could a great *sannyasi* like Lord Chaitanya, who would not even look at a woman, and who rejected one of His *sannyasi* associates simply for begging rice from a woman, declare the method of worship deployed by the *gopis* of Vrindaban to be the topmost devotional service? Such worship is greater than the cultivation of knowledge, greater than mystic yoga, greater than all other yogas.

It is to this Krishna, the Lord and Master of the *gopis,* that Arjuna surrendered utterly, achieving all success. And it is this same Krishna, the beloved of all devotees, who calls us today with His beautiful song of love of God, inviting us to surrender to Him utterly. Hare Krishna.

Glossary

A

ACHARYA: a spiritual master who teaches by his personal example.

ACHINTYA-BHEDA-BHEDA-TATTVA: Lord Chaitanya's doctrine of the "inconceivable oneness and difference" of God and His creation, establishing the Absolute Truth as both personal and impersonal.

AGNI: the demigod controlling fire.

AHAM BRAHMASMI: "I am Brahman." The spiritual identity of the living entity.

AHIMSA: nonviolence.

AKARMA: Krishna conscious activities that carry no reactions, either good nor bad.

ANANDA: transcendental bliss.

ANU: atomic, minute.

ARCHA-VIGRAHA: the incarnation of the Lord in the form of material elements, such as a statue (Deity or *murti*), or painting, or even a mental image. It is manifest to facilitate worship by the devotees in the material world.

ARTHA: economic development.

ASANAS: bodily postures used in yoga discipline.

ASHRAMA: a spiritual order according to the Vedic social system: *brahmacharya* (student life), *grihastha* (householder), *vanaprastha* (retirement), and *sannyasa* (renunciation).

ASTANGA-YOGA: the eightfold path consisting of *yama* and *niyama* (moral practices), *asana* (bodily postures), *pranayama* (breath control), *pratyahara* (sensory withdrawal), *dharana* (steadying the mind), *dhyana* (meditation), and *samadhi* (deep concentration on Vishnu within the heart).

ASURA: not godly; demon, or one opposed to God.

ASURAM BHAVAM ASRITA: one who is openly atheistic.

ATMA: the self, or soul.

ATMA-HANAH: killer of the soul; one who neglects spiritual life.

ATMARAMA: self-satisfied; one who delights in the Self.

B

BALARAMA: Lord Krishna's first expansion, appearing as elder brother of Krishna, manifestation of spiritual strength.

BHAGAVAN: the possessor of all opulences, the Supreme Lord.

BHAKTISIDDHANTA SARASWATI: founder of India's famous Gaudiya Math mission, and spiritual master of His Divine Grace A. C. Bhaktivedanta Swami Prabhupada.

BHAKTIVEDANTA SWAMI PRABHUPADA: founder-*acharya* of the International Society for Krishna Consciousness, greatest exponent of Krishna consciousness in modern times, author of some eighty volumes on the science of *bhakti-yoga*.

BHAKTIVINODE THAKUR: a great devotee, father of Bhaktisiddhanta Saraswati.

BHAKTI-YOGA: linking with the Supreme Lord through devotional service.

BHISMA: a great devotee and senior family member of the Kuru dynasty.

BRAHMA: the first created living being in the universe, empowered by Lord Vishnu to further create the material manifestation and rule the mode of passion.

BRAHMA-BHUTA: state of being freed from material contamination, and transcendentally happy by virtue of devotional service.

BRAHMACHARI: celibate student; the first *ashrama*.

BRAHMAJYOTI: the impersonal effulgence emanating from the transcendental body of Lord Krishna and illuminating the spiritual world.

BRAHMALOKA: the abode of Lord Brahma, highest planet in the material universe.

BRAHMAN: (1) the Supreme Personality of Godhead; (2) the

impersonal, all pervasive aspect of God; (3) the total material substance *(maha-tattva)*; (4) the individual soul.

BRAHMANA: the intellectual, or priestly class, according to the Vedic social system of *varnas*.

BRAHMA-SAMHITA: an ancient Sanskrit scripture of the prayers of Brahma to Govinda.

C

CHAITANYA-CHARITAMRITA: scripture by Krishnadas Kaviraj Goswami describing Lord Chaitanya Mahaprabhu's teachings and pastimes.

CHAITANYA MAHAPRABHU: Lord Krishna's incarnation in the age of Kali, appearing in Bengal, India, in the late Fifteenth Century, to inaugurate the dharma of this age: the congregational chanting of Hare Krishna.

CHANDALA: a dog-eater, outcaste.

CHAPATI: an unleavened, pancake-sized whole wheat bread.

D

DAL: a soup made from beans.

DHARMA: true nature, religious principles; the rendering of service to God.

DHRITARASHTRA: the father of the Kurus. *Bhagavad-gita* was related to him by his secretary, Sanjaya, as it was being spoken on the battlefield.

DHRUVA MAHARAJ: a great boy-devotee, renown for his firm determination and penance. He later ruled this planet and was finally given the polestar, Dhruvaloka.

DURGA: the personification of the material energy.

DURYODHANA: the chief of the evil-minded sons of Dhritarashtra. To establish Duryodhana as world-king, the Kurus fought the battle of Kurukshetra.

DUSKRITINA: miscreant; one who does not surrender to Krishna.

DVAPARA-YUGA: the third age of the cycle of *yugas*. It ended with the disappearance of Lord Krishna from this earth, five thousand years ago.

G

GANESH: one of the demigods, son of Lord Shiva, often worshipped for success in material affairs.

GARBHODAKASHAYI VISHNU: the Vishnu expansion of the Supreme Lord entering each universe to create diversity.

GAU-MATA: mother cow.

GOPAS: the cowherd boy friends of Krishna, highly elevated devotees who enjoy sporting with Krishna in Vrindaban.

GOPIS: the cowherd girl friends of Krishna, highly elevated devotees who enjoy transcendental feelings with Krishna in the conjugal *rasa*.

GOVARDHANA HILL: a hill near Vrindaban lifted by Lord Krishna to protect His devotees from the torrents of Indra.

GOVINDA: name of Krishna, meaning one who gives pleasure to the cows.

GRIHASTHA: householder; the second *ashrama*.

GUNAS: the three material modes, or qualities, of the material universe: goodness, passion, and ignorance.

H

HALAVAH: a dessert made from toasted grains, butter, and sugar.

HARE: the spiritual energy of the Lord by which the Lord is reached.

HARI: the Supreme Lord, Krishna.

HATHA-YOGA: a system of bodily postures (*asanas*) to help control the senses and mind and thereby aid meditation.

HIRANYAKASIPU: a great demon, father of the devotee Prahlada Maharaj, killed by Krishna in His incarnation as Nrishingadeva.

HRISHIKESHA: master of the senses, Lord Krishna.

I

INDRA: a great demigod, the king of heaven and presiding deity of rain.

ISHOPANISHAD: one of the most important of the 108 *Upanishads*, establishing the proprietory right of the Supreme Personality of Godhead.

J

JAPA: chanting of the holy names of God.

JIVA, JIVA-ATMA: the individual soul, or living entity.

JNANA-YOGA: the predominantly empirical, intellectual process of linking with the Supreme, generally executed when one is still attached to mental speculation.

K

KACHORI: a fried pastry filled with potatoes and peas.

KALA: the manifestation of Krishna as eternal time.

KALI: a goddess personifying the ghastly form of material nature.

KALI-YUGA: the age of quarrel and ignorance, the fourth and most degraded age in the cycle of four *yugas*. Five thousand years of this current Kali-yuga have expired; 428,000 years remain.

KALKI-AVATARA: incarnation of Krishna, manifest at the end of Kali-yuga. Appearing on a white horse, He will annihilate all the demons with His sword.

KAMA: desire, lust.

KARANODAKASHYI VISHNU: the Maha-vishnu who lies within the causal ocean and breathes out innumerable universes.

KARMA: (1) material action performed according to scripture; (2) the chain of action and reaction.

KARMA-KANDA: the division of the *Vedas* dealing with fruitive activities performed by materialists for purification and material success.

KARMA-YOGA: linking to God by dedicating the fruits of action to Him.

KARMI: a materialist; one attached to the fruits of his labor.

KRIPANA: a miser; one who does not spend his life on spiritual realization.

KSHATRIYA: a warrior or administrator in the Vedic social system. Literally, a *kshatriya* is one who protects others from harm.

KSIRODAKASHAYI VISHNU: the Supersoul entering into the heart of every living being. He exists in and between every atom, and He is the source of many incarnations.

KUNTHA: the material universe. Literally, the place of anxiety.

KUNTI: (1) mother of the five Pandavas, and great devotee of Lord Krishna; (2) neckbeads worn by initiated disciple of spiritual master.

KURUKSHETRA: place of pilgrimage, north of modern New Delhi, where *Bhagavad-gita* was spoken and the great battle between the Kurus and Pandavas took place. .

KURUS: the one hundred sons of Dhritarashtra.

M

MAHABHARATA: the great epic of 100,000 verses composed by Vyasadeva, narrating the history of the Pandavas and including *Bhagavad-gita*.

MAHAMANTRA: the great chanting for deliverance: Hare Krishna, Hare Krishna, Krishna Krishna, Hare Hare, Hare Rama, Hare Rama, Rama Rama, Hare Hare.

MAHA-TATTVA: the total material energy.

MAHATMA: a great soul who understands that Krishna is everything and therefore surrenders unto Him.

MAHAVISHNU: the Karanodakashayi Vishnu who lies within the causal ocean and breathes out innumerable universes.

MANGAL-ARATIK: early morning (4:30 a.m.) offering to the Lord in the temple, accompanied by chanting and bells.

MANU: the father of mankind, the demigod who set forth *Manu-samhita*, the law book for humanity.

MAYA: illusion; the external energy of Krishna that deludes the living entity into forgetfulness of Krishna.

MAYADEVI: personification of the illusory material energy.

MAYAVADI: impersonalist or voidist maintaining that God is ultimately formless and without personality.

MAYAYAPAHRITA-JNANA: one whose knowledge has been nullified by the influence of the illusory material energy.

MOKSHA: liberation from the cycle of birth and death.

MUDHA: hard-working ass; gross materialist.

MUKUNDA: the granter of liberation *(mukti)*, Krishna.

MUNI: sage or self-realized soul.

N

NANDA MAHARAJ: a great devotee, who served as foster father of Krishna in the Vrindaban pastimes.

NARADA: one of the Lord's greatest devotees, author of *Narada-bhakti-sutras*. He spreads love of God throughout the universe.

NARADHAMA: lowest of mankind; those without religious principles.

NARAYANA: four-handed expansion(s) of Vishnu presiding over the Vaikuntha planets.

NITYO: eternal; refers both to the Lord and the living entity.

NRISHINGADEVA: incarnation of Lord Krishna in the form of half-man, half-lion, savior of Prahlad Maharaj.

O

OM TAT SAT: the transcendental syllables chanted by *brahmanas* for satisfying the Supreme when chanting Vedic hymns or offering sacrifices. They indicate the Supreme Absolute Truth, the Personality of Godhead.

OMKARA: Om; the transcendental syllable representing the impersonal aspect of Krishna.

P

PANDAVAS: the five sons of King Pandu: Yudhisthira, Arjuna, Bhima, Nakula, and Sahadeva.

PANDU: the younger brother of Dhritarashtra, who died early, leaving his five young sons, the Pandavas, under the care of Dhritarashtra.

PARAM-BRAHMA: the Supreme Brahman, the Personality of Godhead, Sri Krishna.

PARAMATMA: the Supersoul, the localized aspect of the Supreme Lord within the heart of all living entities, accompanying everyone as witness and guide.

PARAMHAMSA: topmost devotee of the Lord. Literally, swan-like.

PARAMPARA: the disciplic succession through which spiritual knowledge is transmitted.

PATALA-LOKA: lowest planet in the material universe.

PAVITRAM: pure.

PRABHUPADA: see BHAKTIVEDANTA PRABHUPADA.

PRAHLADA MAHARAJ: a great devotee, persecuted by his demonic father, Hiranyakashipu, and saved by Lord Nrishingadeva.

PRAKRITI: material nature. Literally, that which is predominated.

PRASADAM: food offered in devotion to Lord Krishna. Literally, mercy.

PREMA: pure, spontaneous love of God.

PUJA: worship.

PURANAS: the eighteen historical supplements to the *Vedas*.

PURI: a puffy wheat bread fried in ghee.

PURUSHA: the enjoyer, the dominator, the Supreme Lord. Sometimes the word refers to the individual soul.

R

RADHA(RANI): eternal consort of Krishna, His own internal pleasure potency.

RAJA-GUHYAM: the king of education: Krishna consciousness.

RAJA-VIDYA: the king of knowledge, the confidential knowledge of devotional service, explained in the Ninth Chapter of *Bhagavad-gita.*

RAJASUYA: great sacrifice performed by Maharaj Yudhisthira.

RAMA: (1) a name of God meaning the enjoyer; (2) Lord Ramachandra, the incarnation, hero of Valmiki's *Ramayana*; (3) Lord Balarama, the expansion of Krishna.

RASA: (1) Lord Krishna's transcendental pastime of dancing with the *gopis* in the forests of Vrindaban; (2) relationship.

RISHI: saint or sage.

RUPA GOSWAMI: one of the principal disciples of Lord Chaitanya Mahaprabhu, author of many authoritative books on *bhakti-yoga,* including *Bhakti-rasamrita-sindhu.*

S

SADHANA-BHAKTI: devotional service executed by regulative principles, as opposed to spontaneous love.

SADHU: holyman or sage.

SAHAJIA: a type of impersonalist who takes things cheaply and mistakenly identifies the finite living entity with Krishna.

SAMADHI: trance, absorption in Krishna consciousness.

SANATANA-DHARMA: the eternal religion; devotional service.

SANJAYA: the secretary of Dhritarashtra who related *Bhagavad-gita* to Dhritarashtra as it was taking place at Kurukshetra.

SANKHYA-YOGA: (1) analytical discrimination between spirit and matter, soul and body;(2) devotional yoga taught in *Srimad-Bhagavatam* by Lord Kapila, son of Devahuti.

SANKIRTAN-YAJNA: the congregational chanting of the names of God, the prescribed sacrifice for this age of Kali.

SANNYASA: the renounced order of life, the fourth *ashrama* in the Vedic social system.

SAT-CIT-ANANDA: eternal being, knowledge, and bliss.

SATYA-YUGA: the age of goodness and wisdom, first of the four ages of the universe, characterized by virtue and religion.

SHANKARACHARYA: (788-820 A.D.) the great philosopher who established the doctrine of *advaita* (nondualism), stressing the impersonal nature of God and the identity of all souls with the undifferentiated Brahman.

SHANTI: transcendental peace.

SHASTRA: scripture.

SHIVA: Qualitative incarnation of Krishna in charge of the mode of ignorance and responsible for the annihilation of the material universe; demigod worshipped commonly for material benedictions.

SHYAMASUNDARA: a name of the original form of Lord Krishna as manifest in the Vrindaban pastimes.

SIDDHALOKA: a higher planet inhabited by perfected yogis.

SIKA: tuft of hair on the head of Vaishnavas.

SLOKA: a Sanskrit verse.

SRIMAD-BHAGAVATAM: the scripture composed by Vyasadeva to explain and describe Krishna's pastimes.

SUDHA-SATTVA: purified goodness above the three *gunas*.

SUDRA: a member of the working class in the Vedic social system.

T

TAPASYA: penance or austerity voluntarily accepted for spiritual progress.

TILAK: clay markings worn on the forehead and other places to sanctify the body as a temple of the Supreme Lord.

TRETA-YUGA: the second age in the cycle of yugas, renown for great sacrifices.

V

VAIKUNTHA: the eternal planets of the spiritual sky. Literally, without anxiety.

VAISHNAVA: a devotee of the Supreme Lord.

VAISHYA: the merchant or farmer class according to the Vedic social system.

VANAPRASTHA: retired life, in which one quits home and travels to places of pilgrimage in preparation for the renounced order of *sannyasa*.

VARNA: social class, or occupational division.

VARNASHRAMA: the Vedic social system arranged into four occupations *(varnas): brahmana, kshatriya, vaishya,* and *sudra;* and four spiritual divisions *(ashramas): brahmachari, grihastha, vanaprastha,* and *sannyasa.*

VASUDEVA: Krishna, the son of Vasudeva.

VEDANTA: the philosophical system based on the *Vedanta-sutra,* the treatise written by Vyasadeva.

VEDAS: the four original scriptures *(Rig, Yajur, Sama,* and *Atharva).* Also, in a larger sense, their supplements, the *Puranas, Mahabharata, Vedanta-sutra,* etc.

VIKARMA: unauthorized or sinful activity performed against the injunctions of revealed scriptures.

VIRATA-RUPA: the universal form of Lord Krishna, as described in the Eleventh Chapter of *Bhagavad-gita.*

VISHNU: the Personality of Godhead.

VISHNU-TATTVA: innumerable primary or Vishnu expansions of Krishna.

VRINDABAN: the transcendental abode of Lord Krishna. Also called Goloka Vrindaban or Krishnaloka.

VYASADEVA: literary incarnation who compiled the *Vedas* and wrote the *Puranas, Mahabharata,* and *Vedanta-sutra.*

Y

YAJNA: sacrifice

YAJNA-PURUSHA: Krishna, the Lord and enjoyer of all sacrifices.

YAMARAJ: the god of death; demigod who punishes sinful living entities after death.

YAMUNA: Holy river flowing by Vrindaban, site of Krishna's pastimes. Also spelled Jamuna.

YOGA-MAYA: the internal energy of the Lord, which hides Him from one's material vision.

YUDHISTHIRA: the eldest Pandava brother, the son of Dharma. To install him on his rightful throne, the battle of Kurukshetra was fought.

YUGAS: the four ages of the universe: Satya-yuga, Treta-yuga, Dvapara-yuga, and Kali-yuga. As the ages proceed from Satya to Kali, religion and goodness decline, and ignorance predominates.

Index

A

Abortion, 230

Absolute Truth, *see also* Krishna
realization of, 100
unknowable through material senses, 15

Acharya, see also Spiritual master
necessity of, 49
necessity of becoming, 35

Achintya-bheda-bheda-tattva,
102,177, 201, 252

Action, *see also* Duty, Work
as complement of renunciation, 61, 83
as liberating, 251, 252
better than inaction, 32
five factors of, 251
in knowledge, 234
three factors of, 49

Activity
determined by Nature (of person), 263
in modes of nature, 243
natural for soul, 250

Aghasura, 144

Agni, 156

Ahaituki apratihata, 121

Aham Brahmasmi, 39, 66, 68, 97, 181

Air, 98

Akamah sarva-kamo va, 110

Akarma, 23, 49, 50

Alcohol, 239

Anger, 40, 75, 76, 233, 234

Angira Muni, 73

Animal, 91, 179, 206

Animal-killing, 179, 207, *see also* Cow-killing

Aratik, 180, *see also* Regulative principles

Archa vigraha, see Krishna as Deity

Arjuna, *see also* Pandavas
as conqueror, 112

as conqueror of wealth, 55, 268
as devotee, 5, 131, 265
as disciple of Krishna, 92, 93
as Krishna's friend, 33, 117, 131, 156, 169, 265
as Krishna's instrument, 167, 258, 263
as nonenvious, 132
as perfect disciple, 154
as perfect yogi, 198
as pure devotee, 156, 165
as Savyasacin, 167
as son of Bharata, 222
as son of Kunti, 125
as warrior, 31
asks forgiveness, 169, 226
bewilderment of, 31, 50, 175
Bhagavad-gita confirmed by, 154
Bhagavad-gita understood by, 147, 156, 268
chose Krishna, not army, 167
declares Krishna's promise, 145, 146
directed by Krishna, 33
eternally liberated, 5
fearless, 128
meditation impractical for, 91
nonenvious, 156, 266
prayers of, 153, 154, 155, 156
prefers Krishna's two-armed form, 170
protected by Krishna, 5
represents all men, 31
success of, 56, 269
surrender of, 269
victorious, 269
wanted to retire from life, 32

Armchair generals, 257

Aroma, example of, 195, 218

Artha, dharma, kama, moksha, 266

Asana, 83

Asita, 154, 155

283